filmadelphia

by Irv Slifkin

Middle Atlantic Press
Moorestown, NJ

Copyright

First edition

1 2 3 4 5   09 08 07 06 05

Cover and interior designed by Desiree Rappa

Dedication:

To my wife Margie and daughters Sarah and Rose, Philly and movie lovers all.

table of contents

introduction

To many Philadelphians — and the rest of the country — the first time they saw Philly onscreen was when they watched "Rocky" for the first time.

Sure, there were a few bits and pieces of the city in other films, but it wasn't until that 1976 movie with Sylvester Stallone that moviegoers got such an all-encompassing view of the City of Brotherly Love.

Here was a city in all of its splendor, from the gritty streets of Kensington to the fruit vendors of the Italian market to the Art Museum steps. This was the real deal. That the movie, a low-budget underdog, featured a former area native and went on to win the Academy Award for Best Picture, made it so much sweeter.

Of course, "Rocky" wasn't the first movie shot or set in these parts.

It just seems that way. The problem was that the most famous film B.R. (Before "Rocky") was another Oscar winner, 1940's "The Philadelphia Story," but it had just a few scenes actually shot in the area. Most was shot on a Hollywood soundstage.

A.R. (After Rocky), however, things began to change. The Delaware Valley found starring roles in such major features as "Blow Out," "Philadelphia," and the works of locally-based M. Night Shyamalan. In addition, scores of independent productions were shot in and around the area, while the city has also served as a popular location for TV shows, concert filming, and commercials.

Although so-called experts will tell you that Philly doesn't rank high as a film town, local movie fans know better. In fact, the city's filmmaking roots were established at the birth of the industry, and, at one time, Philadelphia was something of the Hollywood of the east — even before there was a Hollywood.

Never Say Never Again (1983) James Bond (Sean Connery): Well, to be perfectly honest, there was this girl in Philadelphia ...

It was Sigmund "Pop" Lubin, a European émigré and former optician, living in Philly, who invented a motion picture projector, opened some of the country's earliest movie theaters, and ran one of the most successful movie studios in the world from the late 1890s into the early part of the 20th century.

Philadelphians love for movies was triggered by Lubin's efforts, and has remained enthusiastic ever since those times. The city has been the site of 20 grand movie palaces, noted for their awe-inspiring architecture. Although you wouldn't know it now, a trip downtown at one time offered wonderful film — going experiences, with grandiose single — screen theaters all over Center City. And Philly's neighborhoods had impressive film showcases, too, as did its suburbs.

Believe it or not, Philadelphia had its own "Hollywood Row" at one time as well. Many studios and production companies made their headquarters along Vine Street, between 8th and 13th Streets. Leaving Chinatown and seeing the familiar Universal-International globe atop a building, then the various studio logos up on buildings and down the street, served as a reminder that Philadelphia indeed mattered as far as the film industry was concerned.

Filmadelphia is intended as a celebration of Philadelphia and its filmmaking and film-going heritage. It encompasses the movies shot and set here, as well as the talented people whose lives were touched by the city before they contributed to the world of movies and television.

The major part of *Filmadelphia* has been dedicated to the movies shot or set in the Delaware Valley. They have been rated from 1 to 4 Liberty Bells 🔔🔔🔔🔔 in order to serve those who wish to use the book as a movie guide. In addition, each entry in this chapter features a "Local Moments" section that points out facts about the movie's production and what locations were used during its filming. Whether you agree or disagree with the Philly film's evaluation, it's likely you will learn something new by reading these sections that will give you insight into a particular movie's history.

Another section of the book, called "Shore Things," focuses on movies shot and set at the Jersey shore. Since the Jersey shore is such a part of many Delaware Valley residents' experiences, it seemed only natural to include pictures shot or set in and around the South Jersey shoreline.

"Filmadelphia" also offers extensive biographies of locally-born — or at least groomed — people who have made an impact in Hollywood, whether they be actors, directors, writers, producers or executives. We're guessing that you'll be surprised at some of the people you didn't realize came through these parts.

A note is in order about locating the films spotlighted in this book. I can honestly say that I managed to find all but one movie mentioned in *Filmadelphia* (if anyone has a copy of "The Block" from 1964, please contact my publisher immediately!). Many are available now on DVD, had been available on VHS, and play regularly on cable and satellite TV. If you do have trouble tracking any of these films down at your local rental store or reliable mail order sources such as *www.moviesunlimited.com* (full disclosure: I work there) or *www.amazon.com*, I suggest you type the name of the film and the desired format in your favorite Internet search engine. Odds are you'll find it, somewhere.

So, throw on that "Iggles" jersey, run down to 9th and Pashyunk for a cheesesteak wit', and grab a six-pack of Schmidt's at the local taproom.

I hope youse like my book.

Irv Slifkin
September 2006

10th & Wolf (2006)

Based on an idea by Joseph Pistone,

the man who inspired "Donnie Brasco," this South Philly-set crime story covers a lot of the same turf you've seen before in better films like "The Godfather," "GoodFellas," and, well, "Donnie Brasco."

James Marsden plays a marine who leaves fighting in the Middle East behind and heads back home for family business in Philadelphia. Seems that the family business is crime and unstable brother Brad Renfro and hotheaded cousin Giovanni Ribisi are involved in a war over turf with a Sicilian mobster. Federal agents Brian Dennehy and Leo Rossi enlist Marsden to go undercover in order to get the goods on the foreign hood. Of course, this means infiltrating his own family feuding as well. Directed by Bobby Moresco, the Oscar-winning cowriter of "Crash," "10th & Wolf" features a pretty bizarre supporting cast that includes bits by Dennis Hopper, Val Kilmer, Tommy Lee, and Lesley Ann Warren. It's bloody, with some disturbing violence, but it's also a mess, muddled to the max, with barely a character of interest in the entire film.

> "Seems that the family business is crime ..."

Rating:

1776 (1972)

After a successful run on Broadway,

Peter Stone and history teacher Sherman Daniels' 1969 play about drafting the Declaration of Independence was brought to the big screen under the guidance of (then independent) producer Jack Warner and Peter H. Hunt, who helmed the musical on Broadway. Shortly before the film was to be released, a panicked Warner lopped out 25 minutes of a 180-minute film, then ordered the negatives destroyed. The $4 million film was a disappointment when it opened in November 1972 as Columbia's big Christmas movie. Today, with several major parts painstakingly restored, the film remains a surprisingly solid effort: intelligent, absorbing, and extremely witty, mixing historical fact with rich character study and a buoyant musical score. The story is set on the days leading up to July 4, 1776, when the Second Continental Congress convenes in Philadelphia's Independence Hall. The main characters are John Adams (William Daniels), a stubborn, often dislikable statesman from Boston; Benjamin Franklin (Howard Da Silva), the brilliant jack-of-all-trades Philadelphian; and Thomas Jefferson (Ken Howard), the young and idealistic newlywed (to young Blythe Danner) dynamo from Virginia enlisted to draft the Declaration. The film has been criticized as overdrawn and talky, and it certainly rewards patience. But those willing to put the thought and time into "1776" will be entertained and are likely to learn something In the process. Though Hunt's direction Is fairly simple, the film's dialogue and musical numbers are often complex, commenting on the politics of the era, the struggles of trying to unite the 13 colonies and, yes, the sexual prowess of Jefferson and Franklin. The cast members are all game, with Da Silva's likable, ego-driven Franklin a particular standout. And while the score doesn't deliver any truly memorable numbers, it contains several witty, multi-layered tunes. In fact, "Cool Considerate Men," sung by David Madden (as John Dickenson), John Cullum (playing Edward Rutledge), and David Ford (John Hancock) was clipped by Warner because President Richard Nixon thought it was too critical of conservatives. It has been added to the DVD version.

> **... the film remains a surprisingly solid effort ...**

Local Moments:

Except for a few flashbacks and other small moments, the entire film of 1776 takes place in Philly, but its hard to discern the real thing from the reel thing here … Warner had built a full-scale copy of Independence Hall and its environs at the Columbia Ranch … For authenticity, the producers imported bricks from Philly… Oh, well. At least Philadelphians will get the feeling local hero Ben Franklin is cooler than ever thanks to Da Silva's memorable portrayal here.

Rating:

The 13th Child:
Legend of the Jersey Devil (2002)

Local Moments:

Lots of Pine Barrens material means lots of trees, dark woods, dilapidated cabins … Local radio personalities Michael Tearson and Steve Freidman (with a funny dubbed, deep voice) make appearances here … Trenton gets a scene because that's where Down works.

Rating:

Hey, kids. Know what time it is?

It's Jersey Devil time! The legendary Pine Barrens monstrosity is rolled out again in this chintzy horror yarn that appeared in local theaters around Halloween 2002, and promised a sequel, but, as of this date, hasn't delivered on its threat — we mean promise. A surprisingly classy cast has been recruited for the film, which may draw in some serious horror fans. Political official Lesley-Anne Down recruits underling Michelle Maryk to go to the isolated Pine Barrens in hopes of solving the mystery of her father, missing since he went in search of the Jersey Devil 20 years ago. His partner Robert Guillaume survived the incident, but has been relegated to a mental hospital ever since. Spare body parts and slaughtered deer found regularly in South Jersey help light a fire under Maryk to solve the mystery, and with help from "The Blue Lagoon's" Christopher Atkins, she encounters hermit (and Oscar winner) Cliff Robertson, a creepy Devil disciple. Eventually, Maryk and the audience meet the critter, and it looks just like the accounts in the books: body of a kangaroo, jaws of a horse, wings, horns, hoofs, breath in dire need of a gallon of Scope, and "Alien"-like drool. Most of the scenes with the imposing Jersey Devil are in the dark, which is either a budgetary matter or an attempt to make things scary. While the film does have some creepy atmospherics, and it's fun to watch screenwriter-coproducer Robertson chew the scenery, the movie is dreary and slow. Really slow. How slow is it? Glad you asked. Let's out it this way: M. Night Shyamalan's "The Village" feels like it was directed by Michael Bay in comparison.

> **"A surprisingly classy cast has been recruited …"**

The 4th Dimension (2006)

Somewhere between David Lynch,

"The Twilight Zone," and "Pi" lies "The 4th Dimension," an ambitiously stylish sci-fi mystery that had definite cult potential. The film centers on an eccentric genius named Jack (Louis Morabito), who toils with trinkets in the back of an old antique store. One day, he's given a broken vintage watch. At the same time, we meet another Jack (Miles Williams), a young boy whose mother is sick and has what may be an unhealthy obsession with Albert Einstein's theories. We learn eventually that both characters are the same — but do they exist at the same time? And we also discover that adult Jack has Obsessive Compulsive Disorder. What all these seemingly disparate elements have to do with one another remains a hypnotic puzzle shot in black-and-white, until the film's surprising and haunting ending. As first time film directors, local boys Tom Mattera and Dave Mazzoni have done quite well, making a shadowy and often riveting calling card into their dark, surreal world.

> " ... an ambitiously stylish sci-fi mystery that had definite cult potential ... "

Local Moments:

The only film granted permission to shoot in the now-demolished Philadelphia State Hospital (aka "Byberry"), the film offers a creepy look behind closed doors of the facility ... The filmmakers say their locations were inspired by the book "Weird Pennsylvania," so there's lots of offbeat locales here ... Among them: Holmesburg Prison and the shuttered Wycombe Train Station, plus several Bucks County locales.

Rating:

Animal Factory (2000)

The movie was shot almost entirely in Holmesburg Prison on State Road in Philadelphia … Holmesburg was chosen over San Quentin and a prison in Canada after a deal was struck to use convicts from nearby Curran-Fromheld Correctional Facility as extras.

Rating:

Character actor Steve Buscemi's follow-up to his quirky 1996 "Trees Lounge" directorial debut is a solid prison drama than packs an unconventional punch. Edward Furlong plays a young convict sent to the slammer for ten years on a drug-trafficking charge who is befriended by veteran prisoner Willem Dafoe. The two become close friends, as Dafoe mentors Furlong on how to navigate the politics of jail life, where he faces threats on a daily basis. But the viewer is never certain that Dafoe will want for his help, and whether Furlong will survive the violence, threats of rape, and prison guard badgering that surround him. Working with a script cowritten from his own novel by ex-con Edward Bunker (Mr. Blue in Reservoir Dogs), Buscemi, who also helmed an episode of HBO's "Oz," shoots the drama without pretension, keeping the anecdotal proceedings moving at a quick pace. He's helped immeasurably by John Lurie's atmospheric bluesy score and solid work in the acting department across the board, from the reliable Dafoe and believable Furlong in the leads to supporting bits from Danny Trejo (himself an ex-con), Tom Arnold (as a potential rapist), John Heard (as Furlong's ineffectual father), and Mickey Rourke (as a transvestite named Jan the Actress!).

> **But the viewer is never certain that Dafoe will want for his help …**

Philly's Movie Pioneer

Sigmund "Pop" Lubin
was a filmmaking force to be reckoned with around the world in the early stages of the moviemaking industry. Born in Germany (in an area that is now part of Poland), Lubin started his lifelong interest with lenses as an eyeglass maker, opening a store at 237 N. 8th Street, then moving to 21 S. 8th Street where he began experiments that led him into the film industry and developing his own film projector. In the late 1890s, he began producing movies. Among his first efforts were capturing simple demonstrations like a pillow fight between his daughters or a horse eating hay. Then he began restaging historic events for curiosity seekers who attended the peep shows sprouting up throughout the country and, in particular, Philadelphia. Lubin enlisted railroad workers to play the principals in Corbett-Fitzsimmons boxing match, which drew large crowds. He would go on to produce a series dedicated to "A Passion Play" and "The Battle of Gettysburg." And when filming the reenactment of important events wasn't good enough, he'd just take another filmmaker's work — like Georges Melies'"A Trip to the Moon" — rename it (in this case "A Trip to Mars") and put his company's logo (which featured the Liberty Bell) on the front of it. In other situations, Lubin would remake a popular film scene-by-scene. So he did his own version

of Edwin S. Porter's "The Great Train Robbery," which Thomas Edison produced. His version of the story became "The Bold Bank Robbery." Lubin opened studios at 9th and Arch, then Philly's red light district, above The Dime Museum, a place where human oddities were exploited and hoaxes like "The Jersey Devil" were displayed. He built a studio on the rooftop in order to take advantage of the natural sunlight. Later, he opened his main studio at 20th and Indiana, and turned a 500-acre property near Valley Forge into the Betzwood Studios, where he was able to stage elaborate battle scenes and lavish period-based pictures. The thriving company also had production facilities in New Mexico, California, and Florida at one time. At the same time, Lubin was an exhibitor, opening the first theater built just for movies. The idea blossomed out of Philadelphia, and he eventually owned 100 theaters on the East Coast. Throughout his career, Lubin was entangled with Thomas Edison in a patent war that would eventually be settled with Lubin and other companies holding joint rights to making films. The company prospered throughout the early part of the 20th Century, but an explosion in 1914 destroyed almost all of his company's

films, said to be worth $1.5 million. Further bad luck occurred when World War I struck. Many of Lubin's profits were derived from foreign distribution, but he was unable to export films to Europe because of the war. Financial problems prompted Lubin to sell his failing company to the competing Vitagraph, who also bought Selig and Essaney film companies at the same time. Lubin, in ill health and financial hard times, began dabbling with radios and even went back to the optical business. He died in Ventnor in 1924.

Annapolis (2005)

Philly stands in for Maryland as James Franco and Jordana Brewster jog along the Delaware in "Annapolis."
© Buena Vista/The Kobal Collection

What's a movie called "Annapolis" doing in a book about Philadelphia?

The answer is that Philly subbed in several instances for the film's Maryland locales. Unfortunately, this formulaic drama isn't a great showcase for anyone or anything. The story centers on James Franco, a shipbuilder and amateur boxer, who gets accepted to the Naval Academy in Annapolis after pleading with his Congressman to pull some strings. Once there, Franco must prove himself to his disparaging father (Brian Goodman), the Navy recruiter (Donnie Wahlberg) who let him join the swabbies, his fellow crewmates, a tough-as-nails sergeant on loan from the Marines (Tyrese Gibson), and a beautiful upperclassman (Jordana Brewster), who not only becomes his commanding officer but also his romantic interest. Ultimately, Franco wins over all in the boxing ring, when he takes on the hard-ass Gibson. The movie plays out just like its trailer suggests, a dollop of "An Officer and a Gentlemen" spiked with a punch of "Rocky." And although "Annapolis" looks good and features attractive performers, it seems strangely pared down and, ultimately, clichéd.

> **"Ultimately, Franco wins over all in the boxing ring ..."**

Local Moments:

Pennypack Park near Verree Road doubles as a Maryland training spot for the recruit ... The Philadelphia shipyard was used in some scenes as were some piers along Columbus Boulevard ... Because the film wasn't supported by the Navy, several scenes were shot in and around Girard College.

Rating:

Baby, It's You (1982)

No film shot in and around Trenton would be complete without the Lower Trenton Delaware River Bridge with the saying "Trenton Makes — the World Takes," and this film has it … There's a trip to Asbury Park in off-season and other location filming took place in Lawrenceville and Bellville … The now-defunct Roadside Diner in Robbinsville, Mercer County, is featured in a scene.

Rating:

John Sayles' first — and, possibly, last — directing job for a major studio is a romantic dramedy with lots of memorable moments, interesting characters ,and frustrating moments. The story centers on Jill Rosen (Rosanna Arquette), a Jewish middle-class high school student, romanced by a fellow nicknamed Sheik (Vincent Spano), an Italian slickster with an affection for Sinatra. Throughout the last few years of high school in Trenton, Sheik shows his rebellious side by bucking teachers, his working class parents, and her friends in trying to win over Jill. His pursuit leads to the revelation that he is, in fact, in love with Jill, and she with him — but not in "that kind of way." Post high school, they go their separate ways: He to Miami to make it as a lounge singer, she to Sarah Lawrence College to study acting, but they occasionally stay in touch, hoping to figure out if their attraction is worth pursuing further. The chemistry between the two lead performers is genuine, especially in the earlier stages of the film set in high school. The film takes some odd turns in its second half, as Jill moves into a free love stage and tries to find herself, but Sheik stays the same, steadfastly believing the three most important people in his life are "Jesus Christ, Frank Sinatra, and me." And the script, written by Sayles and producer Amy Robinson, who attended high school in Trenton, remains affecting and realistic until the film's upbeat fade-out, which seems tacked on. (Studio interference, perhaps?) A supporting cast that includes early roles for Matthew Modine, Robert Downey, Jr., Tracy Pollan, and Fisher Stevens and a first-rate soundtrack that mixes period greats like "Woolly Bully" and "Baby Love," Sinatra standards, and a bunch of Springsteen cuts help make "Baby, It's You" an ambitious and winning — but imperfect — film.

> " … **interesting characters and frustrating moments.** "

Birdy (1984)

The award-winning book by William Wharton
set during World War II is updated to the Vietnam War era in Alan Parker's unsettling adaptation. West Philadelphia friends Al (Nicolas Cage) and feathered-friend-obsessed Birdy (Matthew Modine) are sent to Nam where both are wounded: Al returns with his face blasted and in bandages while the already eccentric Birdy has moved into a catatonic state. Al is called on to try to draw his pal out of his private world and, hopefully, out of the hospital. He also wishes that through therapy-like sessions with

> **"The acting by Cage and Modine is superior ..."**

Birdy, he'll be able to deal with his own traumatic experiences. During the sessions, the men revisit their past, confront the horrors they faced in war, and attempt to rekindle their friendship. Director Alan Parker ("Angel Heart," "Jacob's Ladder") is not known for his soft side, but he handles the relationship with surprising sensitive, aided by its compelling male bonding story line. The acting by Cage and Modine is superior, and cinematographer Michael Seresin captures Philly with both a nostalgic glow and grubbiness. The film is no easy sit, however, as Birdy and Al delve into their fears, anxieties and depressions, and take the audiences with them. In the end, however, "Birdy" is a flight worth taking.

Local Moments:

Birdy and Al chase pigeons along the 63rd Street El stop ... There are scenes shot along Parkside Avenue and near the West Philly studio where "American Bandstand" was shot, at 46th and Market Streets ... The gym at Woodrow Wilson Jr. High School in Northeast Philly is featured ... An old PCC trolley is seen in two scenes: early on, it's on Luzerne Street, and later at Old York and Pike Street.

Rating:

The Blob (1958)

Local Moments:

The famous scene at the movie theater was shot at the still-operating retro theater, the Colonial, located in Phoenixville, the site of the annual "BlobFest" celebration … After the movie, the space organism makes way for the Downingtown Diner, which has since been replaced by Chef' diner in Downingtown. The location is actually miles away from the movie theater … The school where the fire extinguishers are found to freeze the Blob is Phoenixville's Samuel K. Barklay School … Jerry's Market, a supermarket where the Blob visits, became a Drug Emporium, then morphed into Sly Fox Brewery and Eatery … For more details on "The Blob," we suggest checking out the *www.theblobsite.filmbuffonline.com* website.

Rating:

A chintzy but effective sci-fier,

"The Blob" was a huge success on a small $250,000 budget because it so effectively mixes cheap thrills and teenage angst. Steve McQueen's career was launched playing Steve Andrews, a teenager who tries to save his small Pennsylvania town — and possibly the world — of an icky, interstellar protoplasm that keeps growing bigger and bigger. The goo comes from outer space, whizzing over the head of Steve and girlfriend Jane (Aneta Corsaut, aka Helen Crump of "The Andy Griffith Show"), eventually landing near an old-timer whose flesh begins to disintegrate into an ugly skin condition even Desitin can't cure. Steve takes the poor guy to the local doctor, but the goo doesn't even spare the kindly medic or his faithful nurse. Eventually, the alien gook terrorizes an audience at a packed movie theater showing "Daughter of Horror" (narrated by Ed McMahon). Steve must stop it, but how?! The Blob itself isn't really scary — it looks a melting, pulsating superball, but when spiked with trouble-making kids bucking the local fuzz by racing their cars, a frenzied audience running from a movie theater, and a handsome young 28-year-old star-to-be playing a levelheaded teen hero it doesn't really matter. Proof is in the pulsating pudding: Producer Jack H. Harris has squeezed big bucks out of the film, oversaw an oddball 1972 parody sequel (directed by Larry Hagman), had it remade in 1988, and is eyeing another reworking in the future. Beware of the Blob indeed!

> " … a huge success on a small $250,000 budget … "

Philly on TV

Philadelphia has had an enduring spot in TV Land as well as in the movies. Here are some prominent TV shows shot and/or set in and around the City of Brotherly Love

TV SERIES

"Action in the Afternoon" (1953)
Western adventure and singing cowboys from WCAU studios on City Line.

"Amen" (1986-1991)
with Sherman Hemsley as a North Philly deacon, produced by Johnny Carson.

"American Bandstand" (1952-1964)
"The Philly Years."

"American Dreams" (2002-2005)
Produced by Dick Clark.

"Angie" (1979)
Donna Pescow as a waitress.

"Atom Squad" (1953-1954)
Fifteen minute sci-fi show for kids.

"Big Top" (aka "Sealtest Big Top") (1950-1957)
The best circus act performed in Camden, then Philly, for ringmaster Robert Sterling and clown Ed McMahon. Hi-yo!

"Boy Meets World" (1993-2000)
Kid grows into man, first on ABC, then the ABC Family Channel.

"Brothers" (1984-1987)
Groundbreaking Showtime series in which one sibling is a former Eagles placekicker, another is gay.

"Chelsea D.H.O." (1973)
Frank Converse is a sensitive district health official.

"Cold Case" (2003 —)
Philly detectives investigate unsolved crimes.

"Dance Party USA" (1986-1992)
Cable dance-show sporting Kelly Ripa as a regular and Frank Stallone and Dave "Phillie Phanatic" Raymond on occasion.

"Diver Dan" (1961)
Underwater adventures with scuba expert and fish with moving lips.

"Double Dare" (1986-2003)
Nickelodeon kids chase show shot at WHYY.

"Extreme Championship Wrestling" (1997-2001)
Live…from Soth Philly…and they bleed!

"Fat Albert and the Cosby Kids" (1972-1984)
Bill Cosby's animated childhood adventures.

"Finders Keepers" (1987-1989)
Children's scavenger hunt on Nickelodeon with Harvey and Joe Conklin announcing.

"Hack" (2002-2004)
David Morse as ex-cop-turned-cabbie.

"It's Always Sunny on Philadelphia" (2005 —)
Raucous comedy set in Philly bar.

"Meet Me at the Zoo" (1953)
Featuring The Philadelphia Zoo and its inhabitants.

"Miss Susan" (1951)
Paralyzed actress Susan Peters plays handicapped lawyer.

"The Mike Douglas Show" (1965-1978)
Our version of Merv Griffin that helped make Philly a celebrity stop.

"Philly" (2001-2002)
Kim Delaney as single mother lawyer in Philly firm; Steve Bochco produced.

"The Real World: Philadelphia" (2004)
Live – from third and Arch! 'nuff said.

"Ryan Caulfield: Year One" (1999)
Short-lived saga about rookie Philly cop.

"Starstuff" (1980)
WCAU-produced kid show in which kid uses a computer to see into the future.

"Strong Medicine" (2000-2006)
Lifetime series set in a woman's health center with Janine Turner and Patricia Richardson, produced by and sometimes featuring Whoopi Goldberg.

"thirtysomething" (1987-1991)
Incisive drama or weepy whiners?

"The Tony Randall show" (1976-1978)
Tony Randall is a family court judge.

"Trading Spaces" (2000 —)
Hit Learning Channel show has competing families remodel each other's homes.

"TV Teen Club" (1949-1954) "Bandstand" precursor hosted by bandleader Paul Whiteman.

"What in the World" (1951-1965)
College profs discuss art with a panel of experts.

"You Bet Your Life" (1991)
Say the secret word and Bill Cosby hosts this misfire based on the Groucho Marx quiz show.

TV MOVIES

Benjamin Franklin (1974)
Innovative miniseries consisting of different plays in which Ben is played by different actors. Among those who play him: Willie Aames (at age 12), Beau Bridges, Lloyd Bridges, Eddie Albert, Melvyn Douglas, and Richard Widmark.

Echoes in the Darknness (1987)
Top-notch chronicle of the William Bradfield-Susan Reinert-Jay Smith case, based on Joseph Wambaugh's book. The cast includes Peter Coyote, Stockard Channing, Robert Loggia, and Peter Boyle.

Flying Blind (1990)
Coming-of-age drama with Richard Panebianco, Maura Tierney, and Emily Longstreth includes scenes shot on the Frankford El.

The Garbage Picking Field Goal Kicking Philadelphia Phenomenon (1998)
Tony Danza is a garbageman recruited by the Eagles to kick field goals after he proves he's got strong legs developed on his job. Jeff Lurie plays Danza's pal.

George Washington (1984)
Fine miniseries with Barry Bostwick doing the time warp as the father of our country, and an all-star cast that includes Patty Duke (as Martha Washington) and Hal Holbrook (as John Adams) partaking in the Philly location shooting.

Gia (1998)
The sad but true tale of Gia Caragni, the Philadelphia superstar model who became of one America's top posers, but died of AIDS at the age of 26 after years of drug abuse. Angelina Jolie garnered lots of attention and a Golden Globe Award for her lead performance in this HBO production.

The Hunt for the Unicorn Killer (1999)
The story Ira Einhorn, Philly's least-favorite fugitive, and search to find him. That's Naomi Watts as Holly Maddux, Gregory Itzin as Arlen Spector, and local writer Bruce Graham adapting ex-*Philly Mag* staffer Steven Levy's book.

Blow Out (1981)

Like a mad scientist in an old Boris Karloff movie, Brian De Palma mixes the premises of Michelangelo Antonioni's 1966 arthouse puzzler "Blow Up" and Francis Ford Coppola's 1974 paranoid masterpiece "The Conversation" with a dose of Watergate conspiracy, a healthy sprinkling of cynicism, and images reminiscent of the Ted Kennedy Chappaquiddick incident to make one helluva Frankenstein thriller. The film offers John Travolta in his first adult role, playing a soundman working on low-budget horror movies who can't get the proper scream for his new project. He heads out to the Wissahickon one night to record natural sounds, but witnesses a car accident and rescues the woman in the car, but is unable to save the driver. It turns out that it's Nancy Allen (De Palma's wife at the time), a prostitute, and the dead driver was the governor of Pennsylvania who happened to be a presidential candidate. Meanwhile, sleazy photographer Dennis Franz was on the scene to shoot pictures. Travolta sniffs

> **" The film offers John Travolta in his first adult role ... "**

a conspiracy and attempts to discover what really happened by piecing the sounds together that he has recorded. Of course, this opens a Pandora's Box of suspicion, fear, and murder, leading to the uncovering of a Watergate-type coverup and conspiracies reminiscent of the JFK assassination. Add all this to a subplot involving a serial murderer loose in Philly and an impending "Liberty Day" celebration, and it's whole lot of stuff for a movie — and audience — to handle. But De Palma, who also wrote the complex script, does a masterful job, getting the most out the stunning cinematography by the great Vilmos Zsigmund, his actors (this could be Travolta's and Allen's best performances), and cutting and pasting the integral elements together in a way that's sharp, fresh, and nasty. When it comes to mad doctors of the movies, Brian De Palma proves himself a diabolical genius with "Blow Out."

Local Moments:

The movie is filled with some of Philly's finest screen moments … Travolta's production office is above the Apollo Theater, located near City Hall on East Market Street … City Hall, Independence National Historic Park, the Liberty Bell and Wanamaker's Department Store get screen time … Mummers were recruited to partake in the fictitious "Liberty Day" parade festivities … The Delaware Riverfront near the Port of History building is shown near the film's finale … The Wissahickon Bridge is the scene of the car accident, but the water-based shooting had to be done at a tank in Burbank because the river was too shallow … WPVI weather caster Dave Roberts, "AM Philadelphia" host Claire Carter, TV announcer Sid Doherty, disc jockey Michael Tearson and local character actor Tom McCarthy all get screen time … The producers were local products Fred Caruso and George Litto.

Rating:

The Burglar (1957)

A crackerjack crime thriller that came relatively late in the film noir cycle that permeated the 40s and 50s, "The Burglar" is a great Philly film that relatively few people have seen. The story begins "Citizen Kane"-like with newsreel footage centering on the death of an industrialist who left his Philadelphia estate to phony psychic Sister Sara (Phoebe Mackay). Turns out Sister Sara has also inherited some priceless jewelry in the deal, too, and it's much desired by a gang comprised of master criminal Nat (Dan Duryea), gem expert Blaylock (Peter Capell), grotesque enforcer Dohmer (nightclub entertainer Mickey Shaughnessy), and comely blonde Gladden (Bryn Mawr's attention-getting Jayne Mansfield), who cases the estate for the crew. The crooks pull off the heist of a diamond necklace, but a series of bizarre incidents, a crooked cop (Stewart Bradley) , and a femme fatale (Martha Vickers) lead to a showdown in Atlantic City amidst the Steel Pier, the Boardwalk, and a funhouse. "The Burglar" seems complicated on paper, and it's filled with nifty twists and turns, but it remains relatively easy to follow. The first film of local filmmaker Paul Wendkos, Philly-native producer Louis Kellman, and Delaware Valley noir specialist author-screenwriter David Goodis ("Dark Passage") plays against expectations, too, offering good guys who aren't so good and Duryea's gang leader who is both loyal and sensitive. "The Burglar" is striking, salt-of-the-earth Philly stuff if you can find it.

> **" … and it's filled with nifty twists and turns … "**

NOTE: Though filmed independently, "The Burglar" was sold to Columbia Pictures. It has shown regularly at repertory theaters around the country, but has never seen a DVD release. It is available from a few web sources on VHS.

The Buried Secret of M. Night Shyamalan

(2004)

Two of Philly's most notable filmmakers

collaborated on this film that turns out to be an impressively put together but unmitigated disaster. On paper, the project concerns Nathaniel Kahn, director of the brilliant "My Architect: A Son's Journey," who is enlisted by the Sci-Fi Channel to make a documentary about M. Night Shyamalan, the Philly area auteur of "The Sixth Sense." Kahn heads to Chester County with his crew where Night is shooting "The Village," his latest supernatural opus. But Kahn is given limited access to the director, and goes off the map supplied by a publicist in terms of what he can ask his subject and who he can talk to. He soon learns that M. Night Shyamalan is, in fact, connected to "the other side" and that eerie things occur whenever Night is involved. Now, for the unmitigated disaster part: The feature length documentary is bogus, a hoax, a publicity stunt to hype Night and "The Village" a week before Disney released it in the summer

> " ... M. Night Shyamalan is an otherworldly presence ... "

of 2004. The Sci-Fi Channel came clean about the phony nature of the proceedings a few days before it aired in hopes of doing some damage control. It didn't work. "The Village" turned out to get generally negative reviews and disappointing box-office results. That said, the documentary is well put together, and interesting to watch. Along with real-life appearances by the likes of Deepak Chopra, Johnny Depp, and Adrien Brody, who co-stars in the "The Village," actors were recruited to play purported real people like a cloying publicist and a kid who gave Kahn a creepy Ouija board demonstration. Of course, this didn't help at all to perpetuate the notion that M. Night Shyamalan is an otherworldly presence with connections to a higher consciousness. It did prove, however, that Night has a lot of P.T. Barnum in him, but in this case, not many suckers were buying what he and Kahn were selling. Why the talented and reputable Kahn got involved in this fiasco remains the biggest mystery surrounding this film.

Local Moments:

Along with the location footage of "The Village" in Chester County, there's lots of downtown Philly stuff … City Hall figures prominently … Kahn and Night limo to South Street, eat cheesesteaks at Jim's, and hit a pool hall where Night is asked to sign autographs for eager women … Film commish Sharon Pinkenson and Mayor John Street catch some screen time … A stop at TLA Video allows some its employees to pontificate about M. Night.

Rating:

Clean and Sober (1988)

Rating:

While it won't make anyone forget "The Lost Weekend," "The Man with the Golden Arm," or even "Trainspotting," the surprisingly gritty and intelligent take on addiction is effective and, thanks to star Michael Keaton's self-effacing humor, surprisingly light on its feet. Keaton is the lost-soul realtor whose life has gone to a drug stronger than pot — cocaine to be precise. He's on the skids with a fellow addict found dead in his bed and $92,000 in hock for money he embezzled from a business account. In order to save himself, he enlists in a Philadelphia Alcoholics Anonymous center where he meets the likes of no-nonsense Morgan Freeman, AA sponsor M. Emmet Walsh, and abused addict Kathy Baker, with whom he gets romantically involved. The blueprint of the film isn't much different from addiction movies of the past — will he or won't he stay on the wagon? — but the odd coupling of director Glenn Gordon Caron ("Moonlighting") and screenwriter Todd Caroll (a "National Lampoon" alumnus) brings dark humor and gravitas to the proceedings, and manages to make most of the film fresh. Of course, it's Keaton's show and here for the first time, he shows us his darker side on-screen. Perhaps this is the film that persuaded Tim Burton to cast him as the caped crusader in the Batman films.

> " ... surprisingly gritty and intelligent take on addiction is effective ... "

Condition Red (1976)

It's been shown in the past that foreign directors often have good insight in American ways, so it should come as little surprise that Finnish director Mika Kaurismaki (brother of the more famous Aki Kaurismaki) has found success with this gritty prison picture. James Russo plays Dan Cappelli, a prison guard at Holmesburg Prison, who lands in the female block of the facility after getting in trouble for his violent tendencies on the men's side. The short-fused Cappelli has a fiery, verboten affair with inmate Gidell (Cynda Williams), a singer with a scary boyfriend named Angel (Paul Calderon) for whom she's taken the rap. When Gidell tells Dan that she's pregnant, he tries to spring her from the big house, but his plans add even more problems to his life. Stylishly shot and consistently downbeat, "Condition Red" is an appropriately gritty drama that gets more intense as it goes along. The acting is uniformly fine, especially from its three leads. Surprisingly direct and often squirm-inducing because of its depiction of prison life, "Condition Red" is well worth seeking out.

> **"Finnish director Mika Kaurismaki has found success with this gritty prison picture."**

Local Moments:

Great use of made of Holmesburg Prison, from its grungy yards to its striking octopus-like design and its harrowing interior … Cappelli lives in South Philly although we never see him commute to the Northeast Philly prison.

Rating:

Philadelphia (1993)
Joe Miller (Denzel Washington): We're standing here in Philadelphia, the, uh, city of brotherly love, the birthplace of freedom, where the, uh, founding fathers authored the Declaration of Independence, and I don't recall that glorious document saying anything about all straight men are created equal. I believe it says all men are created equal.

Susan Seidelman: Huntington Valley's Hip Shooter

Susan Seidelman was born on Kerper Street in Northeast Philly, but raised mostly in Huntington Valley, where she attended Abington High School. At Drexel University, she studied fashion design, but her interest in filmmaking led her to New York University where she enrolled in the NYU film school.

Seidelman's first feature was 1982's "Smithereens," centering on the exploits of a young girl from Jersey trying to make it in the punk world of Greenwich Village. The film was accepted at the Cannes Film Festival, and its indie success led to 1985's "Desperately Seeking Susan," the hip comedy with Rosanna Arquette as a neglected North Jersey housewife who gets amnesia and mixes identities with downtown gal Madonna. The film was a big success, leading Seidelman to "Making Mr. Right" (1987), "Cookie" (1989), and "She-Devil" (1989), a big-budget pairing of Meryl Streep and Roseanne Barr.

Since the studio films, Seidelman has been busy making movies for cable TV and has helmed early episodes of "Sex in the City." Her latest feature is "The Boynton Beach Club," a comedy about seniors in a Florida retirement community. It was hatched from an idea by her mother Florence.

"My mom lives in Boynton Beach and I have been making films for 20 years," says Seidelman. "My mother has always been approaching me with ideas. Some of the ideas were interesting, but not right for me, or I was busy.

"About two years ago, she told me about single seniors who were back in the dating game in this community that had a lot of single seniors — you know, they were widowed or divorced or they never married. They were looking for companionship, love, romance, sex, friendship."

Seidelman says that "a light bulb went off" when her mother told her the film's premise. And she realized "the front end of the baby boomer generation was hitting sixty. The idea of what it's like to be older needs to be changed and the way we see that in movies needs to change."

"There was something in those 100 pages that were really authentic," says Seidelman. "She knew these characters. She knew who they were and their voices. There were these wonderful details that I would not have known not having lived in Boynton Beach and being that age. Suddenly, when I read it I realized what this movie could be."

The movie was eventually made with an ensemble cast that includes Dyan Cannon, Brenda Vaccaro, Joseph Bologna, Sally Kellerman, Michael Nori, and Len Cariou.

Does Seidelman think it's unusual that she's gone from chronicling young, hip characters in "Smithereens" and "Desperately Seeking Susan" to senior citizens in "The Boynton Beach Club"?

"The one thing that I tried to do is be ahead of the game," says Seidelman. " 'Smithereeens' was one of the first, new-wave punk things about New York. I didn't think I was joining the bandwagon, but I thought it was one of the first to talk about that subject. The same with 'Desperately Seeking Susan.' It was an early film about downtown Manhattan … Madonna gal pal. The same with 'Sex and the City'. So I kind of felt like I found something new with 'Boynton Beach Club,' the idea of seniors and sex with seniors because nobody's talking about them."

David and Lisa (1962)

Local Moments:

The film was shot on the Main Line with the Isaac Clothier Estate in Wynnwood serving as the institute where David and Lisa meet and reside … To flee the hospital after an argument with David, Lisa hops a local train from the Wynnwood Train Station that takes her into a bustling nighttime Chestnut Street in Center City … David, Lisa, and other patients visit the Art Museum and the final poetic scene takes place on the museum's steps.

Rating:

Frank Perry and screenwriter wife Eleanor Perry's adaptation of Dr. Theodore Isaac Rubin's book is a fondly remembered drama about two distant, emotionally troubled people who eventually find each other. Keir Dullea plays David, a smart 16-year-old brought to an austere mental institution on the Main Line because of his fears of being touched by others. He's cared for by the understanding Dr. Swinford (Howard Da Silva), who attempts to get to the bottom of David's psychosis. One of the other patients at the institution is Lisa (Janet Margolin), a teenage girl with multiple personalities, who speaks only in rhyme. The two teens form a bond that seems to be helpful to both, but an incident sends Lisa AWOL to downtown Philly, which she unprepared to deal with. Shot for under $200,000 in stark black and white with heavy use of extreme angled shots, "David and Lisa" often resembles a film noir. But director Perry gets maximum impact from his edgy style despite the threadbare budget and delivers a memorable film that manages to be haunting and lyrical at the same time. It's also bolstered by attention-getting performances from its three principals: Dullea, who was 26 when he played the teenage part, is appropriately jerky-jerky as the tormented David; Margolin uses her expressive saucer eyes to hint at the turmoil going on behind her innocence; and Da Silva scores waves of warmth as the diligent doctor. "David and Lisa" was a breakthrough film for both its sensitive depiction of mental health problems and its financial record, bringing in over $1 million on a miniscule budget.

> **"a breakthrough film for both its sensitive depiction of mental health problems …"**

Dead Poet's Society (1989)

Manic Robin Williams turns down his shtick a few notches and notched an Oscar nomination for his efforts, portraying John Keating, an English professor at a New England prep school in the 1950s. The iconoclastic Keating is a poetry and Shakespeare specialist, and in order to connect to his male students he tells them to *Carpe diem* or "seize the day," and get the most out of life. They're encouraged to use Keating's lessons in their own lives, and they bond together to form a secret society known as — you've guessed it! — the Dead Poet's Society. The students Keating affects are played by such young up-and-coming actors as Ethan Hawke, Josh Charles, and Robert Sean Leonard, a Wilmington native. Directed by Peter Weir ("Witness") from an Oscar-winning script by Tom Schulman, "Dead Poet's Society" is a handsomely crafted, well-meaning film

> **" ... the focus falls on his students and their predicaments ... "**

that, frankly, doesn't spark the same interest in its audience in that way Keating ignites in his students. Actually, Williams' Keating has sparse screen time, and the focus falls on his students and their predicaments, none of which are all that interesting. And the meeting of the secret society appear to be little more than poetry readings and bulls**t sessions among its so-called enlightened members. In other words, it's "The View" with preppy guys.

Local Moments:

Standing in for the Vermont school is St. Andrew's School on Noxongtown Pond Road in Middletown, Delaware ... The scene featuring a play was shot at Middletown's Everett Theater ... Location work was also done in Rockland and New Castle.

Rating:

The Demo Crew (2002)

You've got to admire the chutzpah of John E. Vitali who maxed out 22 credit cards and put his house up against the budget of his dream project. Sometimes, these stories work out — remember Robert Townsend's "Hollywood Shuffle"? — and sometimes they don't. Unfortunately, "The Demo Crew" has flown under the radar since it was completed and hasn't worked out as Vitali had planned. Certainly, it's not for lack of effort or even talent. Vitali, a local actor and comedian, wrote, directed, and stars in this tale set against the backdrop of "dek hockey"— or "street hockey" to the people in my neighborhood. He plays Anthony, the main man of a group of childhood friends from Catholic school who find their lives slipping aimlessly away. One night they go out and have their kind of fun, knocking over street signs and smashing doors off of cars. They're arrested, but luckily they also help save someone getting beat up by a gang, so their given a reprieve in lieu of jail time. The veteran cop (Tony Devon) okays the proposition that Anthony and his pals form a hockey team and play together in hopes they learn something and straighten out their lives. Their team initially stinks, but gets better as time goes on, then an accident occurs leaving the fate of one of the players — and the team — in the air. "The Demo Crew" should be commended for its earthy Philly atty-tude and "Rocky"-esque inspiration. You can tell it was shot on pennies with friends and mostly amateur actors, but in this case, rawness helps. Hockey fans especially will enjoy the game sequences and others should be able to get into the human element here as well. This is "Rocky" hockey, and we mean that in a good way.

> **"The Demo Crew should be commended for its earthy Philly atty-tude ..."**

Disk-O-Tek Holiday

(1964/1966)

This musical oddity is a real lark that follows an aspiring teen-idol singer (Casey Paton) around the country in search of getting his big break on radio. Along with his girlfriend (Katherine Quint), Casey tries to push his single "East is East" on a number of Top 40 disc jockeys of the time. One of the stops the duo make is Philly, where they meet none other than legendary DJ Hy Lit. The plot seems to exist to show off a series of pre-MTV promotional music videos featuring the likes of Freddie and the Dreamers, Peter and Gordon, The Merseybeats, The Bachelors, and others. If the film appears put together with Scotch tape and a chainsaw, it's because it probably was. Originally a British production made to highlight British Invasion acts, it was Americanized by adding footage of the American groups and disc jockeys. A very weird but very enjoyable musical time capsule excursion indeed!

> **"A very weird but enjoyable musical time capsule excursion in deed! ..."**

Local Moments:

We catch some sights and sounds of Philly with a stroll through Center City and location footage of Independence Hall ... Hy Lit does his "Hyski O'Rooney McVoutie O'Zoot", shtick at the WIBG studios.

Rating:

Downtown (1990)

Philadelphia and the western suburbs get lots of screen time here … Location scouts in North Philly must've picked out the worst streets they could find, giving areas of Diamond Street an ominous screen presence with graffiti, burned-out buildings, and trash all over the place … Conversely, Bryn Mawr and other Main Line locations sparkle … How did they film that wild chase scene on I-76 near the airport? … Lots of footage was shot near the Delaware where some of the illegal car maneuvering takes place … A good line — Whitaker to Edwards: "Where were you born? Alaska?" Edwards' reply: "Haverford."

Rating:

If you know anything about the way the police in the Philadelphia operate,

you will immediately dismiss this film as being bogus. Now, get over the fact that Philadelphia shares the same police force as Bryn Mawr — that Philly and its nearby suburbs all operate as one central law enforcement entity, like Los Angeles — then maybe, just maybe you'll enjoy this buddy cop comedy spiked with drama that's cut from the same 1980s cloth as "Running Scared," "48 Hours," or "Beverly Hills Cop." Here, Anthony Edwards of "ER" does his best Judge Reinhold impersonation playing a milquetoast cop in the cushy suburbs who gets transferred to the Diamond Street Police District — or "Downtown" as the film's title implies — after he stops David Clennon, a close friend of the police department, on a moving violation. Once downtown, Edwards encounters a crime-ridden precinct in which he's not cut out to uphold the law — even his prized, lime green Volkswagon convertible is stripped by hoods when it's parked in front of the police station. Of course, the laid-back Edwards is soon teamed with a partner who is his opposite: Hard-nosed, no-nonsense plainclothes vet Forest Whitaker. And soon they're on a case involving a car theft ring whose participants are linked to both Edwards' former Bryn Mawr stomping ground and Whitaker's North Philly beat. There's nothing new or surprising here, and the mix of the serious (a cop is killed, urban blight is all over the place) and silly (Edwards' fondness for Beach Boys music is adopted by Whitaker's family and neighbors) is uneasy at times, but the film remains fairly diverting throughout, with some exciting car chases and easy-going direction by Richard Benjamin.

> **… just maybe you'll enjoy this buddy cop comedy spiked with drama …**

Eddie and the Cruisers
(1983)

Raised from the theatrical ashes by a burgeoning cable and video rental market,

this ode to Jersey bar rock has garnered an astonishing following over the years, and helped make Michael Pare a star in the mid 1980s. The story concerns Eddie Wilson (Paré), a rocker who leads a South Philly band called the Cruisers. After a hit album, Eddie has an accident on a bridge in 1964 and vanishes into thin air, leaving a legacy of unfulfilled promise as well as a tape of a new, more sophisticated album, that will also disappear after the accident.

> **"... this ode to Jersey bar rock has garnered an astonishing following over the years ..."**

Eighteen years later, magazine writer Maggie Foley (a brown-haired Ellen Barkin) wants to get to the bottom of the story. She corners Drank Ridgway (Tom Berenger), the Cruisers' piano player and lyricist, now working as a school teacher. Frank doesn't want to be bothered at first, but eventually he revisits his past by meeting up with Sal Amato (Matthew Laurance), another ex-band member. A possible reunion and the fate of those missing tapes are discussed, much to the reporter's delight. The music from South Jersey's John Cafferty and the Beaver Brown Band smacks of Springsteen, down to the Clarence Clemons-inspired sax solos, and even the tinkling incidental music will remind Bruce fans of Roy Bittan's work on the "Born to Run" LP. Pacing is "Eddie and the Cruisers" biggest problem, as writer-director Martin Davidson ("The Lords of Flatbush") has problems mixing the procedural "contemporary" scenes with Berenger and Barkin and the more energized period stuff. The film is helped immeasurably by Paré's brooding South Philly rocker. Inspired by both Jim Morrison and Elvis, Pare has lots of South Philly swagger, and an air of mystery that helps fuel the plot's intrigue about his disappearance.

Local Moments:

Tony Mart's, a well-remembered defunct nightclub in Somers Point where Bob Dylan reportedly saw The Band play for the first time, is the location for several concert scenes ... Ocean City serves as the site for a flashback to the early 1960s ... Eddie and the Cruisers play a gig at preppy Haverford College on Lancaster Avenue ... Mount Holy, Vineland, and Atco also get scenes in the film, and Ocean City is the location for the boardwalk and beach sequences.

Rating:

Eddie and the Cruisers II: Eddie Lives! (1989)

Local Moments:

Not much real location stuff although a jam session with blues great Bo Diddley supposedly takes place in Lakehurst, NJ … A quick trip to the Boardwalk, this time it's Asbury Park near the Stone Pony for its one new Jersey shore scene.

Rating:

Hey, what's with all these French names in the opening credits?

And I'm not talking about Michael Paré either! Seems that Eddie Wilson really does live — he's relocated to Canada for this six-years-later sequel, inspired, no doubt, by the original's video and cable popularity. We're reminded right from the start that Eddie has, in fact, survived the supposedly fatal car crash of the first film, and is alive and well and working as a construction worker in Montreal. The Jersey boy has gone Canuck — big time! Taking the monicker "Joe West," he's grown a mustache and even attends Montreal Canadiens playoff games and drinks beer! Well, those long lost tapes of his last album, "Season in Hell," have been found and released to amazing success. Eddie and the Cruisers rock once again on the charts and on the radio, so the real Eddie decides to join another group of musicians to get back into the music scene. Amazingly, people don't recognize him until his mustache gets clipped and he plays a gig at a big rock festival in Montreal. The rabid fans of the first "Eddie and the Cruisers" film seem to really hate this outing. Without key performers (and characters played by Tom Berenger, Ellen Barkin, and Helen Schneider from the original), this looks, feels, and smells like a rip-off. But at least it's a tackily enjoyable one, foiled with illogical events and situations. For example, how can a Freddie Mercury-style 1980s mustache camouflage Eddie Wilson beyond recognition? It's also funny how rotten the more dour-than-ever Eddie treats his new band mates. And enough of that "Dark Side" song already. We get the picture: He sounds just like Springsteen — only, he's from Canada now, eh?

> " … this looks, feels, and smells like a ripoff … "

Michael Paré Talks "Eddie and the Cruisers"

Through some strange coincidence, Michael Paré's career is linked to Philadelphia. Two of the films that the prolific Brooklyn-born actor made early in his career were set in and around Philly: 1983's "Eddie and the Cruisers," in which he plays a rock star who has vanished from public life after a car accident, and 1984's "The Philadelphia Experiment," a science-fiction film that finds him as one of two sailors from the World War II era who are transported to modern times because of a time warp. In addition, Paré appeared in 1989's sequel "Eddie and the Cruisers II: Eddie Lives!"

Q. Since the music of "Eddie and the Cruisers" sounds like Bruce Springsteen, did you model the character Eddie Wilson on "The Boss"?

A. Not really. The two people I was thinking of Jim Morrison and Elvis Presley. I wanted to get some of Morrison's mystery in Eddie and some of Presley's showmanship, too. John Cafferty and the Beaver Brown Band did the music, but that wasn't decided on until we were into production on the film. Kenny Vance was the guy who helped me, and director Martin Donovan was into the music. You know, Kenny was with Jay and the Americans, and produced lots of big groups. And some of the songs in the film were around years before the movie.

Q. What do you remember about making "Eddie and the Cruisers" in the area?

A. We were staying at the Rickshaw Inn in Cherry Hill for weeks. I can tell you that if you watch the film closely enough you'll see me and Ellen [Barkin] and Tom [Berenger] scratching ourselves once in a while because the place was overrun by lice. It was awful! But we stayed there and commuted all over the place — the Jersey shore, the Main Line, wherever we were shooting.

Q. How about "Eddie and the Cruisers II: Eddie Lives!"? Most of that was set in Canada.

A. That movie sucked. My agent at the time signed me up for it before I read the script. Most of it was shot in Canada — maybe there was a day or two at the Jersey Shore. The director didn't know what he was doing and never staged musical numbers before. He couldn't speak English. And he was having this thing with the lead actress. He would get all of these cranes and elaborate pieces of equipment and lighting people for a concert scene, then use them to get better shots of the actress.

Q. Ever think of doing another "Eddie and the Cruisers" movie?

A. There has been talk over the years, but it hasn't happned. I thought of a reality show, though, where me and a producer go around the country and audition the best bar bands. The winner of the contest would get on TV and a recording contract. We've pitched it to companies. Who knows? I think it's a good idea.

Fallen (1998)

Best described as "Silence of the Lambs" meets "The Hidden," "Fallen" delivers the promised chills by mixing police suspense conventions with supernatural thriller scares. Released in the wake of "Se7en," the film stars Denzel Washington as a Philly cop on the trail of a killer who has taken on the same idiosyncrasies of a murderer recently put to death in the gas chamber. As bodies pile up, Washington and his big galoot partner John Goodman discover that a demonic fallen angel is the culprit and his spirit is willing to continue his crimes and implicate Washington in the process. Working with Nicholas Kazan's inventive script, which begins "Memento"-style at the end of the story, director Gregory Hoblit ("Primal Fear") makes the most out of his Philly locations, accenting the dark

> **" ... delivers the promised chills by mixing police suspense conventions with supernatural thriller scares. "**

and mysterious locations of the city that appear striking and quite unsettling at night. It's no surprise that Washington delivers a fine performance as the confident cop who eventually becomes unnerved by the increasingly creepy situation. The game supporting cast includes a pre-"Sopranos" James Gandolfini as a fellow cop and Embeth Davidtz as a theology student. Using the Rolling Stones song "Time is My Side" as its theme, "Fallen" works as a nightmare for hypochondriacs: It's a paranoiac allegory about AIDS that shows how even casual rubbing against another person can be an awfully fatal distraction.

Local Moments:

Eastern State Penitentiary is the prison where protestors try to stop the gas chamber death of killer Edgar Reese ... The City Hall courtyard gets a cameo ... Local newscasters Steve Highsmith, Elleanor Jean Hendley, Byron Scott, Pat Ciarrocchi, and Kent Manahan make appearances ... Director Sal Mazotta ("Mafioso: The Father, The Son") turns up in a scene ... Local character actor Thomas McCarthy is briefly spotted on TV ... Geno's Steaks, with it attention-getting neon, looks great in a nighttime sequence.

Rating:

Fighting Back
(Death Vengeance) (1982)

Local Moments:

There's interesting geography afoot here. Skerritt's hyperactive character lives in South Philly, but the El appears nearby. Confusing for Philadelphians familiar with the turf, but soon they'll catch on that the movie is juggling Kensington and South Philly locations, making them one big, bad neighborhood … McPhearson Park in Kensington is the hubbub of much activity … Rock disc jockey Debbi Calton is heard over the radio on WYSP in the beginning of the film … The Italian Market and several of its stores are prominent … Camden doubles for Philly in some scenes … Fire in Kensington! A factory catches on fire thanks to an arsonist whom D'Angelo tries to track down … "Fighting Back" presents one of the ugliest showcases of Philly ever. It's shown as a town overrun by hookers, pimps, burglars, purse snatchers, robbers, crooked politicians, and drug dealers. Oh, yes, the good guys are bat-wielding, gun-toting vigilantes, In other words: Philly — The City That Hates You Back.

Rating:

In this based-on-a-true-story Philly version of "Death Wish," Tom Skerritt's John D'Angelo kicks ass first, and takes names later. His character is a deli owner tired of the crime in his South Philly neighborhood. After a violent incident with a pimp in which his wife Lisa (Patti LuPone) has a miscarriage and a robbery at a pharmacy that leaves his mother and friends shot, D'Angelo decides to go after the culprits himself. Along with help from Vince Morelli (Michael Sarrazin), he begins the Peoples Neighborhood Patrol, a watchdog group that sicks itself on local thugs, particularly those causing problems in a nearby park. Producer Dino De Laurentiis also gave the world the "Death Wish" opuses (at least the first few) and he mines the same vigilante turf here. Unlike Charles Bronson's Paul Kearsey, however, Skerritt's D'Angelo is a rumble-stirring street fighter who wins over friends, the media and politicians with his strong-armed tactics, and doesn't face many repercussions when he takes things a little too far. There are questions aplenty here in light of D'Angelo's responses — "If he's not racist, why does he target the brothers?" is the one question broached by community leader Yaphet Kotto in a few scenes — but it's never explored in a satisfying way. Likewise, why does Lisa, D'Angelo's wife, push for the family to move after encountering one harrowing episode after another, then drop the idea so quickly? You'd be best to watch "Fighting Back" strictly for what it on the surface — a gritty, button-pushing action yarn — but drop the questions.

> " … a gritty, button-pushing action yarn ….. "

A Gentlemen's Game (2001)

Local Moments:

The film was shot in Media and Paoli with the bulk of it at Rolling Green Country Club on State Road in Springfield.

Rating:

More "The Legend of Bagger Vance" than "Tin Cup," this heartfelt coming-of-age tale is a gorgeously filmed ode to the game of golf that may not win over converts to the sport, but should please its fans. Twelve-year-old Timmy Price (Mason Gambles) shows an aptitude for the game, and at the urging of his father (Dylan Baker), he gets a job caddying at a local country club. There he meets other working-class young men earning cash by caddying for the rich.

> " ... gorgeously filmed ode to the game of golf ... "

At the urging of club patron Charley Logan (Phillip Baker Hall), he gets an education on the sport and life from Foster Pearse (Gary Sinise), a pro who quit the game. Debuting writer-director J. Mills Goodloe and cinematographer Conrad Hall, Jr., lovingly translate Tom Coyne's novel to the screen. Like the game itself, "A Gentleman's Game" is leisurely paced and methodical in the way its spins its life lessons fable, but if you didn't know Tiger Woods from Tony the Tiger you may have trouble relating to this.

Shakiest Gun in the West (1968)
Jesse Heywood (Don Knotts): I'm in teeth. And I came out here all the way from Philadelphia, single-handed, to fight oral ignorance.

The Great Cheesesteak Debate (2003)

Local Moments:

The "Rocky" theme opens up the proceedings and Elton John's "Philadelphia Freedom " closes things down … A nice city montage, and lots of footage of Ninth and Passyunk … Want to know what a real Philly dialect is? Check it out.

Rating:

The debate has been raging on for decades and,

as evidenced Scott Vosbury's film (available on the DVD compilation entitled "Full Frame, Documentary Shorts, Vol. 1"), there's no end in sight. In this corner … the supposed originator of the Philly Cheesesteak … from 9th and Passyunk … Pat's, King of Steaks! And in this corner … the contender … from across the street … Geno's Steaks! It's a knockdown, drag-out battle captured on video, as supporters of both sandwich emporiums discuss (and often shout out) which place they prefer, and other important things, like the arguments for and against Cheez Wiz. But wait! There are other joints jumping into the ring as well.

> **"It's a knockdown, drag-out battle captured on video …"**

There's the South Street-based Jim's and relative newcomer Tony Luke's, which is picking up steam (pun intended), even among Pat's and Geno's loyalists. "The Great Cheesesteak Debate" is great fun, and when the filmmaker heads to 9th and Passyunk for a late night quiz with Pat's and Geno's mostly inebriated patrons, there's danger in the air, along with the scent of smoldering onions. We would have liked to have seen a longer documentary on the subject — where's D'Allesandro's? John's Roast Pork? Steve's?— but what's here is choice.

The Hamster Factor And Other Tales Of Twelve Monkeys (1997)

Former Temple students Keith Fulton and Louis Pepe turn in nothing less than one of the finest films about making a film with this fascinating peek behind the scenes at director Terry Gilliam and the making of 1995's Bruce Willis-Madeleine Stowe sci-fi starrer "Twelve Monkeys." Given unlimited access to the mostly shot-in-Philly production, the filmmaking team gets into the mind of the eccentric genius Gilliam, the American member of the Monty Python comedy troupe, whose dealings with Hollywood lean toward the disastrous ("Brazil," "The Adventures of Baron Munchausen") and struggles with his dealings with producer Charles Roven. "The Hamster Factor," named after one of the scenes in the film which reflects Gilliam's

> **" ... one of the finest films about making a film ... "**

obsession with detail, was commissioned by Gilliam as insurance to protect himself against studio interference, and takes the viewer through many of the steps filmmaking, from preproduction to shooting to editing to promotion (we follow Gilliam as he goes on "Late Night with David Letterman") to marketing to showing the film to the public. Like Fulton and Pepe's other film about Gilliam (2002's "Lost in La Mancha"), "The Hamster Factor" offers an absorbing survey of filmmaking from the inside out.

NOTE: This 90-minute film is available as part of the bonus features on the "Twelve Monkeys" DVD.

Local Moments:

The local sites are similar to what you'd find in "Twelve Monkeys": power generator plants around the city, City Hall, Kensington, and Eastern State Penitentiary.

Rating:

The Happiest Millionaire

(1967)

Local Moments:

The entire film looks and feels (and was) shot on a back lot. Some of the sets reportedly even doubled for the London of "Mary Poppins" … Cordy is sent to the Wingfield School for Young Ladies in Lakewood, New Jersey … The cover of The Evening Bulletin announces "Wilson Re-Elected."

Rating:

Those Biddles of Philadelphia sure were wacky! That's the point of this lavish musical comedy about the eccentric Biddle family, led by Anthony J. Drexel Biddle, played by Fred MacMurray. Set mostly on the Main Line (although the soundstage sets appear to be more of an Old City locale) in 1916, the film focuses on the zany Biddle, who is into boxing, dieting on chocolate cake, martial arts, and tending to a group of alligators that roam around and near his mansion. In the film, Biddle, a religious World War I combat veteran, has a wife (an underused Greer Garson), two sons (Paul Peterson and Eddie Hodges), and daughter Cordy (Lesley Ann Warren), who plans to marry the automobile-obsessed Angier Duke (John Davidson), but the young man's mother (Geraldine Page) seems to

> **" … lavish musical comedy about the eccentric Biddle family … "**

have a problem with both the Biddles and Philadelphia. In the middle of all this scampers John Lawless (British comic Tommy Steele), the Biddles' optimistic new butler, who gets an opportunity to make things right with Cordy and Angier and the rest of the clan. Walt Disney had hoped he'd hit "Mary Poppins" gold again, and enlisted "Poppins" composers Richard and Robert Sherman for the score. They deliver a nice batch of tunes, but the film's inter-familial antics don't quite click now — and imagine how it played in the "Generation Gap" world of the late 1960s? The film's full 172-minute version is now available on DVD, after various truncated editions have been available for several years. While the film's restoration is to be applauded, it's not likely kids today will survive a three-hour family musical comedy no matter how odd the lead characters are.

Happy Birthday, Gemini (1980)

Something not so funny happened on the way to adapting Albert Inaurato's hit off-Broadway play to the screen. Canadian writer-director Richard Benner, the filmmaker of the drag queen comedies "Outrageous!" and "Too Outrageous!," was enlisted for the job, and the result is … well, really outrageous. The broad face and pathos of the story don't translate well here because all actors and dialogue are done in a feverish pace, and the characterizations come across cartoonish and, ultimately, phony. That said, there are some things to appreciate in the story of

> **" … the characterizations come across cartoonish … "**

Francis (an almost unrecognizable Alan Rosenberg), a Harvard student from South Philly, whose life gets rattled when he's visited by brother and sister acquaintances from school: Judy (Sarah Holcomb), whom he should be attracted to, and Randy (David Marshall Grant), to whom he actually is attracted. The gay romantic angle is just a part of this timpani of a movie that also involves Francis' butcher father (Robert Viharo) and his secretary (Rita Moreno), and the nymphomaniac next-door neighbor (Madeline Kahn) and her SEPTA-obsessed genius son (Timothy Jenkins). Everyone seems to be huffing and puffing to make the material work on screen — it just doesn't. At least there are real South Philly locations and the actors' accents seem authentic.

Local Moments:

South Philly gets a nice showcase, including Pat's Steaks, the Italian Market, and the shops on Passyunk Ave … You'll get a kick out of the kid who impersonates the sounds of trolleys at various stops … An interesting concept we're not familiar with is introduced here: A cheesesteak truck that rides around the neighborhood like Mister Softee. Too bad it doesn't have its own theme song … The finale takes place at the now-defunct Crossroads Diner, a once-popular breakfast spot.

Rating:

High School (1968)

Local Moments:

The film opens with a camera moving down a Northeast Philly driveway as trash cans roll around and Otis Redding's "Sitting on the Dock of a Bay" plays … All of the film was shot in Northeast High classrooms, corridors, and gym … There is a sequence involving testing for the NASA-sponsored "SPARC" program, which continues today.

Rating:

When I arrived for orientation at Northeast High School

sometime in the early 1970s, I had a question to ask every teacher or counselor I encountered: "What do you know of a film called 'High School,' directed by Frederic Wiseman?" The parties I queried were mum across the board. If they knew something, they weren't talking. I was fascinated with the fact that a major, highly acclaimed documentary was shot at the Northeast Philly learning institution I was about to attend, but nobody — and I mean nobody — would discuss this or even recognize this. The best I could get from a shop teacher was "I think I heard something about it." Years later, while attending Temple University, I finally had a chance to see "High School," and I realized some of the instructors I had asked about the movie on orientation day were actually in it. The movie came with its own group of legendary rumors, among them: It was forbidden to be shown in the city of Philadelphia because of an ordinance by either City Council or the school district president Mark Shedd; the local chapter of the Fraternal Order of Police banned it because of the way it depicts the son of a police officer; and director Wiseman didn't want it screened in the area because he didn't want to deal with its controversial nature, especially after "Titticut Follies," his previous film about a mental hospital, was banned from being shown in Massachusetts. The screening at Temple's Annenberg Hall was packed, and the audience included many Northeast High teachers. Rumors swirled that Wiseman was in the audience and that once the lights went down and the film came on the screen, the print was going to be seized. To this day, it's never been confirmed that the filmmaker was there at the first public screening in 1979, and the film unspooled problem-free. And though there was another packed public screening at the

> **"The movie came with its own group of legendary rumors …"**

continued on page 42

Prince Music Theater in 1998 and a broadcast of it on PBS around the same time, "High School" still remains difficult to see. Like all of Wiseman's documentaries, it can only be sold or rented to schools or institutions, and at a hefty rate. So, what is the big stink about, anyway? Well, based on a number of sources (including radio personality and unofficial Northeast High School historian Joel Gibbs), it seems that a lot of people were angry about Wiseman's bleak look at the school — including the city, the school board and, possibly, the FOP. All were in favor of the filming at Northeast, but they expected the result to be a positive one — after all, this was one of Philly's top academic schools, located in a safe, middle class white (and predominately Jewish) neighborhood. The result of Wiseman's findings observed in the film, however, was that Northeast was a place where creativity was stifled, kids are bored, and teachers either tried to press their often old-fashioned values on the pupils body or offer hypocritical words of wisdom that confused students. For example, a demonstration of proper and improper fashion tips for girls regarding mini-skirts and weight probably seemed ludicrous the second after it was shot; the school disciplinarian tells a reprimanded student that he should take his punishment like a man; a guest gynecologist informs students that teenage sex leads to bad marriages; a teacher reads "Casey at the Bat" to a classroom of kids whose attention seems miles away; and a girl argues about the length of her prom skirt only to be told by an advisor that she shouldn't be so "individualistic." "High School" is anecdotal in nature, moving from class to class to class and incident to incident in seemingly random fashion. The _cinema verite_ approach often makes the audience a fly on the wall, as the movie appears objective, telling it like it is, "High School" drones on because school drones on, and to some it may be a chore to sit through. But this is precisely Wiseman's point, and he underlines it subtly, with such an attentive lens, that he enraged a lot of people.

"The _cinema verite_ approach often makes the audience a fly on the wall ..."

A History of Violence
(2005)

Local Moments:

Real Philadelphians know Hurt's accent is more Brooklyn than South Philly, and we're not sure what dialect Mortenson is speaking in the last twenty minutes of this film … There's a shot of a sign on the Schuylkill Expressway, but all the location work was done in Toronto, and it shows.

Rating:

Leave it to Canadian director David Cronenberg ("The Fly"):

The guy knows how to get under your skin. Consider this film, an intense examination of violence in America, filtered through the prism of a seemingly happy family. Dad, played by Viggo Mortenson, owns a little luncheonette in a small Midwestern town. Mom (Norristown's Maria Bello) is a lawyer. Son (Ashton Holmes) and daughter (Heidi Hayes) seem like perfectly happy, well-adjusted kids. But something unsettling is going on. It involves Dad's past. A couple of seedy characters led by Ed Harris are making their presence known, and begin menacing the family. There's talk that Mortenson may not be who everyone thinks he is. Something about an incident back in Philadelphia. A violent altercation brings attention to Mortenson, who is then forced to head back to Philly and face his past, as well as his criminal brother, played by William Hurt. It's all chilling, thought-provoking stuff that get sunder your skin, and Bello and Mortenson should be complemented for some pretty racy sex scenes. But Hurt's psychotic sibling — a role for which he was Oscar-nominated — throws everything off balance with his overacting and faux Philly accent.

> **"It's all chilling, thought-provoking stuff …"**

Steven De Souza:
From Cartoon Corners to Hollywood

Steven E. de Souza is best known for scripting some of Hollywood's biggest actioners. With credits like "48 Hours," "Die Hard," "Commando," and "The Running Man" under his belt, de Souza has been tagged a specialist in mixing action with irony comedy — to the tune of over $2 billion.

But before de Souza became a name to be reckoned with in Tinseltown, he made a film in Levittown called "Arnold's Wrecking Co.", a pot comedy that remains one of the lost films of the 1970s and predated Cheech & Chong's "Up in Smoke" by six years.

De Souza was born in Rolling Hill Hospital and raised in Oxford Circle on Knorr and Rutland Streets near his father's travel agency. The de Souza family moved to Levittown when Steven was six.

"I had been a professional writer when I was in high school," says de Souza, who attended Neshaminy High School. "I was writing for the men's pulps. I was having my lunch money stolen from me, then I would go home and write a story for *Rogue Magazine*."

De Souza worked his way up to *Crawdaddy*, a *Rolling Stone*-like music magazine, which led to bylines in *The New York Times*. He attended Penn State University and joined the Army Reserves. During the summers, he toiled at TV stations in the Philadelphia area.

"I had worked already at all the stations in Philly in my checkered career," says de Souza. "I had worked at WCAU — I did a show there called 'Datebook,' a talk show with Muhammed Ali as a recurring host. I directed

> **"Eventually, he wound up producing more than writing, and decided in 1972 it was time to make "Arnold's Wrecking Co." his own movie."**

an episode of 'Bowling for Dollars' on Channel 29. One of their directors was a semi-pro Triple A ballplayer. I had to fill in for him when he went on the road. I was the pinch director. I was on 'The Gene London Show' as an alien who invaded Cartoon Corners.

De Souza considers his first "real" job in show business was for the burgeoning New Jersey Public Television. "I made the rounds," he recalls. "Finally, there was this full-time job in Trenton. I walked into the bowling alley and the only guy there was at the desk. He was the one who was hiring people for the TV station. They are literally ripping up the bowling alley. This guy's only experience was being in charge of all the tape recorders, slide projectors and tape recorders for the prison system. So that's kind of like show business."

De Souza impressed the man with his *New York Times* clips and old-time radio scripts. Eventually, he wound up producing more than writing, and decided in 1972 it was time to make "Arnold's Wrecking Co.", his own movie.

"We went out and raised private money from a half dozen people, primarily a guy who made a fortune in software in Princeton," recalls de Souza. "We made the film and took it to the Atlanta Film Festival where it won the Special Jury Prize, the one the audience liked. It was a big deal and we got attention and got a distributor. It would have been a happy ending if the distributor didn't go out of business the month they released the movie."

The film is virtually impossible to see today. Even de Souza isn't sure if he has a copy.

"It actually played in theaters — maybe nine to a dozen theaters in opening weekend," says de Souza. "Then it went to drive-ins. I'm in the film."

So, what's the premise?

"It's basically like the city mouse and country mouse. The hip, cool Philadelphia guy played by me is visited by his country cousin who is a dork and cramps my style. The country cousin discovers the city cousin smoking marijuana, but rather than being shocked — he was the guy who had a newspaper route — he applies his Horatio Alger business acumen to the marijuana business. So the cousins sponsor a Little League team and go down the whole slippery slope of this Horatio Alger Americana story and they go boom and bust.

"I was thinking silent pictures. There was a style to it to play up physical comedy and sight gags.

It was inspired by *Mad Magazine*, especially the little side cartoon panels that come between the main features."

> **"The hip, cool Philadelphia guy played by me is visited by his country cousin who is a dork and cramps my style."**

Eventually, de Souza made his way out to Los Angeles and, through a series of happy coincidences and strong script samples, he landed as a staff writer on "The $6 Million Man" TV show.

Meanwhile, "Arnold's Wrecking Co." was really talked never about again in his professional career, except for once instance. "I didn't show the movie to anyone, but somebody involved with "Deep Throat 2" [aka "Linda Lovelace for President"] saw it," says de Souza. "I was up to direct 'Deep Throat 2.' And I was introduced to Linda Lovelace. They said they wanted to open it up to an R rating, and I said ok. But then it evaporated. Sometimes you may see my name associated with it, but it was because I had a meeting about it, but nothing else."

Home of Angels (1994)

It's supposed to be well-meaning and maybe even a little sugar-coated,

something administered to go down easily with family consumption. But there's an element to this fable that is downright unsettling: It's like "It's a Wonderful Life" meets "The Warriors"!? Directed by Nick Stagliano ("The Florentine"), the story tells of Billy (Lance Robinson), a young boy who fondly recalls going fishing with his grandfather (Abe Vigoda). But now Grandpa is in a Philadelphia nursing home with Alzheimer's disease, and Billy decides it's time to spring him from the place and take him home to Long Island. So, Billy takes a train to Philly and, with help from some of the facility's patients, gets Pops out of the joint, only to face a series of oddball characters and scary incidents along his journey

> **"It seems like he's supposed to be an angel or something..."**

home. Their main obstacle is a group of punks who steal money from the grandfather and bully Billy. Then Billy and Gramps come across a box city populated by homeless people where they meet Buzzard Bracken (Philly native Sherman Hemsley), a former boxer. What's odd about this low-budget effort is that each time it gets a sweet tooth — a genuine yearning to make audiences happy — along comes those pesky hoodlums to mess things up, and not only for Billy and company, but for the audience as well. Then there's former heavyweight champ Joe Frazier in a bizarre role, popping up in the middle of the action every once in a while, and not doing a whole lot. It seems like he's supposed to be an angel or something, but his role is never clarified. One could imagine that Frazier had something to do behind-the-scenes since with the film's production company is "Cloverlay Productions," and Frazier's management team was "Cloverleaf." The film also takes an odd look at Alzheimer's disease and surmises things can indeed get better, just let love do it's thing. Sadly, this notion is not based in reality, even though the idea helps "Home of Angels" try some last minute tugs of the heart to win audiences over.

Local Moments:

North Philly is the location for the box city, inhabited by homeless helpers … 30th Street gets some screen time … And of course Hemsley and "Smokin' Joe" are area legends.

Rating:

House of God (1983)

Local Moments:

Graduate Hospital is extensively used throughout the movie … The interns meet along the banks of the Schuylkill in one of the film's better scenes … Lunch is at Famous Deli on 4th Street and then-owner David Auspitz even gets a cameo … The young physicians hang out at Dr. Watson's Pub on 11th Street.

Rating:

If Robert Altman had directed the great Paddy Chayefsky-penned 1971 satire "The Hospital" it would play something like this little-seen look at the trials and tribulations of young doctors at an inner city healing facility. Based on a book written under the pseudonym Sam Shemm, "House of God" centers on a group of interns led by Fats (Charles Haid), who are getting a rude awakening to the medical profession. They're learning first-hand how to deal with death, mishaps, and the annoying GOMERS — a code word for elderly patients who don't want to die — that populate their rooms. Like "The Hospital," comedy mixes with tragedy here and the tone is often pitch-black and cynical. And like an Altman film, there's a sizable cast, anecdotal situations, overlapping dialogue, and offbeat incidents. The film was actually filmed in Philly in 1979, but sat on the shelf for four years before getting dumped into a handful of theaters. Despite an impressive but eccentric cast — many of the members of the ensemble in very early roles in their careers — the film has never even landed on VHS or DVD, but occasionally shows on cable. Check out the players here: Tim Matheson, Bess Armstrong, James Cromwell, Joe Piscopo, Howard Rollins, Jr., Sandra Bernhard, Gilbert Gottfried, and Ossie Davis. The lineup alone should warrant a release, especially since the film is much better than the treatment it received from its caregivers.

> **" … comedy mixes with tragedy here. "**

I Don't Buy Kisses Anymore (1992)

Can a chubby Jewish guy obsessed with chocolate candy find true love with an Italian college student who's an aspiring singer? That's the premise of this (appropriately) sweet comedy that offers the unlikely pairing of Jason Alexander and Nia Peebles. He's Bernie Fishbine, an overweight shoe salesman who buys candy kisses each night and lives at home with his overbearing mother (Lainie Kazan) and acerbic grandfather (Lou Jacobi). She's Theresa Garabaldi, a grad student who works at an office and sings standards part-time at a restaurant.

> **"This is definitely a sleeper, well worth searching for ..."**

The two meet while waiting for a SEPTA bus, and an unlikely romance blossoms. Bernie tries to lose weight to impress her, but he doesn't know that she's also using him as the subject of her thesis entitled "A Psychological Study of An Obese Male." When he does find out, the relationship's future is threatened. Although its setting is contemporary, "Kisses" seems old-fashioned in a lot of ways. Alexander's Bernie wears bow-ties and a Jess cap and seems so polite he appears to have stepped out of a 40s film. And Peebles is quirky in a sweet and innocent way — that is, until her plan involving Bernie is revealed. This is definitely a sleeper, well worth searching for.

Local Moments:

Not as many as one would hope. Except for the SEPTA bus (Featured in a few scenes), there are some background shots of the Ardmore shopping area and a couple sequences featuring city backgrounds.

Rating:

The **In Crowd** (1988)

Local Moments:

Tons on view here. Locations include Upper Darby's Tower Theater doubling as the exterior of WPHY-TV's studios, the Allen's Lane train station, the Ben Franklin Parkway, Huntington Valley, Cheltenham, and Cheltenham High School … You can't miss Sally Star in her cowgirl regalia in a scene, but did you catch Peter Boyle, playing his father and "Pete's Gang" kiddie show host Pete Boyle in the same scene? … The dance sequences were choreographed by veterans of the Wagner ballroom and other teen dance sites, and include kids doing "the Popeye," "Mickey's Monkey ," and "The Soul Street" … One radio station is tuned to WIBG with Hy Lit on the air; another is tuned to WIP, then middle-of-the-road music … There's a teen dance in Wildwood … A character wears a Temple University t-shirt … Pantoliano gives an impassioned spiel about Dick Clark going to L.A. with "American Bandstand" and leaving Philly behind.

Rating:

Local screenwriter-made-good Mark Rosenthal
(he co-penned "Mighty Joe Young" and "Godzilla," and "Planet of the Apes" remakes) makes his directorial debut by going back to his roots with this exuberant look at the music and dancing that thrilled local teens in the mid 1960s. Meshing elements of "Grease" and "West Side Story," the film features Donovan Leitch (son of the folk singer Donovan) as Del Green, a Cheltenham High School student who really, really wants to dance. And he gets his chance when he's paired with Catholic school girl Vicky (Jennifer Runyon) on the afternoon "Dance Party" TV show, hosted by the fast-talking disc jockey Perry Parker (Joe Pantoliano). As Del struggles with coming-of-age matters like deciding about furthering his education and dealing

> " … it has energy and aims to please … "

with peer pressure, he strikes a romantic relationship with Vicky. But where can it go? Kudos go to cinematographers Anthony Richmond and Jeff Jur for capturing the look of teen films of the mid 1960s with a washed-out Eastmancolor look, as well as the music coordinators who picked such dandies as "Land of 1,000 Dances," "Cast Your Fate to the Wind," "A Wonderful Dream," "I Do," and, of course the title track. The movie gushes Philly atmosphere, from Pantoliano's hyperactive homage to Jerry Blavat (who reportedly tried to stop the film's release with a threatened lawsuit) to its parade of local personalities, locations, and affectations. Alas, the movie sank quickly at the box office, and, sadly, a soundtrack was never even issued. "The In Crowd"'s drama is fairly inert and the romantic elements never really click, but it has energy and aims to please and you always feel that you're getting the real Philly deal while watching it.

In Her Shoes (2005)

On paper, this romantic dramedy had lots going for it: a top-notch cast, an acclaimed director, a best selling book served as the inspiration, and great Philly locales. But for some reason, the film didn't click at the box office. By the sound of it, "In Her Shoes" seems like prime chick flick material. When a reporter mentioned the term "chick flick" to co-star Shirley MacLaine, she begrudged the term and referred to the film as a "relationship movie." We're inclined to agree, so it's safe for ladies and men. A tale of two sisters, the film stars Toni Collette as the good sibling, a slightly plump (though not as plump as in the book) Philadelphia attorney whose career is doing swell, but has no love life to speak of. Sister Cameron Diaz is a floozy, a blonde beauty with few aspirations who hops from bed to bed and is dependent upon Collette to bail her out of jams. An incident involving Collette's boyfriend and Diaz separates the two, prompting Diaz to move to Florida, where she tracks down her long-lost maternal grandmother (MacLaine). While in the Sunshine State, Diaz struggles to get herself together, while Collette attempts to change her lonely life in Philly. The story has been done many times before, but director Curtis Hanson ("L.A. Confidential", "8 Miles") and screenwriter Susannah Grant ("Erin Brockovich") bring a freshness to the proceedings. They're helped by expert work from an all-around exceptional cast: Collette, an Aussie who played the worried mother in "The Sixth Sense" shines in a complex part; Diaz adds depth to the demanding party-girl-gone-wrong role; and MacLaine excels as the sharp, cynical granny. Lots of help is also afforded from a host of scene-stealing senior citizens who share a Florida retirement community with her.

Above: Toni Collette goes dog-walking at the Art Museum in 2005's romantic drama "In Her Shoes."
©20th Century Fox/The Kobal Collection/Baldwin, Sidney

Left: Cameron Diaz steps out of a center city brownstone while filming "In Her Shoes."
© Scott Weiner

Local Moments:

Rittenhouse Square is the place where Collette takes her dogs for a walk … South Street's funky Jamaican Jerk Hut features prominently in key scenes … Jennifer Weiner, who wrote the book, stands with agent Jennifer Pulcini behind Toni Collette in a scene shot at the Italian Market.

Rating:

Invincible (2006)

Much of the film was shot in and around the city, and uses many local actors … Franklin Field plays Veterans' Stadium in the movie, complete with benches and outside track markings … The exterior of the Vet is done with Hollywood wizardry through computer generated images … Real Philadelphians will note the following inaccuracies: a steak sandwich place that's obviously Pat's is called Columbo's and a TV station shown frequently throughout the film is "Channel 11." Why? Our guess is legal reasons … There are some shots of the real South Philly as well as the Kensington area and the Frankford El … There are a few cracks about how tough Philly sports fans can be, including a line about them throwing snowballs at Santa Claus … Late local legend Jim Croce sings "I Got a Name" over the opening credits … Steak sandwich legend Tony Luke, Jr., has funny moments as the Eagles fan who wears a cape.

Rating:

The story of Philadelphia Eagles wide receiver Vince Papale is a "Rocky"-esque fable that is so Philly it smells like a cheesesteak with fried onions, which is why it makes for a rousing movie, especially if you have an affection for this area and "the birds." Mark Wahlberg plays the real-life bartender/ substitute teacher who — down in the dumps because he's been let go at his school and walked out on by his wife — goes for a tryout with the Eagles. They're in the middle of an overhaul with unconventional new coach Dick Vermeil (Greg Kinnear) leading the way. It's Papale's grit, determination, and running speed that eventually land the former street ballplayer a spot on the Eagles as a wide receiver and special teams member. That's pretty

Greg Kinnear scores as Philadelphia Eagles coach Dick Vermeil in 2006's "Invincible."
© Disney Enterprises/The Kobal Collection/Phillips, Ron

much the story, but debuting director Erickson Core and screenwriters Brad Gann (and an uncredited Mike Rich) know their football and obviously have an affection for the working class milieu of the city. Most of the film is set in and around a South Philly bar and training camp, where he's dished by vets and continually pooh-poohs the possibility of making the club while rookie skipper Vermeil — fresh out of UCLA — struggles with adapting to the NFL. The story is an real upper, an underdog saga not unlike "Rocky." And since Papale is a real person, some liberties were taken with his tale. The most alarming is the fact the film overlooks Papale's brief stint playing for the short-lived World Football League's Philadelphia Bell before hooking up with the Eagles. Other incidents regarding his personal life (he's from Glenolden, not South Philly) have been tinkered with, but it doesn't lessen the impact of this study of a hero who could have only been part of Philly sports lore.

Reel-Life Philly

Philly is not only home to a wide range of features, but the city and its environs play a part in several documentaries as well.

Andrew Dice Clay: The Diceman Cometh (1989)

The bad boy of comedy with the leather jacket, ever-present cigarette and dirty limericks performs at the TLA just before he hit it big. "Hickory dickory dock…"

Confessions of a Suburban Girl (1992)

Produced by the BBC, this real-life film centers on director Susan Seidelman ("Desperately Seeking Susan") who returns to her Huntingdon Valley neighborhood to reminisce with old friends about growing up in the Philly 'burbs.

Crumb (1994)

Terry Zwigoff's marvelous but disturbing documentary about Philly-born cartoonist Robert Crumb, creator of "Fritz the Cat," Zap Comix, and the bearded "Keep on Truckin'" character, includes sequences featuring his emotionally troubled brother Charles, who continued to live in Philly, and committed suicide in 1995, not long after Zwigoff filmed interviews with him.

Curtain Call (2005)

This inspiring feature looks at the Curtain Call Creations program in which a group of kids get together to write, produce, and act in a musical play. Run by former schoolteacher Maureen Mullin, the South Philly-based troupe consists of 50 or so kids who buck financial restrictions to produce a big show, and director James Doolittle follows their efforts over a period of several hard-working months. Any kid — or parent of a kid — interested in the arts should watch this fine documentary.

Girls Like Us (1997)

An eye-opening look at four girls from South Philly, tracing their lives from 14 to 18 years. Directed by Jane Wagner and Tina DeFelici-antonio, the film studies the young women's thought on sex, school, and their future. Reminiscent of Michael Apted's "Up" series, the film makes you want to see a follow-up on what has happened to Lisa, Anna, Raeline, and De'Yona since this was completed.

I Am A Promise: The Children Of Stanton Elementary School (1993)

A year-in-the-life look at the children in North Philadelphia's Stanton Elementary school is an affecting slice of "cinema verite". Written and directed by Alan and Susan Raymond ("An American Family"), the film masterfully weaves together stories of kids dealing with troubled backgrounds, poverty, and other hurdles, and how they and their teachers and Principal Deanna Burney try to cope and educate each other and themselves. Part of the "Docurama Worlds Collection, Vol. 2" DVD.

In the King of Prussia (1982)

Radical filmmaker Emile de Antonio helmed this fact-based sage of the trial of war activist, known as the "Plowshares Eight," who protested nuclear arms by breaking into a Westinghouse King of Prussia weapons plant. Daniel and Philip Berrigan play themselves and Martin Sheen plays a judge.

Investigative Reports: Peace, Love, and Murder: The Ira Einhorn Story (1998)

Cable TV special on Philly counterculture fugitive Ira Einhorn and the murder of girlfriend Holly Maddux.

The Last Party 2000 (2001)

A follow-up to 1993's "The Last Party," which was hosted by Robert Downey, Jr., this political documentary features Philip Seymour Hoffman surveying the political climate of the 2000 election, with reports from the Republican Convention at the First Union Center, and segments shot in North Philadelphia, the Marriott in Center City, and the Kensington Human Rights Center.

The Maestros of Philadelphia (1993)

Local favorite Blythe Danner returns home to narrate this PBS study of the City of Brotherly Love's greatest musical talents, including Riccardo Muti, Deanna Durbin, and Eugene Ormandy.

Nina Simone: La Legende (1992)

This British documentary on the jazz legend includes a stop at the Curtis Institute of Music.

Poverty Outlaw (1997)

A no-nonsense look at a woman struggling to stay afloat as she and her children move from welfare to abject poverty in Kensington. Nominated for the Grand Jury Prize at the Sundance Film Festival.

The Show (1995)

Filmed at the Civic Center and produced by local guy Mike Tollin, this high energy "rapumentary" showcases Notorious B.I.G., Run DMC, Dr. Dre, Naughty by Nature, and Snoop Dogg.

Sun Ra: A Joyful Noise (1980)

Legendary jazz performer/eccentric Sun Ra and his equally iconoclastic bandmates are profiled in this fascinating but gritty documentary by locally-based filmmaker Robert Mugge. This guy claims he came from Saturn and, by film's end, you may believe him.

Tommy Davidson: Illin' in Philly (1991)

A regular on "In Living Color tears the house down — the Schubert Theater in this case — with his comedy routine that features riffs on Freddie Krueger, "Friday the 13th," and the erotic elements of a Juicy Fruit commercial.

Yes: Live in Philadelphia (1979)

Art rockers Yes perform such songs as "Roundabout," "I've Seen All Good People," and "Starship Trooper" at the Spectrum.

The Italian Job (2003)

This slick retooling of the Michael Caine 60s favorite stars Mark Wahlberg as the student of murdered master thief Donald Sutherland who plots to lift $35 million in gold bullion from the mansion of Edward Norton, Wahlberg's former associate. To pull of the scheme, which is also a comeuppance for Norton murdering Sutherland, Wahlberg enlists Philadelphia police department safecracker — Sutherland's daughter, in fact — Charlize Theron; computer geek Seth Green; demolitions expert Mos Def; and womanizing gearhead Jason Stathan. To get to Norton's highly secured abode in Los Angeles, the team carries out an

> **"This remake is tailored for contemporary audiences ..."**

intricate plan that involves driving a fleet of Mini Coopers through downtown L.A. The 1969 original was a quirky delight, with veddy British elements and an extremely bizarre ending. This remake is tailored for contemporary audiences by mixing familiar heist elements with a solid cast playing experts in their specific field, a la "Ocean's Eleven." It's not great or memorable, and Norton seems totally bored as the bad guy, but it's an enjoyable time-waster that's been successful enough to spawn a 2007 sequel.

Local Moments:

A shot of the Ben Franklin Bridge, a city skyline, a wild car ride along the Delaware River, and some shots of Spruce Street are featured in the early Philadelphia segment.

Rating:

Jersey Girl (2003)

Local Moments:

Although shot mostly in Paulsboro and Highlands, NJ, the film offers lots of Philadelphia locations. The Forrest Theater on Walnut Street served as the showplace for the "Sweeney Todd" sequence, and interiors were also shot in Berlin, NJ … Other location filming included Havertown and Cherry Hill, NJ … Philly's Will Smith makes a cameo.

Rating:

This was the film that was supposed to put the raunchy Kevin Smith on ice, a sensitive romantic comedy with no Jay or Silent Bob or dick jokes. We all know what happened, don't we? With the Ben Affleck-Jennifer Lopez lovefest garnering all sort of coverage in the press, Lopez's part was clipped (after the "Gigli" debacle the year before) down to cameo status and the film's release date was moved a few times — never a good sign. When it finally made it to theaters, "Jersey Girl" was met with tepid reviews and less-than-enthusiastic box office response, topping off a little over $25 million. Truth be told, the movie is not as bad as some have suggested. Ben Affleck plays Ollie Trinke (what a name!), a New York-based music publicist who tries to juggle raising his daughter Gertie with a chaotic work life after wife J. Lo dies during childbirth. Affleck leaves his slick Manhattan lifestyle for home in central Jersey with curmudgeonly father George Carlin. But Affleck eventually tires of the slower pace, and attempts to make a go of it again in Manhattan, but, with help from cute video store clerk Liv Tyler, discovers he can, in fact, go home again. Smith's fans, accustomed to religious rants, a litany of four-letter words, and lots of profane guy humor, undoubtedly loathed this effort, as it showed off the mushier side of their revered raunchy auteur. But those willing to give Smith a chance to charm, should find it decent, breezy fun, with Affleck at his most winning, Tyler totally winsome, and newcomer Raquel Castro affecting as daddy's little, precocious girl (Carlin however, is mostly cloying as Ben's cranky father). Unfortunately, the film derailed Smith's more serious aspirations, leading to the collapse of a long-in-the-works Green Hornet feature and forced him to return to his old cinematic stomping grounds with "Clerks II".

> **"We all know what happened, don't we?"**

Jesus's Son (2000)

Based on an acclaimed series of stories by Dennis Johnson, this rambling existential road movie is set in the early 1970s and centers on a character called FH (short for "****head"), played by Billy Crudup. The film is about FH's trials while meeting people, falling in love, getting addicted to heroin, and finding himself. We follow FH as he encounters Michelle (Samantha Morton), a junkie with whom he falls in love. She teaches him how to shoot up and he's soon hooked, but when she leaves him in hopes of finding a better life with the older John Smith (Will Patton), he hits bottom. He also begins meeting a series of characters that will affect him in different ways. There's Wayne (Denis Leary), who makes extra cash by pulling stuff out of a house he used to live in and selling it for salvage; Georgie (Jack Black), a hospital orderly hooked on pills; and Mira (Holly Hunter), a disabled woman with whom he becomes close. Directed by Canada's Alison Maclean ("Crush"), the film moves from Iowa to Chicago to Phoenix in free-flowing fashion, keeping the audience surprised by what oddball, screwed-up FH is going to meet next and where the drugs he's ingested are going to take him — and the audience. Darkly humorous and enigmatic at the same time, the loosely structured "Jesus's Son" is well worth discovering if you're looking for a challenging film with an offbeat vibe all its own.

> **Darkly humorous and enigmatic at the same time ...**

Local Moments:

So what does a film set in Iowa, Chicago, and Phoenix have to do with the Delaware Valley. The answer is nothing, although much of it was shot here ... Riverside, New Jersey, with its clock tower and Main Street, USA-type shopping area around Lafayette Street doubles for Iowa City, circa 1971 ... The Delsea Drive-In, currently New Jersey's only drive-in, is featured in a scene, shot before it was reopened a few years ago ... And Philadelphia's Frankford El is showcased in a few trippy sequences, impersonating the Chicago Transit Authority trains.

Rating:

Killing Emmett Young
(Emmett's Mark) (2002)

A great showcase for Philly, the movie is practically a city travelogue, although some of the locales are not so sweet … The Chinatown area is featured in several sequences, including one in which a character gets pummeled with a baseball bat at 10th and Cherry … "Summer of Love," a CD from local group Love Seed Mama Jump gets screen time and one of their songs is on the soundtrack … Roth's character lives in West Philly on 46th Street, and there are trips to Fairmount Park, down Broad Street, and to the Rittenhouse Square area … The late Silk City Diner, 4th Street's Eddie's Tattoo Parlor, and Repo Records on South Street also get the spotlight … Scott Johnston, director of the annual Festival of Independents has a cameo towards the film's end … Philly born character actor John Doman ("The Wire") plays Captain Berman, Young's commanding officer.

Forty-five years after "The Burglar,"

Philly still proves to be an ideal locale for film noir with this moody, highly underrated police thriller. Scott Wolf ("Party of Five") offers a fine performance as Emmett Young, a young Philly detective who discovers he has a fatal disease and not long to live. Young decides to pay a former federal agent Jack Marlow (Gabriel Byrne) $15,000 to have him killed so he doesn't have to go through the pain his disease's tract usually takes. Marlowe in turn enlists down-and-out security officer Frank Dwyer (Tim Roth) to kill the detective. At the same time, however, Young is in hot pursuit of a serial rapist and killer terrorizing Philly, and with time running out, he wants to make his mark (hence, the film's original title) before he's assassinated. The film remains intense and compelling throughout, and offers a dizzying

> " … the acting is uniformly fine … "

view of the city and several of its more colorful — and seedier — neighborhoods. In addition, the acting is uniformly fine, from Wolf's compelling, change-of-pace turn, to Khandi Alexander ("CSI: Miami") as his determined partner, to Byrne and Roth as the shady Irish – and British – accented chaps in the background. While debuting writer-director Keith Snyder (a Wilmington native) falters towards the end, unable to tie up loose ends, "Killing Emmett Young" manages to be a forceful modern noir throughout most of its running time.

Rating:

Kimberly (Daddy Who?) (1999)

The daughter of a legendary Olympic rower, the title character is a British cutey-pie (played by British cutey-pie Gabrielle Anwar of "Scent of a Woman") desired by four buddies who love sculling on the Schuylkill. The men who have fallen for Kimberly include a ladies man (Chris Rydall), a hard-working yuppie (Jason Lewis), a frat boy past his prime (Sean Astin), and a guy with serious commitment problems (Robert Mallhouse). Each of them gets a chance to get cozy with Kimberly, but things get awfully complicated when she becomes pregnant. Who the real father is and how the quartet of boys in mens' clothing deals with the situation make for some fairly amusing screen time, as long as you don't think about such obvious things, like, "Where was a condom when they needed it?" The film is bolstered with some oddball cameos from Patty Duke, Astin's real-life mother playing a doctor, and Molly Ringwald as the commitment-scared guy's gal pal. The first directorial effort from producer-actor Frederic Golchan, the film also offers a nice score by Paul Verhoeven fave Basil Poledouris.

> **"The first directorial effort from producer/actor Frederic Golchan ..."**

Local Moments:

The film may not be top-shelf, but the location footage is … Lots of well-lensed scenes of Schuylkill sculling are pretty as a picture … City stuff includes the funky confines of the Rittenhouse Square-based ad agency MBC … The campus at University of Pennsylvania gets some screen time along with some of South Street's watering holes.

Rating:

Ivy League Cinema

These films were either shot or set in and around Princeton University.

A Beautiful Mind (2001)
Ron Howard's true-life Oscar-winning story of Princeton math professor John Nash (Russell Crowe), whose imagined involvement with a secret government project stems from severe emotional problems.

Class of '44 (1973)
Decent sequel to nostalgic winner "Summer of '42" picks up the further adventures of Hermie, Benjy, and Oscy with Princeton locales standing in for a midwestern learning institution.

Infinity (1996)
Matthew Broderick directs and stars in the tale of physicist Richard Feynman, one of the architects of "The Manhattan Project" and a developer of the atomic bomb.

I.Q. (1994)
Car mechanic Tim Robbins dates Meg Ryan, the niece of Albert Einstein (Walter Matthau).

The Last Embrace (1979)
Everyone recalls the Niagra Falls climax in Jonathan Demme's paranoid thriller starring Roy Scheider as a CIA agent who believes everyone's trailing him since his wife's death.

But other sequences were shot in and around Princeton.

One True Thing (1998)
Anna Quindlen's novel of fractured family matters involved professor William Hurt, cancer-stricken wife Meryl Streep, and guilt-ridden daughter Renee Zellweger. Although the college is actually called Langhorne, Hurt's office is in McGosh Hall on the Princeton campus.

People Will Talk (1951)
Joseph L. Mankiewicz wrote and directed this oddball film, an anti-McCarthy diatribe, during the time of the Hollywood witch hunts, and a quirky character study of gynecologist Cary Gray whose unconventional methods causes colleagues to discredit him through misinformation.

Scent of a Woman (1992)
Hoo-hah! Al Pacino's Oscar win with the blind ex-military man's aide Chris O'Donnell spending time at Princeton University's Holder Court, standing in for a private boarding school, and Rockefeller College getting screen time for some of the opening shots. Hoo-hah!

Varsity (1928)
Now considered a lost film, this part silent, part sound effort tells of a Princeton student who is coerced into robbing a campus fund after getting liqored up. Charles "Buddy" Rogers and Chester Conklin star.

Wilson (1944)
Alexander Knox plays the 28th President of the United States and former head of Princeton University in this valentine to the university that features many locales around the campus and even the rah-rah fight song.

Kitty Foyle (1940)

Throughout the 1930s, Ginger Rogers was best known as Fred Astaire's fleet-of-foot dancing partner, nimbly cutting the carpet with the master hoofer in such classic films as "Top Hat", "Flying Down to Rio", and "Carefree." By the beginning of the next decade, she wanted a go at it alone. And she got her wish big-time, winning an Academy Award for Best Actress for this adaptation of Christopher Morley's novel about a Philadelphia woman confronted with some tough decisions in her life. The film begins in an odd way, with a mostly silent montage about women getting the right to vote.

> **"But Kitty can't help but find herself caught between Mark and Wyn ..."**

Then, we meet Rogers' title character and learn she has a baby and is torn between two lovers, a well-meaning but struggling New York physician, Mark Elson (James Craig), and Wyn Stafford (Dennis Morgan), a would-be entrepreneur with close ties to his snobby Main Line family. In an eerie moment near the film's opening, Rogers' is confronted by her alter ego, and we learn how she got into such a predicament. Kitty is a young working-class woman from Philadelphia, warned by her loving, single father (Ernest Cossart) to beware of Cinderella stories. But Kitty can't help but find herself caught between Mark and Wyn, the lower middle-class and the rich and New York and Philadelphia, which she comes to be fearful of because it reminds her of her past. Directed by Sam Wood ("Pride of the Yankees") and scripted by David Ogden Stewart ("The Philadelphia Story") and future Hollywood Ten blacklisted member Dalton Trumbo ("Spartacus"), "Kitty Foyle" remains memorable mostly for Rogers' fine turn in a fairly demanding dramatic role and its serious depiction of the problems faced by "modern women."

Local Moments:

Although shot mostly on a Hollywood backlot, the film has footage of a debutante ball at the Bellevue-Stratford Hotel on Broad Street; Kitty lives on Griscom Street in the Frankford section of the city, and the designers do a swell job recreating a Frankford home and its environs.

Rating:

Lady in the Water (2006)

Local Moments:

The entire film is set in and around a complex called The Cove. Although a character mentions they are in Philadelphia, the place bears little resemblance to a Philly complex. In fact, the film was shot almost entirely in Levittown.

Rating:

If you thought "The Village" was a step in the wrong direction for M. Night Shyamalan, wait until you

see "Lady in the Water." This mythic tale of weird, ferocious animals, a sea nymph, and finding one's destiny becomes more and more muddled as it goes along until its halfway point. Then it just ceases to be interesting and plays out the rest of its running time in what appears to be perpetual slow motion. The premise held some promise. Paul Giamatti is Cleveland Heep, a maintenance man at a Philadelphia apartment building. He suspects that someone has been swimming in the establishment's pool at night, and, sure enough, that has been going on. The culprit is a sea nymph named Story. Played by Bryce Dallas Howard, who was also the blind girl in "The Village," Story is a monosyllabic woman of ethereal beauty who has risen out the pool and holds the key (literally) for Heep to unlock his troubled past and live freely. Or something like that. But in order for Story to survive, she must return to the water because some ferocious wolflike critters are after her. To send her off to safety in the water, Heep must decipher an ancient story and recruit his neighbors to take part in a weird bon voyage ceremony that could save generations in the future. Still with us? Giamatti is the best thing about the movie, displaying common-guy looks supplemented by nervous tics and a self-effacing sense of humor. It's not easy to feel anything about anybody in the cold fish-out-water saga, but Giamatti works hard to get the audience to have empathy for him. The rest of the culturally diverse apartment dwellers are ciphers, from the aspiring writer (Shyamalan) and his sister (Sarita Choudray); an Asian student (Cindy Cheung) who translates her grandmother's stories for Heep; an animal lover (Mary Beth Hurt); a bodybuilder (Freddy Rodriguez); a crossword puzzle wizard (Jeffrey Wright); a cynical recluse (Bill Irwin); and the complex's newest resident, a pompous film critic

> **"Then it just ceases to be interesting ..."**

continued from page 62

Lady in the Water continued from page 61

> " ... the filmmaker still has a mesmerizing cinematic style ... "

(Bob Balaban). On the plus side, "Lady in the Water" shows that the filmmaker still has a mesmerizing cinematic style — but here it's used to lull its audience to sleep. Shyamalan's shortcomings in the writing department really come to the forefront here as he has fashioned thinly drawn characters — Howard is little more than that "Lady in the Water" — and a story line filled with unexplained incidents and gaps of logic the size of — well, that swimming pool. Credit him, also, for skipping the trick ending this time around, but here he has no real finale as a substitute. The movie just sort of ends. Perhaps Shyamalan expects his fans to go along for the ride without questioning where the filmmaker is taking them. But in the case of "Lady in the Water," there's are major holes aboard the vessel that sink it soon after it hits the water.

The Last Broadcast (1998)

The legend of the Pine Barrens' Jersey Devil has been around for decades, surfacing in several books, ghost stories, and a few movies. But the tale gets an original treatment in "The Last Broadcast", a fresh, shot-on-digital feature from Bucks County filmmakers Stefan Avalos and Lance Weiler. This mock documentary disguises itself as a tacky cable TV reality show called "Fact or Fiction," hosted by Steven (Avalos) and Locus (Weiler). The two plan to track down the Jersey Devil in the Pine Barrens, where they are joined by

> **"There are striking similarities to monstrous hit 'The Blair Witch Project'..."**

a soundman (Rein Clabbers) and oddball psychic (Jim Seward). Things go horribly wrong, and two men are murdered and the other goes missing while the psychic remains alive. After the murder trial, more mysteries linger, leading a documentary filmmaker (David Beard) to investigate. Shot on a shoestring, "The Last Broadcast" makes the best of its lack of funds, using inventive video techniques, the mystery of the then-burgeoning Internet, and an underlying creepiness to its advantage. To take things a step further, the film was projected digitally to several theatres when shown, an early test that may, in fact, become the movie theater standard in the coming years. There are striking similarities to the monstrous hit "The Blair Witch Project," what with its hand-held camerawork, faux documentary structure, disturbing desolate setting, and supernatural overtones. But truth be told, "The Last Broadcast" came first, and while it's never been proven, it probably inspired the makers of "The Blair Witch Project" in more than one way.

Local Moments:

Among the locales used were the Doylestown Courthouse, an old public access TV station, Bucks County Community College, an Upper Black Addy Christmas Tree Farm and the real deal — the New Jersey Pine Barrens.

Rating:

"The Last Broadcast" Marks First Step in Film Revolution

Stefan Avalos and Lance Weiler both grew up in Bucks County and attended Bucks County Community College where they met for the first time while attending film classes.

Thanks to their time at college, the two decided they had all the production exposure they needed and decided to get filmmaking experience on their own. Each went their own way, with Avalos making corporate videos and commercials, while Weiler toiled on music videos, concerts, and, briefly, a show for the Fox Sports Channel.

The two talked about doing a project together, but they had very little money to work with. They got together to conceive "The Last Broadcast" about a tabloid television team's search for the legendary Jersey Devil in the Pine Barrens of New Jersey.

Using "David Holzman's Diary," Jim McBride's seminal faux documentary, and "Paradise Lost," the disturbing 1996 real-life study about Arkansas child murderers, as their inspirations, Avalos and Weiler shot "The Last Broadcast" on video for an incredibly paltry $900.00 budget. The film offered Avalos and Weiler an opportunity to use all of their talents, as they wrote, produced, directed, and costarred in the film.

> **" The showing at the County Theater was a smashing success ... "**

But since it was shot on video, there was no print that could be shown in theaters. So, Avalos and Weiler came up with another idea.

"Right when we were finishing our movie, Texas Instruments had redone their DIP chips and Digital Projection Incorporated was interested in working with us," says Avalos. "We talked to them and there had never been any public screenings with these projections. We talked to the County Theater in Doylestown and we were able to retrofit their projection room so it could take this huge projector. The projector was just at the White House where Tom Hanks had just shown 'From the Earth to the Moon' to Bill Clinton."

The showing at the County Theater was a smashing success, leading Avalos and Weiler to test other unknown waters with "The Last Broadcast."

"From there, Lance and I had done festivals but we stayed in the digital realm," says Avalos. "Nobody had implemented the idea of showing films digitally. We put together the first ever digital release of a movie. It was downloaded to each theater from a satellite from Mountainview, California. It was delivered to theaters the day before and took several hours to download."

Avalos points out that George Lucas has said that "Star Wars: The Phantom Menace" was the first film to be digitally projected to theaters, but "The Last Broadcast" beat it by eight months.

Meanwhile, one of the theaters that projected "The Last Broadcast" was in Orlando, Florida, where Daniel Myrick and Eduardo Sanchez were working as managers. Eventually, the two went on to make the enormously successful "The Blair Witch Project," released in theaters a year after "The Last Broadcast" was screened. The film has many striking similarities to Avalos and Weiler's film.

Avalos says he and Weiler "were in contact with them. They had gotten screeners of the films.

The fact is they were already working on a Blair Witch movie, but they radically changed it after watching 'The Last Broadcast.' They don't deny it. They deny we had any influence on them. Our paths kept crossing. It got disconcerting after a while. We met via email and we met them at the Sundance Film Festival where we did a digital demonstration of 'The Last Broadcast.'"

Did Avalos and Weiler ever consider taking legal action against "The Blair Witch Project" creators?

"Plenty of people advised us to sue them," says Avalos. "Lawyers were calling us advising us. They represented other people with copyright cases. But I never really considered this because I'm not a litigious person.

"They [Myrick and Sanchez] had mouthpieces doing a lot of talking, says Avalos. "The guy I despise out of all this is [producer] John Pierson who would bad mouth us by name. He financed it, but it's a little known fact. It was unseemly I thought. I had read his book ["Spike, Mike, Slackers, & Dykes: A Guided Tour Across a Decade of American Independent Cinema"] and I admired who he was.

"It's very easy for people to go for the most enticing or enraging word they were going to say. When "Entertainment Tonight" or "Extra" would do these stories they would go for the most attention getting things.

"If these guys said they saw the movie and they saw mistakes we had made and tried to make it better, that is one thing. But all this denying got to us. What's ironic was that this whole movie was about discerning between fact and fiction."

In the long run, "The Last Broadcast" did well for both Avalos and Weiler. They struck successful video deals for the film and it was issued in October 2006 in a special edition DVD. They have parted company, but still keep in touch. Avalos, who lives in Los Angeles, has since made "The Ghosts of Edendale," about ghosts in Hollywood. Weiler's creepy psychological horror film "Head Trauma," shot in Doylestown and Scranton locations, was released on DVD in 2006.

The Lost Man (1969)

Sidney Poitier, wearing sunglasses with a dour look on his face, stars in this reworking of Carol Reed's classic Irish Republican Army thriller "Odd Man Out." Here Poitier is Jason Higgs (sounds a little like Tibbs from "In the Heat of the Night," doesn't it?), a cool-as-a-cucumber black revolutionary, who tries to swipe $200,000 from the payroll of a factory reputedly owned by racists. The heist goes bad when a cop and Higgs are shot, forcing Higgs to try to elude the fuzz in the wilds of North Philly. For support of his cause, the radical has a former partner (Al Freeman, Jr.) and a white widowed social worker (Joanna Shimkus, soon-to-be Mrs. Poitier). While dodging the law amidst burned-out houses, abandoned cars, unruly foliage, and an ugly rural landscape close to Temple University, it's revealed that Higgs, in fact, really wants the money to go to the kids of black revolutionaries in prison. Substituting ramshackle Philly streets for shadowy Belfast of "Odd Man Out," "The Lost Man" is strong in its cityscape atmospherics, but its racial-empowerment-meets-classic-heist motif doesn't always blend well. Writer-director Robert Alun Arthur, who went on to coscript "All That Jazz," has everyone play it so solemnly, there's little joy while the actors trying hard to make the proceedings important. Still, for a peek at Philadelphia's urban blight in the late 1960s, "The Lost Man" is worth tracking down.

> **" ... but its racial empowerment-meets-classic-heist motif doesn't always blend well. "**

Local Moments:

North Philly is heavily on display, with a focus on Broad Street and Germantown Avenue … Poitier's Higgs ducks into the long-shuttered Liberty Theater near Temple University to elude the cops … Pier 78 on Delaware Avenue is the setting for the finale … Black-and-white oldfangled Philly cop cars are prominently displayed … A main sequence takes place at a gas station at "8th and Norris."

Rating:

Mad Ron's Prevues From Hell (1987)

Local Moments:

The late, lamented Lansdowne Theater is the locale for all the activity ... "Mad Ron" Roccia and producer-costar James Murray, Jr. are well-known movie collectors and "gore-storians," while Nick Pawlow and happy frequently play comedy clubs in the area.

Rating:

You can practically smell the stale popcorn and Lysol and feel your shoes sinking into sticky candy after watching this homage to the grindhouse horror films of the 1970s. This is essentially a program of some of the most disgusting trailers of all time, coupled with some gross-out special effects and a wraparound featuring a ventriloquist and his ghoulish dummy. In other words, a labor of love. The ventriloquist (Nick Pawlow) and his dummy (Happy) link the coming attractions together with off-color jokes and not-so-witty banter. They're situated in a movie theater where projectionist "Mad Ron" (Ron Roccia) keeps the trailers coming. Come-ons for such classics as The Blood-Splattered Bride, the I Drink Your blood/I Eat your Skin double-bill, The Wizard of Gore, Texas Chainsaw Massacre, and Torso are unspoiled. Meanwhile, a group of zombies and other monstrosities munch on human parts in the theater. Well, at least they don't have cell phones that ring when they're watching the movie.

> **This is essentially a program of some of the most disgusting trailers of all time ...**

All that Jazz (1979)
Audrey Paris (Leland Palmer): Quick. Tell me. What was the name of the girl in Philadelphia, the blonde with the television show?
Joe Gideon (Roy Scheider): Ah, the blonde with the television show. The blonde with the television show in Philadelphia? I remember that girl's name. I remember that girl's name because that girl meant something to me. The blonde with the television show — her name was Sweetheart! Honey? Baby? Can't remember her name.

Malatesta's Carnival Of Blood (Malatesta's Carnival)

(1973)

Philly's long-unseen answer to "Night of the Living Dead" tells of terror in a carnival, but, it's actually about terror in an amusement park. Shot in the long-gone Willow Grove Park, Christopher Speeth's film tells about the Norris family — mother, father, and daughter Vena (Janine Carazo) — who take jobs at a carnival where their teenage son has disappeared. They hope to find out what really happened. We soon discover that the people running the show are up to no good. Mr. Blood (played by Jerome Dempey and whose name should've been a tip-off is the manager of the rundown joint. He looks like Kelsey Grammar and speaks like a third rate Shakespearean actor auditioning for a role in a dinner theater production of *Hamlet*. Little does the Norris family know, however, that Mr. Blood happens to be a vampire, who bears his fangs when the time is right. There's also a creepy old fellow named Mr. Bean (Tom Markus), an excitable transvestite fortune teller (the late Lenny Baker of "Next Stop, Greenwich Village" fame), a dwarf with a French accent named Bobo (Herve Villicheze), and Malatesta (Daniel Dietrich) himself, who enjoys throwing rave parties for his ghoulies in a hidden underground cove where they watch Lon Chaney movies. "Malatesta's Carnival of Blood" scores for its ambition and certainly the Willow Grove Park nostalgia factor, although it's a pretty incompetent production, with amateurish, wobbly direction and shoddy camera work. You can tell it's trying hard to scare you, and it does parade out a slew of icky creatures and offers some truly psychedelic moments, including a hallucinogenic nightmare that looks like a Fillmore West light show filmed in a Saran Wrap factory.

> **"You can tell it's trying hard to scare you ..."**

Local Moments:

There's nothing outside Willow Grove Park here, so enjoy the sights of the once grand entertainment center just three years before it closed ... At this point, the park had actually become "Six Gun Territory" with a western theme, but that's not apparent from the few rides featured in the film.

Rating:

Mannequin (1987)

Local Moments

The nice thing about "Mannequin" is that it uses Philly pretty well and offers a swell showcase of the Grand Court, stock rooms, and nooks and crannies of the late, great Wanamaker's Department Store. The Dorchester Hotel gets a few screen moments … A restaurant scene was shot at DiLullo's, the now-shuttered eatery on Locust Street.

Rating:

This surprise hit reworked a plot very similar to the 1948 Ava Gardner vehicle "One Touch of Venus," adding some modern touches. The result? A healthy audience in theaters, especially among teenagers. A few years after "Porky's" and way before she discovered "Sex in the City," Kim Cattrall plays Emmy, a department store mannequin who comes to life. The backstory tells us that Emmy is the reincarnation of an ancient Egyptian princess. Upon her return as a dummy, Emmy hits it off with Jonathan (Andrew McCarthy in a part reportedly conceived for Dudley Moore), a window dresser at the Philly department store called Prince and Company who is inspired by Emmy's advice and beauty. While Cattrall and McCarthy at least make a pretty (albeit bland) couple, everyone else badly overacts in this film.

> **"Add up all these elements an you have an extra large hoagie of a 1980s headache."**

Among them: James Spader is a not-be-trusted young store manager; Meshach Taylor a flamboyantly gay window-dressing associate of McCarthy; and G.W. Bailey, a redneck security guard. Then there's the theme song, the Starship's bombastic "Nothing's Gonna Stop Us Now." Add up all these elements and you have an extra large hoagie of a 1980s headache. Still, there's no denying that this movie remains popular, even all these years after its release. Just look at the "User's comments" on *www.imdb.com*.

Mannequin On the Move
(Mannequin 2: On The Move)  (1991)

If ever a sequel was unnecessary it's this follow-up to the inexplicably popular Kim Cattrall/Andrew McCarthy romantic fantasy. Meshach Taylor as flamboyant designer "Hollywood" Montrose is back, as is Wanamaker's as Prince and Company Department Store and the total innocuousness of it all, but the leads have changed. Now, Kristy Swanson (the movie world's "Buffy, the Vampire Slayer") plays Jessie, a blonde peasant girl frozen by a spell 1000 years ago who resurfaces as a window dummy at the Market Street's Prince Department Store. Jason ("Fright Night"'s William Ragsdale), a department store assistant and descendant of a prince who loved Jessie, helps to break her curse, and before you can ask "Who cares?," she's smooching him, taking bubble baths, riding in his Jeep along South Street and sucking down cheesesteaks from Jim's. Meanwhile, Hollywood is given the task to design the medieval-themed store display and the mysterious Count Spretzle (Terry Kiser, aka the corpse from "Weekend at Bernie's"), a reincarnated evil sorcerer, wants to kidnap Jessie and take her to … Bermuda (?). Boasting labored comedy, unfunny, way-over-the-top gay stereotypes, little chemistry between the romantic leads, an annoying villain backed by a group of muscle bound, spandex-clad cohorts, the sequel to "Mannequin" is every bit the dummy its ancestor was.

> **the sequel to 'Mannequin' is every bit the dummy its ancestor was.**

Rating:

Philly Fill-Ins

Philadelphia has stood in for several cities in films, here are the movies for which Philly has done the switcheroos for.

The Age of Innocence (1993)

As a stand-in for a New York opera house and its 19th century streets envisioned by writer Edith Wharton, Martin Scorsese recruits the Academy of Music and the surrounding Broad Street.

Amazing Grace (1974)

Philly stands in for Baltimore in this political comedy with Moms Mabley (a regular on "The Merv Griffin Show") as a plucky ghetto inhabitant who helps get fomer convict Moses Gunn elected mayor in order to get the city out of crooked white men's hands. West Philly High School and the Master Theater in West Philly are featured, while two prominent Philly African-Americans had their hands in this one: "Sesame Street" veteran and Holly Robinson Peete's father Matt Robinson produced and wrote it while Stan Lathan ("Beat Street"), father of Sanaa Lathan, directed.

Beloved (1998)

Jonathan Demme directed and Oprah Winfrey costars in and produces this haunting adaptation of Toni Morrison's award-winning saga about slavery. Lancaster County doubles for rural Ohio, and Old City Philly is 19th century downtown Cincinnati, while soundstages at the Civic Center and Old New Castle were used for locations as well.

Dressed to Kill (1980)

Brian De Palma's psycho-thriller with Michael Caine and Angie Dickinson utilizes the Philadelphia Museum of Art in favor of the Metropolitan Museum of Art in it signature sequence.

The Last of The Red Hot Lovers (1972)

Neil Simon's neurotic romantic comedy stars Alan Arkin as a randy restaurant owner whose midlife crisis leads him to affairs with Paula Prentiss, Renee Taylor, and Sally Kellerman. Because of union problems in New York, Rittenhouse Square and, in a memorable scene, the exterior of the Dorchester Apartments were substituted for Manhattan locales.

Marnie (1964)

Long considered in the middle of the pack as far as Alfred Hitchcock movies are concerned, "Marnie" has picked up steam over the years, and is now recognized as one of Hitch's flawed but fascinating efforts. The film stars Tippi Hedren as the title character, a kleptomaniac who shifts her identity as she moves around the U.S. stealing cash from her employers. After pulling a swindle as a blonde, she goes to brown hair and gets a job working for a company headed by dashing Main Line widower Mark Rutland (Sean Connery). He recognizes Marnie from her last job, in which she swiped cash from his business associate, and catches her taking money from him, too. But rather than prosecute his new employee, Mark marries Marnie, and sets out to understand her many neuroses — including the fear of thunder and lightning, the color red, and sexual relations. Using crimson tinting and Bernard Herrman's brazenly lush score to underline the psychological aspects of the story, Hitchcock digs as deep as Connery to investigate Marnie's psychoses. What he finds are unsettling truths in her past, and the uneasy feeling that husband Mark is as unstable as his unhinged spouse — he's irrationally driven to find out what makes Marnie tick, even at the expense of her emotional stability. Marnie may not be prime Hitchcock, but it's one of the master of suspense's most unsettling works. Good evening, indeed.

> **" ... but it's one of the master of suspense's most unsettling works. "**

Local Moments:

All the exteriors of "Marnie" were shot on soundstages in Los Angeles, but there are several recognizable location shots in the film ... Rutland and Company is located in an undisclosed location in Center City where the Ben Franklin Bridge is visible in the background, via a matte painting ... 30th Street Station is highlighted in one scene. Rutland's estate on the Main Line is located in Woodwyn. Were they thinking Wynnwood? ... Connery drives Marnie in his Thunderbird onto what appears to be the rearscreen version of the eastbound Schuylkill Expressway via the City Line entrance. They end up at a Howard Johnson's for lunch. Does this guy know how to treat a dame, or what? ... Connery's father, played by Alan Napier (Alfred the butler in the 1960s "Batman" TV show), says he likes tea and cake from Horn & Hardart's in the film ... Rutland and Marnie attend the races at Atlantic City Racetrack.

Rating:

Mikey and Nicky (1976)

Local Moments:

More than half of the movie's 100-day shooting schedule was in Philly, while the rest was shot in Los Angeles. This makes for an odd mix, in which some of the locations are unmistakably Philadelphia, and others don't look like anything here at all … There's talk about a movie theater located on 14th Street. Perhaps an inside joke from native May who knows there is no 14th Street in Philly … The movie theater, which is showing a double feature of a kung fu film and "The Laughing Policeman," was actually the Nixon, located at 52nd and Ranstead Streets … Schmidt's Beer has a prominent spot in a bar where Cassavettes and Falk go … And the bar they went to was the Ebony Lounge, Broad and Oxford Streets … The sleazy hotel where Cassavettes holes up was formerly the Essex House, located at 11th and Filbert Streets.

Rating:

Taking a page out of her leading actor's book,

Elaine May tips John Cassevettes' intimate, independent, improv-heavy, cinema verite style with this jazzy gangster drama. Cassevettes plays a Philly hood paranoid of leaving his hotel room at night, fearful of being bumped off by a hitman (Ned Beatty) enlisted by a mob boss (played by noted acting coach Sanford Meisner). Cassavettes seeks help throughout the night from lovers, cohorts, and especially best friend (and frequent real-life collaborator) Peter Falk, who works for the same boss and actually has other plans for Cassavettes. To watch what transpires over one night's time in grimy Philadelphia neighborhoods will remind viewers of the quirky nocturnal escapades of "After Hours" and the

> " … will remind viewers of the quirky nocturnal escapades of 'After Hours' … "

philosophical ruminations of the seminal 60s film "The Swimmer," in which Burt Lancaster reevaluates his life, swimming from pool to pool across his suburban neighborhood. The movie offers an uneasy mix of downbeat drama and dark humor, but it seems that May and company are out to make audiences uncomfortable here, and to that, they succeed splendidly. In fact, there isn't a likable character in the film and it's to May and the actor's credit that the unpredictable ranting and raving Cassavettes turns out to be the most sympathetic of the bunch. "Mikey and Nicky" had a tortuous production history — an extremely long shoot (for such a low-budget film) coupled with months of editing and then reediting by distributor Paramount to make it releasable. On DVD, we get to see May's cut of the film. It's a disquieting, problematical work, but one senses that was its intent.

Money Power Respect

(2006)

An impressive first film from West Oak Lane native Jamal Hill, this urban crime story wears its inspirations on its sleeve, but still manages to be exciting and absorbing. With obvious reverence to "Scarface," "New Jack City," and "Dead Presidents," "Money Power Respect" tells the tale of Levi (Kyle Schell), a slick, young operator who gets tangled up dealing coke in Philly. He gets into cahoots with the brother of his girlfriend, and moves out from his Philly cooperative to Cherry Hill. But he can't seem to handle the heat supplied by his mother, girlfriend, and business associates. Shot in just two weeks on a miniscule budget, "Money Power Respect" has some amateurish acting, but it also has real energy and drive, and works best as a solid urban actioner about the downside of dealing and gangbanging and is a great calling card for writer-director Hill.

> **"Shot in just two weeks on a miniscule budget ..."**

Local Moments:

Lots of location work in and around Germantown Avenue, and some Oak Lane locales are on view.

Rating:

Music From the Inside Out (2005)

The musicians are shown at their homes in and around the city … The Academy of Music is featured as is the area around the Art Museum.

Rating:

"Classical Musicians Are People, Too"

could be the subtitle of this often joyous, occasionally painful investigation into the lives of members of the Philadelphia Orchestra. What makes these masters of music tick? And, aside from excelling in playing their instruments, what else is going on in their lives? Both questions are answered in fascinating fashion as director Daniel Anker zeroes in on several of the players and their private time. Among those we meet are a trombonist who digs salsa music and plays it in his off hours; a French horn player who gave up jazz for classical and enjoys running marathons; a violist with the unique talent of witnessing colors as sounds; and a violinist from Japan who filters her frustrations about her mother through her music. Strangely absent from the interview sessions are maestros Wolfgang Sawallisch and Charles Dutoit, but it's easy to see why Anker preferred to focus on the performers, proving, well, "classical musicians — but, perhaps, not conductors — are people, too."

> **"... often joyous, occasionally painful investigation into the lives of the members of the Philadelphia Orchestra."**

David Morse's Philadelphia Code

David Morse wasn't born in the Philadelphia area. He was born in Hamilton, Massachusetts. But the busy actor, who played Dr. Morrison in the hit 1980s TV series "St. Elsewhere," and has been featured in such films as "Inside Moves," "The Green Mile," "Proof of Life," "16 Blocks" "Down in the Valley," and the shot-in-Philly TV series "Hack," now makes his home in Chestnut Hill.

Q. Why do you live in Philadelphia?

A. My wife [Susan Wheeler Duff] grew up here. Her father was involved politically here. We lost our house [in Los Angeles] in the 1994 earthquake and moved to the area."

Q. How do you like working close to home, like you did with "Hack" in which you played a disgraced ex-cop who drives a cab and helps others in trouble?

A. I love to bring work here. It's a great thing "Hack" was shot here. I loved being in the neighborhoods here and all over the city. Every place I go, people tell me how they love that show.

Q. The show did well with critics and had a solid following, but seemed to get bad time slots. How do you feel it was handled?

A. I knew when we went to Saturday night we didn't have much longer to go. Les [CBS chief Moonves] kept saying that if he had a night to put it on, he had confidence it would find an audience. He left it on for two years and had enough confidence in it to leave it on while he yanked other shows, which I appreciate. It didn't get enough of an audience to keep it on. But I was actually told that if I took it to Toronto, we would keep shooting. I didn't want to do that. I felt it was a Philadelphia show — a lot of the crew were from here and my character was a Philadelphian, plus my family's here. It didn't make sense.

Q. You've directed a few episodes of "St. Elsewhere" and some other TV shows. Do you have any aspirations of directing a movie?

A. I was ready to make a movie last year [2005], but the financing didn't come together.

Q. Can you tell us about it?

A. It was something different than you'd expect from me. It was going to be shot in Philly.

My Little Girl (1987)

This well-meaning, undervalued drama

stars Mary Stuart Masteron as Franny Bettinger, born and bred in the posh 'burbs, who decides to make a difference by joining the staff of a downtown Philly center for troubled and underprivileged kids. Idealistic and strong-willed, Franny soon learns that funding and politics have more to do with helping these kids than her good intentions. At the center, she comes in contact with a number of the residents, including Joan (Philly actress Erika Alexander), a black woman who barely speaks, and Alice (Tracy Lind), a teenage prostitute who can't seem to stay out of trouble with the center's director, Ike Bailey

> **We follow Franny as she struggles with her parents …**

(James Earl Jones). We follow Franny as she struggles with her parents — who don't understand why she would do such altruistic work to begin with — attempts to help Joan when she abandons the center and is arrested, and dodges the advances of Alice's pimp (Peter Gallagher). If this sounds a bit like the female version of "To Sir with Love" or any other teacher-makes-good-with-tough-student effort, you're right, but "My Little Girl" seems genuine and it is honestly affecting at times. Additionally, the acting is fine all-around, from the 20-year-old Masterson (who looks a lot like Molly Ringwald here) to a supporting cast that includes Geraldine Page (in her last film role), Anne Meara, George Newborn, and, yes, that's an 18-year-old Jennifer Lopez in her film debut as Myra.

Local Moments:

If the center in the film and its parking lot look familiar it's because it's the Southern Home, located on Broad Street near Packard, a building whose parking lot faced what is now Chickie's & Pete's … The interior shots at the center were filmed in Norristown State Hospital … Kensington and the Frankford El are showcased in several scenes, and Franny gets Joan an apartment next to the Tioga El Stop.

Rating:

My Architect: A Son's Journey (2003)

A heartfelt, emotionally-packed personal documentary, "My Architect" chronicles filmmaker Nathaniel Kahn's search to find his father, renowned Philadelphia architect Louis Kahn. In reality, Nathaniel knew his father only fleetingly, from irregular visits he made at his home at night. You see, for all of his accolades, awards, and reverence from fellow architects, Louis Kahn was a cipher, and Nathaniel's family was one of three that the architect had. Muddying the waters of his memory even more is the fact that Louis died as an anonymous, penniless person with no name on his passport in New York's Penn Station in 1973, when Nathaniel was 11 years old. The further Nathaniel gets in to his crusade to uncover the secrets of his father, the more complex the puzzle and his father become. He travels around the world, from Trenton to New Hampshire to California to Texas to India and, finally, to Bangladesh to see examples of Dad's work and talk to coworkers who may recall meeting him. He interviews fellow architects like I.M. Pei and Frank Gehry to get their views, and engages city planner Ed Bacon in a heated exchange about Louis's rejected plans for the city (imagine parking garages all along Vine Street and people walking into Center City sans traffic!). Finally, Nathaniel meets some of his blood relatives for the first time, and commiserates with them about the lives Louis affected and left behind. Five years and a lifetime in the making, the highly personal "My Architect: A Son's Journey" offers a lyrical look at the life of an enigmatic artist who refused to compromise, even if the fate of his wife, lovers, and children were at stake.

> " ... offers a lyrical look at the life of an enigmatic artist who refused to compromise ... "

Local Moments:

Louis Kahn's office is located at 1501 Locust Street in both archival footage and contemporary footage ... The film offers a veritable travelogue of the city, through newsreel and newly shot sequences ... Of particular interest are the sketches Kahn made of the city and its environs ... The Richards Medical Tower, one of Kahn's few local public buildings, located on the Penn campus, is showcased ... There are segments of a symposium Kahn gave to Penn student sin the 1960s ... Kahn's Trenton Bath House in Ewing, NJ is visited.

Rating:

Nasty Habits (1977)

Local Moments:

Though most of the interiors were shot in England's Elstree Studios, there's plenty of local color here … A few great aerial shots of Philly allow us to catch the skyline when City Hall was its highest building and Vine Street before there was an expressway … A scene with Penhaligon is shot on the University of Pennsylvania campus … Talk show host Mike Douglas does a nice bit playing himself, as does newscaster Jessica Savitch … The Eagles lose a game heard over the radio in the last minute … The bathroom in Wanamker's plays a part in the plot.

Rating:

Maligned when it was first released,

"Nasty Habits" holds up better in retrospect. A keen satire on Watergate with nuns standing in for Nixon and his cohorts, the film stars Glenda Jackson as a duplicitous sister who will do just about anything to gain power in her Philadelphia-area abbey — including blackmail and wiretapping. When an elderly abbess (Edith Evans) dies, her successor is not determined. Sister Alexandria (Glenda Jackson), a British import who assumed she'd take the job, attempts to keep Sister Gertrude (Melina Mercouri) away on missionary work. She has another competitor in Sister Felicity (Susan Penhaligon), a young sister with ideas to modernize the church and the convent who happens to be having an affair with a local Jesuit. The increasingly paranoid Jackson and followers Sister Walburga (Geraldine Page), Sister Mildred (Anne Jackson), and sister Felicity (Sandy Dennis), go all-out to thwart

> **"A keen satire on Watergate with nuns standing in for Nixon and his cohorts …"**

Felicity's attempts at running the show by having the place bugged (by plumbers, of course), and smearing Felicity by making her trysts public. But their efforts don't quite work out as planned. At times clever and inspired and other times flat-footed and obvious, "Nasty Habits" is a fairly complex spoof of Nixon's downfall, and would make a great double bill with "Dick," the 1999 comedy with Kirsten Dunst and Michelle Williams. Here Jackson turns in a fine lead performance as the treacherously Nixonian nun and she gets able support all-around, from her all-star female costars and bits by Eli Wallach, Rip Torn, and Jerry Stiller. Directed by Michael Lindsay-Hogg, best known for chronicling the Beatles demise in "Let It Be," and based on the British novel by Muriel Sparks, the film may be a little too complicated for its own good, but "Nasty Habits" hits most of its targets pretty squarely, whether they be religious or political in nature.

National Treasure (2004)

Improbable and messy, "National Treasure" shouldn't work at all, especially if you read its meandering story line before seeing it. Yet it does work in spite of itself and, for a good half-hour, it serves as a cool travelogue of Center City Philly. Nicolas Cage is Benjamin Franklin Gates, a wide-eyed history buff and explorer, who has been trying to track down ages-old secrets about a mysterious treasure that have been related to him by his father (Jon Voight) and grandfather (Christopher Plummer). Gates and his team of fellow explorers find a key piece to the historical puzzle when they come across a boat frozen in water in the Arctic. The discovery of the vessel and an antique pipe leads to a parting of ways between Gates and villainous team member Ian Howe (Sean Bean) and his cronies. It also spirals into a wild chase for the goods that involves the Declaration of Independence, the Freemasons, and special secret codes, and sends the former team members to Washington, Boston, New York, and Philadelphia. High in several concepts as well as dopey plot machinations, "National Treasure" still manages to entertain — even enthrall at times — thanks in part to Cage's winning turn as the nerdy action hero, and fine support from Dianne Karger as the brainy security-expert love interest and Bartha as the put-upon sidekick. Typical of a Jerry Bruckheimer production, the technical stuff is top-notch, with daredevil stunt work and a handsome look (Philly natives Caleb Deschanel and William Goldenberg did the cinematography and editing, respectively). The high point of the film, however, is the Philly section, spotlighting many of the city's most recognizable landmarks, some of them part of an elaborate chase sequence.

Nicolas Cage prepares for a scene from "National Treasure."
© Scott Weiner

Local Moments:

A SEPTA bus poster for "Liberty Bank" helps Cage connect the dots to his puzzle … The Franklin Institute, Independence Hall, and the Liberty Bell are integral parts of the plot … Somehow, a chase that begins at 5th and Chestnut winds up at the Reading Terminal Market … Cage's car is parked at Head House Square.

Rating:

One Last Thing ... (2005)

A high school kid with cancer declares his last wish is to spend a day with a supermodel. Sounds bad already, right? But this movie is deftly handled with sensitivity and dark humor, and turns out to be surprisingly affecting, a rare film that could likely elicit tears from the staunchest man's man out there. Michael Angarmmo ("Sky High") is Dylan, the Marcus Hook, Pennsylvania boy with little time to live, who decides to go out without feeling sorry for himself, but finds time to consul his widowed mother ("Sex in the City's" Cynthia Nixon) at the same time. When asked what he really wants by wish-granting organization on TV, Dylan says a date with Nikki Sinclair (Sunny Mabray), a petulant model with a serious drinking problem. Along with her manager (Gina Gershon), Nikki stops over for

> **" But this movie is deftly handled with sensitivity and dark humor ... "**

a brief visit to Dylan's house, but that's not enough for him. With some much-needed cash supplied from a fundraising cable access auction, Dylan and his two gung-ho pals head to the Big Apple to track Nikki down in what may possibly be Dylan's last fling. The results of the film are not altogether predictable, and equally sweet and edgy — there are strippers, pot-smoking, and some other nonsaccharine elements. Produced on a lean budget by entrepreneur Mark Cuban, and directed by Alex Steyermark and written by Barry Stringfellow, two area natives, "One More Thing ..." offers some nice, unassuming surprises, especially for big boys who don't usually cry.

Marcus Hook ... Or Bust!

Local Pals Team for "One Last Thing ..."

Friends since they were twelve years old, Alex Steyermark and Barry Stringfellow always figured that some day they'd work together on a project. After being raised in the Wilmington, Delaware area — just a stone's throw from Marcus Hook, Pennsylvania, where Stringfellow's father worked at a refinery — the two men went their separate ways, but in the same business. Steyermark became a music supervisor and music producer, working on scores for a diverse slate of films like "The Ice Storm" and several Spike Lee films, while Stringfellow found steady work writing scripts for such TV shows as "Perfect Strangers" and "The Angry Beavers."

The two childhood friends kept in contact, telling each other about what they were working on, until Stringfellow wrote a script called "One Last Thing," which centers on Dylan, a Marcus Hook teenager, dying of cancer, who is given an opportunity to have his final wish fulfilled. The teen surprises everyone when, on national TV, he proclaims he'd like to spend a weekend with a supermodel.

"Barry sent me the film while he was writing it," says Steyermark, who had directed the feature "Prey for Rock & Roll" with Gina Gershon. "When he told me about his problem getting the studios interested, I asked if I could take it to the people at HDNet [the cable company]. We set it up for about $2 million and shot it on high definition video. I shot 'Prey for Rock & Roll' that way. If you do it right, it looks like film. It's a beautiful format."

Stringfellow says much of the material in "One Last Thing" ... comes from his experiences growing up in the Philadelphia suburbs. "My dad worked in Marcus Hook for 36 years, I worked there for awhile and the town always intrigued me.

"For a while, it looked like we weren't going to be able to shoot there. When we shot location photos, we got pulled down to the pokey. It was post 9/11 concerns. It was a little nerve-wracking. I told them my dad worked there and I worked there. Then Alex showed them the script and it said 'Marcus Hook'.

"But there was [still] a question whether we could film there. The script mentioned documentary and a kid with cancer, and I realized this is not going to happen. I got my mother to come to Marcus Hook and meet with the city council. My mother met my father at the refinery where she was a secretary, which is in the film. We talked to the council and told them we wouldn't be here except for Marcus Hook, and it's all done with respect. Before all this happened, the location scouts were all over New York and New Jersey, and Alex wouldn't settle because he knew the uniqueness of the town."

Eventually, the "One Last Thing" ... cast and crew got to shoot exteriors in Marcus Hook, but only for a day. The rest of the film was lensed in New York City, where, in the film, Dylan and his two friends [played by Matt Bush and Gideon Glick] try to track down the supermodel after her initial, brief visit to Dylan's home.

"My arc is like the arc Dylan [the lead character] went through in movie," says Stringfellow. "I grew up going to church and I learned some good stuff, then I hit my 20s and I was not so sure and kind of skeptical. Then my father died, and things that happened around his death convinced me that there was something else, and put me on a search.

Add sSteyermark: "Certainly it's autobiographical for Barry and in ways it captures what we were like growing up. We've known each other since we were twelve, so we liked the idea of filming in Marcus Hook. At night, you could see the city from where we lived, and you could see the skies glowing from the refineries. It always had an amazing visual sort of quality to it. I always wanted to go there and take pictures. "

Philadelphia (1993)

There are a plethora of Philly sights and sounds to be found in the film … The Mellon Bank Center at 1735 Market Street plays the Wheeler Building, Hanks' former law firm … Pickwick Pharmacy, located across Market Street, is where a person attempts to pick up Washington, believing he is gay … Denzel's law office is 1901 Chestnut Street … The University of Pennsylvania Arts Library doubles as the law library in the film… Scenes were also shot at The Racquet Club, Mt. Sinai Hospital (where Washington's wife gives birth) at 4th and Reed, and The Spectrum … The courtroom where the final trial goes down is Room 245 in City Hall.

Rating:

Jonathan Demme's film was a breakthrough, the first Hollywood film dealing with AIDS. Tom Hanks won an Academy Award for his bravura portrayal of Andrew Beckett, a Penn grad, who becomes a successful lawyer in a Center City blue-blood firm headed by powerful Charles Wheeler (Jason Robards, Jr.). When it's discovered Beckett has contracted AIDS, he's dismissed from his job. Forced to fight his former employers in court, Beckett has trouble finding an attorney to take his case. Eventually, Joe Miller (Denzel Washington), an African-American with his own antigay agenda, decides to take Beckett as a client, setting the stage for a courtroom showdown. "Philadelphia" is a solid piece of social drama that features superb acting, intense courtroom sequences, expert cinematography by Tak Fujimoto, superior musical contributions by Neil Young and Oscar winner Bruce Springsteen, and local color to spare. But it also is politically correct in a comic book sense at times, and — blame Demme's ambitiousness here — tries to cram too many characters into its proceedings. Demme and screenwriter Ron Nyswaner should be applauded for trying to examine how the disease and the case has affected Beckett's life, but the sequences involving his family (his mother is played by Joanne Woodward) and lover (Antonio Banderas) appear way too brief. Still, "Philadelphia" is to be commended for tackling a taboo subject with class and intelligence. Stanley Kramer, the filmmaker who gave us such socially conscious works as "The Defiant Ones," "On the Beach," and "Guess Who's Coming to Dinner," would have certainly approved.

Tom Hanks won an Academy Award for his role as an AIDS-stricken lawyer in "Philadelphia."
© Columbia/The Kobal Collection/Regan, Ken

"... to be commended for tackling a taboo subject with class and intelligence."

The Philadelphia Story
(1940)

It's quite talky, sexist in spots, and features some primary characters that border on the unsavory. Yet "The Philadelphia Story" remains a classic screwball comedy boasting some uproarious moments and a dream cast that's tough to beat. The pretentiousness of Main Liners in particular is skewered by director George Cukor ("The Women," "A Star is Born") and the screenplay, adapted by David Ogden Stewart from Phillip Barry's hit play. Repeating her comeback stage role is Katharine Hepburn as Tracy Lord, a socialite recently divorced from C.K. Dexter Haven

> **" ... a classic screwball comedy boasting some uproarious moments and a dream cast ... "**

(Cary Grant) and about to marry stuffy nouveau riche fellow George Kitteridge (John Howard). But Haven has plans to derail the nuptials and they involve reporter Mike Connor (James Stewart) and photographer Liz Imbrie (Ruth Hussey), who work for *Spy Magazine*. The witty dialogue is spewed fast and furiously by the charming but somewhat smug Grant, the spoiled but oddly appealing Hepburn, and the well-meaning nice guy Stewart, who won his only Academy Award for this role. One of the film's pleasures is picking out the modus operandi of its main characters, then watching them as they try to pull off their ingenious little schemes. At the same time, the backdrop of a huge Main Line estate, where the Lord-Kitteridge wedding is about to take place — looking orderly and proper as belies its upper crust denizens — is the center of wacky predicaments, unruly behavior, drunken interludes, and illicit sexual encounters. The Philadelphia Story is a frantic farce that continually asks the question "What's Love Got to With It?" And even when it comes up with the answer, it never seems quite certain — in a good way.

Local Moments:

Except for some quick exteriors, including a shot of the North Philadelphia train station and the Main Line, "The Philadelphia Story" was shot on the MGM lot in Culver City, California.

Rating:

The Pride of the Marines (1945)

Local Moments:

It comes as a big surprise that a studio film (Warner Brothers) in this case would do so much location filming, but this movie is filled with Philly sights … It opens with an aerial view of the skyline, takes us on a quick montage tour of such historic sites as Independence Hall, Constitution Hall, and the Betsy Ross house, then arrives where Al Schmid is renting a room, on Tulip Street near Hellerman in Tacony … 30th Street Station is showcased a few times in the film. There are several interesting exterior shots of a train stop at 20th Street overlooking the Schuylkill River, Boathouse Row, and the Philadelphia Museum of Art.

Rating:

While William Wyler's 1946 Oscar-winner "The Best Years of Our Lives" is generally considered the first film dealing with the problems of returning World War II veterans, this true story from 1945 beat it to the punch by a year. It remains a pretty powerful and compelling story, centering on Al Schmid (John Garfield), a Type A Philadelphia factory worker who boards with a family in Tacony. A confirmed bachelor, Schmid gets cozy with Ruth Hartley (Eleanor Parker) just as the Japanese bomb Pearl Harbor. Schmid enlists in the Marines, and soon finds himself at the Battle of Tenaru River in Guadalcanal. After fierce exchange with enemy troops, a Japanese soldiers drops a grenade near Schmid, blinding him. Transferred to a naval hospital in San Diego, Schmid has

> **" … the first film dealing with the problems of returning World War II veterans …"**

problems dealing with his loss of eyesight as well as how to handle his relationship with Ruth, despite the better efforts of an understanding Red Cross nurse (Rosemary DeCamp) and fellow Marine (Dane Clark). In many ways, "The Pride of the Marines" is an unusual film. It's a war film, but the intense, ultra-realistic combat sequence is relegated to ten minutes or so. It also has moments of pro-American propaganda as "The Halls of Montezuma" ("Marine's Hymn") swells in the background during a scene, but doesn't pull any punches relating to the nature of war or to the plight of those who fought and have been affected by it. At the same time, Al Schmid is anything but likable: hyper, motor-mouthed, sour, and eventually bitter, Garfield reportedly played him close to the real Schmid — the actor spent time with him to get the portrayal right. It's interesting to note that both Garfield and screenwriter Albert Maltz were targeted by Joseph McCarthy in the 1950s and blacklisted as Communists.

Primal Scream (1987)

An oddball, amateurish mix of pulp detective conventions and science fiction a la "Blade Runner", this low-budget project tells of a sleazy private dick named Corby McHale (Kenneth J. MacGregor) who trying to find out more about Hellfire, a substance mined from outer space that has the ability to turn its users' flesh into something resembling burnt toast. McHale is enlisted by Caitlin Foster (Julie Miller) to find out more about why her Hellfire-president brother is spying on her, and what his ultimate goals are for Hellfire. The film uneasily moves from one genre to the other, and little help is offered by the convoluted script, uninspired direction, or clunky acting that resembles the sort you'd find in a school project. One positive note: The special effects, mostly shown in the beginning, are decent for a small budget.

> " ... the film uneasily moves from one genre to the other ... "

Local Moments:

Some pretty nondescript locations of what appears to be Delaware County.

Rating:

Renegade (1988)

Local Moments:

This is a faux Philly film, meaning it mixes real location work with Toronto city fill-ins … There is a sequence on the El beginning at the 2nd Street station that's a memorable — and real — Philly screen moment. But check out the route the characters supposedly take: They start at a beauty parlor at 8th and Snyder and somehow end up at 2nd and Market on the El. Nice try … Much of the chase sequences are shot in Canada. Yes, the streets may have *Daily News* and *Inquirer* boxes, but we know Broad Street when we see it, and this ain't it. Nice try, though … Quaker Cab Company gets some screen time.

Rating:

Can a tough Philly undercover detective

with a bad attitude help a Lakota Indian find a priceless relic that was swiped during a Philadelphia jewelry heist? Well, that's the premise of this high-concept actioner that's big on chases and blood and Italian thugs wearing ponytails. Kiefer Sutherland is Buster McHenry, a plainclothes cop with a knack for causing trouble, who gets caught up in the heist of diamonds with ruthless hoods led by Marino (Robert Knepper). During the getaway from the confused heist, Marino spots the relic on display in a museum and decides it would be cool to own it. Visiting tribesman Hank Storm (Lou Diamond Phillips) and his people are not too pleased. Soon, Storm and McHenry — who may or may not be caught up in the gem swindle — team to take down Marino and retrieve the artifact. Also on hand is Jami Gertz as the pretty South Philly hairdresser caught in the middle of the danger. "Renegades" moves along at a bustling pace, thanks to some cool action set pieces from director Jack Sholder ("The Hidden"). It also has a nice sense of humor about itself, even though there's violence aplenty throughout. Unfortunately, whenever the focus moves to the Native American material, "Renegades" gets all self-important and mystical, bogged down with melodramatic music and solemn dialogue. It's more successful in the hit-and-fun motif.

> **" ... big on chases and blood and Italian thugs wearing ponytails. "**

> **"**
> **Die Hard (1988)**
> **John McClane (Bruce Willis):** With all things being equal, I'd rather be in Philadelphia. **"**

Jack Polito: Movie Everyman

Jack Polito has been working in the film industry for nearly 50 years. The brother of character actor Jon Polito, Jack has been involved in many phases of movie and TV production, mostly in lighting and special effects.

He began making corporate films in the late 1950s, when Philly was a center for corporate and business production.

"Doing corporate films, I worked with Mary Tyler Moore, Cliff Robertson, Dina Merrill, Matthew Broderick, James Earl Jones, and Jack Palance," says Polito. "It's amazing how busy Philly was with industrial and corporate films in the early 1960s."

He also worked as first assistant on the long-lost 1964 feature film "The Block" with radio personality Red Benson and James Myers, the writer of "Rock Around the Clock."

Polito recalls that Center City's Vine Street was a center for movie studio offices in the 1950s and 1960s, as well as a place where many production companies had their headquarters.

"Universal, Fox, Warner Brothers, and MGM were all around 13th and Vine," he recalls. "Then you had people like Jack Lopatin and Louis Kellman who had facilities as well."

In the 1960s, Polito went to Hollywood, where he worked on special effects for L.B. Abbott and Irwin Allen at 20th Century Fox Studios. A fan of the original "King Kong," Polito struck up a friendship with Merian C. Cooper, the film's director, and Max Steiner, the legendary composer.

Upon returning to Philadelphia, the "King Kong" fan came across a treasure in a projectionist's home one day: The long-missing footage believed to be lost from the film.

"It was the censored five minutes of film that was cut in the 1930s," Polito says. "Stories had circulated when 'King Kong' was reissued in the 1950s that stuff was cut out. We found the part where Kong pulls Fay Wray's dress and other scenes. Merian Cooper asked if he could have the copy for himself. We took it to a lab to get a copy and within a week, everyone on the West Coast had copies of the footage. The lab had pirated it."

Today, Polito runs the locally based The Production House, and has done extensive animation work for a number of films, TV shows, and commercials. He's also directed "The Dancing Pumpkin," an animated film in which his brother supplied one of the key voices. The film has been optioned to a Hollywood production team and is being readied for a feature-length animated presentation.

W.C. Fields

Ted Wioncek heads the international W.C. Fields Fan Club, a group devoted to keeping the memory and spirit of the Philly-based funnyman alive. Wioncek has been publishing a newsletter and keeping fans in the loop for Fields-related events for 12 years. Here are his thoughts on the comic known as "The Great Man."

Q: What is the appeal of W.C. Fields and your fan club members?

A: He was an everyman, the type of person things happened to. He was usually married to a nagging wife, had a stepson, and a nagging boss. In almost all of his films he was put-upon. In "It's a Gift," he had car problems, he got tomato juice all over him, and he gets an orange branch that's a dud. Because people can relate to him, the films have stood the test of time and people can relate to him.

Q: What do you know about W.C. Fields' connections to the area?

A: He may have been born in Darby, His father was a barkeeper who lost his bar and soled fruit. He worked at Strawbridge & Clothier, which was one of his first jobs. In Atlantic City, he worked at Fortescue Pavilion, where he was a professional drowner. He would make pretend he was drowning to draw a crowd, someone would save him, then vendors would hawk their wares. He also worked in an amusement park in Norristown during his teenage years.

Q: There are lots of stories about Fields being an alcoholic and not being particularly fond of Philadelphia or children.

A: Well, he did have a drinking problem, but he was in a lot of fights when he was a kid, so his large, red nose was because of the fights, the drinking, and a skin problem he had. He really didn't hate Philly. He probably liked it because he liked funny names. Most comedians use their birthplace as a subject in their comedy. And I can tell you that "I'd rather be in Philadelphia" is not on his gravestone. And the story about him not liking children is a myth, just part of his act.

Q: Can you enlighten us on some of things people may not have known about him?

A: He was self-educated and learned from reading encyclopedias. In real-life, hee was shy and not big on formal entertaining. He had a small circle of friends and was estranged from his wife. Carlotta Monti, an aspiring actress, was his mistress for 14 years and wrote a book that became a 1970 movie called "W.C. Fields and Me" with Rod Steiger and Valerie Perrine. Many Fields fans question the accuracy of the book and the movie.

Q: Tell us about the W.C. Fields Fan Club.

A: The members are all over the world, including Sweden, Denmark, Germany, France and Pakistan. It started after I met the grandson of W.C. Fields at a convention for The Three Stooges. We put out a newsletter and keep people informed about everything pertaining to W.C. Fields on our website.

Note: The W.C. Fields Fan Club address is: PO Box 506, Stratford, NJ 08084-0506. The website is at *www.webtrec.com/fields*

Rittenhouse Square (2005)

Produced by Philadelphia's Max Raab

and directed by New York iconoclast Robert Downey ("Putney Swope"), this survey of a year in the life of the city's premiere park offers an impressionistic, anecdotal look loaded with people-watching. Between eavesdropping on attractive female park regulars, Downey takes time to listen to musicians perform, shows snippets of special events, allows patrons and offbeat characters to tell stories, and gets Philly luminaries such as Philadelphia Film Office honcho Sharon Pinkenson, restaurant owner Neil Stein, and late man-about-town Stanley Green to elucidate about what the park means to them and the city. Stealing the show, however, is Caeli Veronica Smith, a 12-year-old violinist, who enchants viewers throughout with her lovely playing. Downey appears throughout, interviewing various subjects, and Raab (he's the man in the white beard) often sits next to him. While structureless and a tad overlong, "Rittenhouse Square" has lots of heart, a warm feel for the city, and lots of attractive women who make their way through the Square that Downey captures with his cameras.

> " ... has lots of heart, a warm feel for the city, and lots of attractive women ... "

Local Moments:

The whole film is shot in Rittenhouse Square, so take your pick. Along with that violinist, we're particularly impressed with the lovely scenes of the park at winter, the fiddling trio called Time for Three, and Harold Brown and his didgeridoo, an aboriginal wind instrument with a haunting sound.

Rating:

Rock School (2005)

Local Moments:

Exterior shots of the "rock school," located near Chinatown … There's a visit to Lancaster area, home of that Quaker rap act, as well as South Philly and Bucks County.

Rating:

It's hard to believe the people who put together "School of Rock," the 2003 Jack Black hit comedy, weren't at least aware of the "Paul Green School of Rock Music," located near Race Street in Philly. After all, the similarities between the "fictional" film and the real deal are strikingly similar, as Don Argott's winning documentary shows. Paul Green, the owner and grand Pooh-Bah of the establishment, is a former rock star wannabe, who teaches tough love to his aspiring Eddie van Halens and Joan Jetts, aged mostly between 9 and 18 years old. In the class captured in the film, his students are an eccentric, wildly varied bunch, ranging from a Quaker rap artist to an emotionally troubled kid to a pint-sized guitar wizard. But they all have one thing in common: They love to rock, and they'd love to ultimately do it for a living. Green, a boisterous chap, whose firmness with the kids borders on the masochistic, preaches the gospel of hard rock, heavy metal, and practice, practice, practice to them. Ultimately, they get a chance to earn their stripes taking on the jazz/metal/rock/electronic space music of Frank Zappa at a tribute concert to the late musician in Germany. A little of the verbose, blustery Green goes a long way, but you can tell that the kids who don't fear him, respect him. And ultimately, this film deserves respect, too, showing that the road to rock stardom is a bumpy ride no matter how early you start the trip.

> **"...showing that road to rock stardom is a bumpy ride no matter how early you start the trip."**

Rocky (1976)

Sylvester Stallone's Rocky Balboa takes a break along the river in "Rocky."
© United Artists/The Kobal Collection

To paraphrase the tagline on the poster,

"Rocky's life was a million-to-one shot." And so, too, were Sylvester Stallone's chances of going from a nobody to a somebody. But he, his film, and his character bucked the odds, and came out winners. And that's why Philly goes ape over "Rocky" in almost any incarnation: We love underdogs. Written by Stallone and directed by John Avildsen, best known for the controversial Peter Boyle drama "Joe" and later heralded for "The Karate Kid" movies, "Rocky" works because it is familiar and fresh. It tells of a Philadelphia club boxer who gives it his all, and gets a chance to get in the ring against a champion, and stands his ground. The film is such an upper than many people actually believe Rocky Balboa (Sylvester Stallone) wins against Apollo Creed (Carl Weathers) in the big finale fight. He doesn't, and Philadelphians either accept the fact he lost by going the distance or just simply don't recognize that he lost. The story is akin to other boxing stories, but the working class surroundings — the refrigerated meat packing unit where Rocky pummels sides of meat, the streets of the Italian Market, the neighborhood pet shop where Adrian (Talia Shire) works, the grunginess of Rocky's confidante Paulie (Burt Young), the corner Kensington gym where the "Italian Stallion" trains — are the film's heart and soul. These things helped make "Rocky" the perfect movie for its 1976 Bicentennial year release. It can and has been argued that "Rocky's" Academy Award opponents — "All the President's Men" and "Taxi Driver" among them — were more worthy for the Best Picture trophy. But "Rocky" made more sense, a low-budget effort, shot on-the-fly, with an unknown actor-screenwriter, filmed in Philadelphia, birthplace of the nation. How could anyone argue with it? And if they did, wouldn't a Philadelphian punch their lights out?

Local Moments:

We have Kensington, that run through the Italian Market, along the Schuylkill River, up the Art Museum steps … Rocky's Apartment is located at 1818 E. Tusculum Street … Rocky eats at Pat's Steaks with Gazzo (Joe Spinell) … J&M Pet Shop, where Adrian works, was located at 2146 N. Front Street, near Front and Susquehanna.

Rating:

" It tells of a Philadelphia club boxer who gives it his all …"

Rocky II (1979)

Local Moments:

Rocky runs through Philly again and up the steps of the Art Museum, but this time he's joined by a group of fans … The Spectrum is showcased in fight sequences.

Rating:

Give Sylvester Stallone credit for trying to stretch his characters with this sequel to the surprise 1976 hit. But, taking over the director's reins from John Avildsen, one can also blame Sly for turning "Rocky II" into a dour affair, filled with awkward, melodramatic moments. The film opens with the end of the match featured in the original, as Rocky Balboa heads to the hospital from the Spectrum in what, to Philadelphians, will appear the strangest route ever taken by an emergency vehicle. Rocky decides to hang up his gloves, as his bad eye requires surgery, but Apollo Creed (Carl Weathers) wants a rematch — this time for the heavyweight belt. Rocky and Adrian (Talia Shire) get married and spend lots of money. Rocky is forced to take a job at the meat-packing place, then with his trainer Mickey at the gym. Meanwhile, Adrian gets pregnant, but complications land her in the hospital, then lands in a coma. Will Adrian ever come out of the coma? And if she does, will she give her hubby the OK to step back into the ring, threatening his eyesight in the process? Can Rocky get in good enough shape to box again, going for the title against Apollo Creed? You know the answers going in, but in order to get to them, you have to sift through a whole lot of soap opera stuff. Except for some expert fight sequences towards the finale, "Rocky II" lacks energy and is often downright dull at times, as Stallone piles up the tragic events to excess.

> **" … filled with awkward, melodramatic moments. "**

Stan Hockman's Rocky Splash

Legendary *Daily News* sportswriter Stan Hochman recalls getting his turn in front of the cameras in "Rocky V." Here's what he remembers about the experience:

"I got a call from a casting director one night, asking if I'd like to appear as a sportswriter in 'Rocky V.' At first, I thought it was a crank call, but I listened politely and she said that auditions would be taking place at a little photo shop in South Philly. I said I'd be there and when I got there I found Elmer Smith, *The Daily News* boxing writer, and Bob Seltzer, *The Inquirer* boxing writer there.

"There was a video camera set up, and the woman handed us a script, said the scene was a post-fight press conference. We read the lines, and then she asked us to improvise, to throw tough questions at a fight promoter and a fighter. We did that for a while, and then she said we'd be hearing from her. I was covering a Penn-Princeton basketball game that night at the Palestra and when I got home, I found a message from the woman, asking me to come to the old Convention Hall at 6 a.m. and to bring a change of clothing in case they didn't like the outfit I was wearing.

"We gathered in a big room set up like a post-fight press conference and director John Avildsen approached us with copies of the script. He pointed to each of us, and said, "You're number one, you're number two, you're number three," and we read the lines for him. Then he shifted us around, changing the order. He settled on the order, and then he saw that we were having trouble with the lines because they weren't realistic. He said, "Go ahead and say them the way you would in a real post-fight conference situation." That's all I needed to hear, so I changed the simplistic, "Let's face it, you fought a second-rate fighter with glass in his jaw ..." to "Let's face it, you fought a second-rate fighter with so much glass in his jaw he tinkled when he walked." Everybody laughed and Avildsen liked it, so he said, "Do it that way.

> **"Everybody laughed and Avildsen liked it, so he said, 'do it that way.'"**

> **"** *The Daily News* had a photographer there and he was taking shots of me delivering my lines when they asked him to stop and tried to confiscate the film. **"**

"It took us 18 takes in the morning, and the first time I said my line with 'tinkled when he walked,' Tommy Morrison [who plays Tommy "Machine" Gunn in the film] was startled, because that wasn't in his script. But he caught on, and we had no trouble after that.

"We broke for a huge lunch, seven desserts as I recall. And then it was back to work. Stallone showed up on the set, insulted the woman playing Tommy Gunn's new girlfriend, who complained about her part. 'Next time, you can be a nun,' Stallone said, and all the extras groaned at

his tone. He sat next to Avildsen and watched on a monitor. After I shouted the line I glanced over and Stallone gave Avildsen the 'I don't know' sign with his right hand. I did it once more the way I'd rewritten it, and then Avildsen came over to me and said, 'can you say, so much glass in his jaw he oughta be a chandelier?' I said, 'Okay, it's your movie,' and that is the way I delivered it from then on. We needed fifteen takes in the afternoon with the cameras shifted behind Morrison and Richard Gant [who plays the flashy boxing promoter].

"I used my own tape recorder in the scene and my own notebook. *The Daily News* had a photographer there and he was taking shots of me delivering my lines when they asked him to stop and tried to confiscate the film. He gave them an empty roll and kept the real film. The shot appeared with my story the next day.

"I got $1440 as a speaking actor, and am still getting royalties. They add up to something like another $1400."

The "Rocky" statue, at it's new home, near the Philadelphia Museum of Art.
© Sally Lindsay

Rocky III (1983)

After the mushy route taken by Sylvester Stallone in "Rocky II,"

the writer-director-star goes for a different approach here, turning this entry into an adrenaline-charged, bigger-than-life action yarn. The decision proves to be winner, as Rocky must rediscover the "Eye of the Tiger" after he decides to retire. But we're getting ahead ourselves here. We discover first that the Philly pug has become a world-famous name brand with his own pinball machine and appearances all over the place — including "The Muppet Show." But two events get him steamed and depressed:

He loses a bout to ambitious upstart Clubber Lang (Mr. T), and loses his trainer when Mickey (Burgess Meredith) dies. What's a Rocky to do? He finds help in both the most likely and unlikely places — support from wife Adrian (Talia Shire) and former rival Apollo Creed (Carl Weathers). With their help and a high-energy training montage, Rocky steps back into the ring for a rematch with Lang. Credit Stallone for getting things back on the right track for this go-round (although his efforts, based on "Rocky IV," were, sadly short-lived) Mr. T is a ball of jive meanness, there's a real punch to the fight sequences, and Hulk Hogan makes an impression as a wrestler Rocky battles called Thunderlips (huh?). Meanwhile, Rocky's mourning of Mickey is touching and not overplayed.

Sylvester Stallone, Butkus the dog, and Talia Shire from the original "Rocky."
© Scott Weiner

 **Local Moments:**

The Rocky statue is revealed, and the Philadelphia Art Museum hasn't been the same since … There is some Philly location work here, mostly of the Parkway and downtown areas, but most of the film was shot in Los Angeles and New York with the Felt Forum in Madison Square Garden highlighted.

Rating:

> " **… adrenaline-charged, bigger-than-life action yarn.** "

Rocky IV (1985)

The "Rocky" series had already been turned into a comic book with the third installment, but with this entry in the series turns the plight of the "Italian Stallion" into a jokebook. After Russian heavyweight Ivan Drago (Dolph Lundgren) pummels Rocky rival Apollo Creed (Carl Weathers) to death, the Rock decides it's time to get back into the ring and fight for the memory of Apollo, his country, and, of course, himself. And since Drago is from the USSR, we know he's dirty. To add further evidence, we see his high-tech training lab where he's even ejected with unknown substances. We all know American athletes would never do that, right? Meanwhile, Rocky trains au natural, in the Siberian wilderness, where he gets all medieval on logs and rocks and other non living things. The showdown in the ring is grueling as expected, with blood, sweat, tears, and jeers. And, of course, there's Brigitte Nielsen, writer-director-star Stallone's then girlfriend and future spouse, on hand as Drago's mouthpiece and wife.

> **"The showdown in the ring is grueling as expected ..."**

Mayor (Gene Crane): Thank you. Thank you, one and all. Every once in a while a person comes along who defies the odds, who defies logic, and fulfills an incredible dream. On behalf of all the citizens of Philadelphia, and the many who have been touched by your accomplishments and your untiring participation in this city's many charity functions, it is with tremendous honor that we present this memorial which will stand always as a celebration to the indomitable spirit of Man. Philadelphia salutes its favorite son, Rocky Balboa!

Rocky V (1990)

Well, the Balboa family has certainly moved on up, haven't they? After the big bout featured in "Rocky V" with Dolph Lundgren's super-villain Ivan Drago, Sylvester Stallone's Rocky, wife Adrian (Talia Shire), son Rocky Jr. (Sage Stallone), and sidekick Paulie (Burt Young) head back to Philly to their spacious Main Line estate for some well-deserved R&R. But they soon learn that Rocky has early signs of brain damage due to his boxing bouts and the Balboa fortune has been squandered away by a sleazy accountant. So, it's back to Kensington for the family, where Rocky has to go the lunch bag route again, Adrian becomes the best-dressed worker at the old pet shop, and Rocky Jr. gets teased at school when he's not hanging

> **"Stallone's overbearing 'dem' and 'dose' dialogue …"**

out with some bad kids. Before long, however, Rocky is befriended by Tommy "Machine" Gunn (real-life boxer Tommy Morrison, a real-life relative of John Wayne), a young pugilist looking for guidance from Rocky. After Rocky offers fighting and training tips, Gunn jumps to flamboyant promoter George Washington Duke (Richard Gant doing Don King), who then tries to set up a showdown between Tommy "Machine" Gunn and Rocky. Original director John Avildsen jumps back in the ring for this installment and he and Sly, who wrote the film, should get credit for trying to get back to the Philly roots that made the first film a classic. But you can also discredit them with the film's maudlin elements, Stallone's overbearing "dem" and "dose" dialogue, and a storyline about boxers that leads to a street brawl rather than a battle in the ring.

Local Moments:

The appearance of the El leads to Rocky's old Kensington home … The now-demolished Philadelphia Civic Center, with its low second level of seats, is used for the fight between Tommy Gunn and Union Cane … The school Rocky Jr. attends is actually the Kirkbridge Elementary School at 7th and Dickenson … Local reporters used in the press-conference sequence include Stan Hochman, Elmer Smith, John Clark, Al Meltzer, Robert Seltzer, and Lauren Woods … As expected, the Philadelphia Museum of Art and the Rocky statue make triumphant appearances.

Rating:

The Shame of the City

(2006)

Local Moments:

A flatfooted Sam Katz attempts to strut like a Mummer; Katz poll workers get beat up early on election day — no cops show up … A who's who lineup of TV radio and newspaper reporters, and political experts are showcased throughout the film, including former *Daily News* editor Zack Stahlberg, reporter Dave Davies and Tyree Johnson, *Philadelphia Magazine* staffers Larry Platt and Sasha Isenberg, radio vets Michael Smerconish and Mike Missanelli, and political commentator Mary Patel … and Philly locales are in the spotlight throughout, including Famous Deli on 4th Street, City Hall, "Two Street," South Philly, Northeast Philly, and the Center City headquarters of both candidates.

Rating:

A funny thing happened while Wynnefield filmmaker Tigre Hill was documenting the 2003 mayoral showdown between incumbent Democratic mayor John Street and Republican challenger Sam Katz: The ongoing wiretapping investigation by the FBI of the mayor's office became public. Almost immediately, Street and his close associates used the earth-shattering revelation to their political advantage. They pointed to race as a reason for the FBI's inquiry, connected President Bush's shaky administration and policies to the City Hall tower, and pointed out that the feds shouldn't be sticking their noses in Philly's own dirty business. The investigation had an immediate impact, as Katz's slight lead was quickly clipped by Street, while flames of racism and timing of the supposed Republican-sponsored inquisition were fanned by national figures like James Carville, Bill Clinton, and Jesse Jackson, stumping for Street. The bugging scandal, however, was a blessing for Hill, an African-American and self-described Republican, given full access for coverage by Katz, but forced to use a hidden camera to capture the internecine movements of Street and company on the way to victory. Using this footage and lots of local newscasts and talking head interviews with local writers and pundits, Hill draws a vivid picture of the treachery of big city politics. We're introduced to such characters as Milton Street, the mayor's bombastic brother; Joe Dougherty, the blustery union chief; and many others. While Hill has clearly stacked the deck in Katz's favor, however, it's hard for the audience to garner much sympathy for Katz in his third losing bid for mayor. While he appears to be well-meaning and in favor of the right things — trying to play ball fairly, veering away

The Famous 4th Street Deli, spotted in many movies shot in Philadelphia.
© Sally Lindsay

continued on page 100

> **"It's a telling moment that captures the essence of Philadelphia."**

from name-calling and using race as an issue — Katz remains terminally bland, and certainly doesn't help his cause by showing ignorance in the way race is sued in city politics. When he confronts persistent name callers at a rally, his anger seems tempered and when he delivers an important speech at crunch time criticizing the oppositions' unsavory race-oriented tactics and their relation to money, he's mechanical and unsure of himself. In some ways, he resembles Philly's version of Al Gore — a decent man with good ideas who lacks the dynamics and authority to win the big one. (And, ironically, Gore is shown visiting Philly in support of Street.) One of the film's final images is its most striking, a post-election clip of Street getting vocally throttled by boobirds at Citizen Bank Park's opening. It's a telling moment that captures the essence of Philadelphia, whether it be sports fans or voters. It's a terrific ironic coda to this often fascinating film about big time mudslinging and its discontents.

Shadowboxer (2005)

Local Moments:

The film is a great showcase for Philly, from its opening scene on … Rose and Mikey's apartment is in a high rise overlooking City Hall … There are several neat montages of downtown Philly showcasing some of its largest and most striking buildings … Pat's Steaks and its environs are highlighted in a key scene … Rose meets the handicapped go-between of her client at the gazebo behind the Art Museum, overlooking the Schuylkill … Boathouse Row, the Waterworks, and Kelly Drive are featured in several sequences.

Rating:

"Shadowboxer" is a great family film —

if your family's last name is Manson. Producer Lee Daniels ("Monster's Ball", "The Woodsman") makes a way-over-the-top directorial debut with this crime drama that pushes the envelope in terms of sex, drugs, and violence. It is the perfect antidote for people who think the state of independent films has become staid. Helen Mirren is Rose, a paid assassin who knocks off people with her adopted son/and sometimes lover Mikey (Cuba Gooding, Jr.). Rose is in bad shape, suffering from cancer and popping Percoset because of the pain. She wants to get out of the business and decides to tackle just one more hit. But something goes awry, and instead of killing the very pregnant Vickie (Vanessa Ferlito), girlfriend of gangster Clayton (Stephen Dorff), she delivers her baby. She also takes her and her newborn son under her wing, gives them a place to stay and takes care of them. Along with Mikey, the new foursome make a truly unique family unit: Call it Two Hit People, a Woman, and a Baby. That's the premise behind

> **" … pushes the envelope in terms of sex, drugs and violence … "**

the film, but it's Daniel's ultra-stylized telling that really counts here. It seems like he's overdosed on Asian crime films, Abel Ferrera ("The King of New York") and Luc Besson movies ("The Professional" comes immediately to mind), and delivers a highly stylized sleaze-out filled with raunchy sex, extreme violence, child abuse, voracious gunplay, incessant drug taking, and some very disturbing characters, like Dorff's unruly hood and Joseph Gordon-Leavitt as a doctor who would creep out Jack Kervorkian. At the middle of all this mayhem is the saga of the dying hitwoman and her patched-together family that is quite compelling despite all the riff-raff.

Michael Dennis Keeps It Reelblack

Michael J. Dennis is a man on a mission.
A filmmaker, screenwriter and promoter, Dennis runs Reelblack, a company dedicated to African-American filmmakers and filmmaking. Dennis and Reelblack's mission is mirrored by the tagline "Good Movies 'bout Black Folks," which appears on the info-packed *www.reelblack.com* website.

Dennis, a one-time buyer for the Video Library video stores, attended the NYU Film School and the American Film Institute. He worked on Jonathan Demme's "Beloved" and directed such films as "A Taste of Lady Alma" and "The Story of Breakout," and was the first filmmaker to capture Chris Rock on film in an early documentary.

Now, Dennis wears several hats. As a filmmaker, he's working on getting the spoof he wrote called "Tupac Is Alive" on screen. He also hosts several screenings of independent films and Hollywood offerings around the city at such locations as the International House and Point of Destination Café. Other projects are a *Reelblack Magazine* and a Comcast TV show.

"The regional film scene is important and Reelblack hopes to establish and nurture an audience for African-American films," says Dennis. " "Many movies are made by studios, but many interesting films are done independently. A lot of this stuff can sit on shelves if people don't know about, so I feel like that's part of our mission.

"Hollywood is like going to McDonald's. If you just eat mainstream films, you'll grow obese with junk food. You have to go beyond this stuff to find something that's good for you."

Does Dennis see things changing for African-American filmmakers since he established Reelblack in 2001?

"Believe it or not, Fox and UPN, which were often criticized for their African-American programming," have proven important to black filmmaking. They've helped get talent in front of the camera, like Jamie Foxx, who have showed they can win Oscars.

"As for the writer and directors, the democratization of film — the idea that video cameras, You Tube, and other avenues are readily available — can only help.

"These two factors have given people a chance. There is still bad work in any spectrum but the possibility for good or great work increases everyday. Audiences appear interested, talented people with names and people with creative ideas now want something different. This is what Reelblack celebrates. "Whenever you see our logo, it tells people something is worth investigating."

Signs (2002)

The less thought given to M. Night Shayamalan's low-tech science fiction yarn the better it plays. Let's face it: Why would aliens pick Earth to visit if one of the planet's primary elements kills them? Other questions abound in the writer-director's screenplay after close inspection, but, hey, the same thing occurs in all of science-fiction. Audiences should skip the analysis and enjoy this sharp, funny, scary and, ultimately inspirational film. In it, perhaps as a tune-up for his "Passion of the Christ" effort, Mel Gibson plays Graham Hess, a former minister and farmer who has lost his faith because of a horrifying car accident that killed his wife (Patricia Kalember) six months ago. He lives with his family members, former baseball player brother Merrill (Joaquiin Phoenix), asthmatic son Morgan (Rory Culkin), and H2O-obsessed daughter Bo (Abigail Breslin), on a Bucks County farm. The family is frightened when crop circles — weird, ornate designs in their cornfields — appear. Morgan thinks they're a sign from God, but Graham suspects something different. It's soon revealed that the signs point to aliens nearby, and it's up to the Hess family in their Buck County farm to ward them off in order to stay alive. Accenting silence and tight, Hitchcockian suspense over big-time special effects like "Independence Day," "Signs" is refreshingly low-tech, commendable for its concentration on the human elements of the story, of how this family comes together in the face of total terror to battle these otherworldly creatures. Shayamalan gets maximum effect out of his pause-filled script, deliberate acting styles, and tingly score channeling Bernard Herman and John Williams. And he also scores some genuinely frightening moments here: One scene in which the family watches footage from around the world of the alien invasion when a monster pops up in a school in Brazil is one of the most jolting things I've ever seen on screen. In the end, however, "Signs" is about Graham Hess getting his groove back, finding his calling through the ordeal he and his family have experienced. Night has given us some of that old-time religion along with the shock and awe.

> **"And he also scores some genuinely frightening moments ..."**

Local Moments:

The Hess farm is located on the premises of Delaware Valley College in Doylestown, PA … Downtown Newton serves as the small town in the movie with Mom's Bake at Home Pizza doubling for "2 Aldos Pizzaria "… The scene in the drug store was shot in Morrisville, PA.

Rating:

Snipes (2001)

A cut above most urban dramas that come down the pike — and usually land quickly on DVD — "Snipes" marks the directorial debut of Rich Murray, a Philly native whose credits include helming a load of music videos and heading RuffNation Films. The plot concerns Erik (Sam Jones III of "Smallville"), a young rapper wannabe who works putting up posters all over Philadelphia for a record outfit headed by Bobby Starr (Dean Winters).

> **" … Snipes remains sturdy and often riveting throughout. "**

The company is sweating bullets because their big star, Prolifik (played by rapper Nell) is delayed in delivering his latest cuts. After Erik and his pal discover two bodies in a recording studio, they discover the tapes to Prolifik's album are missing as is the rap sensation himself. Erik also finds himself in big trouble, with Bobby Starr and others pursuing him, thinking he has some connection to the missing music and the kidnapping. Director Murray gets nice performances from his solid cast — including Zoe Saldana ("Guess Who?") as Erik's coworker and ally, and local rapper Schooly-D — and gets maximum mileage out of the Philly locales. While there are some incredible contrivances in the plot, "Snipes" remains sturdy and often riveting throughout. As far as rap-oriented thrillers go, it's solid; as far as first features go, it's quite impressive.

Local Moments:

West Philly was used extensively, with filming taking place around Al's Love Lounge and a house on 54th Street … The good, old Frankford El gets some screen time … Iglesia Del Barrio, a youth recreation center, on Cambria Street was used … Newscaster Larry Mendte can be viewed onscreen … Graterford Prison gets a shout-out … Other references: 30th Street Station, the Devon Theater on Frankford Avenue, and "A.I." (as in Allen Iverson).

Rating:

The Soldier (1982)

So many people know this film for its opening sequence: Early in the morning, a woman with a baby carriage crosses the Philadelphia Parkway, only to be run over by a speeding car. Four people in the area run to see the damage. Soon, a couple of guys in tight black suits gun down the onlookers, then take off on a helicopter, which flies towards the Art Museum. And that's it for the Philly sequences. The rest of this mostly incomprehensible film about a crack CIA team of killers crisscrosses around the globe, from Tel Aviv to Niagra Falls to Berlin, etc. Good luck trying to figure out this paranoid action thriller that involves plutonium in a Saudi Arabia oil field as well as the KGB, the Mossad, the Communists, and others. There are lots of explosions, bombs, gunplay — in other words, things blow up real good. Writer-director James Glickenhaus specialized in this sort of slick actioner ("The Exterminator" and "Shakedown" were also his), but for all of its bells and whistles, it's that first sequence — set in Philly — that really made an impression on people.

> **" Good luck trying to figure out this paranoid action thriller ... "**

Local Moments:

Only one — see to the right.

Rating:

Stealing Home (1988)

A tearjerker that has welcomed legions of fans on cable TV and home video,

"Stealing Home" provides syrupy "Summer of '42"-style nostalgia to those so inclined. Philly native Steve Kampmann and Will Aldiss ("Back to School," "WKRP in Cincinnati") wrote and directed this saga of Bill Wyatt (Mark Harmon), a down-and-out minor-league baseball player who discovers that teenage friend and mentor Katie Chandler (Jodie Foster) has died. He's been asked to take her ashes and spread them in a special place. This, of course, means that Billy must leave his seedy motel room in Camden and travel back home to Chestnut Hill. It also means it's flashback time, as Billy reminisces about his formative years playing ball, his parents, tragic events in his life, and

> " ... remindful of a Hallmark Hall of Fame entry. "

his relationship with the older Katie. David Foster's overly sentimental score emphasizes the touchy-feely nature of the proceedings remindful of a Hallmark Hall of Fame entry. The cast is filled with interesting faces — Blair Brown, John Shea, Harold Ramis, Richard Jenkins, and Helen Hunt turn up in support — but, sadly, they aren't given much interesting to say or do.

Local Moments:

This has one of the weirdest bits of Philly geography ever: In order to get back to his Chestnut Hill home from a motel on the Admiral Wilson Boulevard, Mark Harmon's Billy takes a bus to Trenton, then a SEPTA train to another bus. No wonder it takes so long … Bob's Diner on Ridge Avenue gets to shine a scene. What, a diner next to a cemetery? Only in Roxborough! … Chestnut Hill Academy is prominently displayed, as is much of Chestnut Hill … The famous "Trenton Makes The world Takes" bridge is displayed … And Veteran's Stadium gets its day in the sun here, too … Margate and Island Beach State Park serve as Jersey shore locales.

Rating:

Perfectly Frank
"Stealing Home" Stories

In 1987, promotions expert Frank Chille was hired by Warner Brothers to act as unit publicist for the film "Stealing Home," which was going to be shot in the Philadelphia area. Chille, who was used to handling public relations when films were finished, got an opportunity to handle the chores this time while "Stealing Home" was shooting from May to the second week of August, 1987. This presented its own unusual situations to deal with for Chille.

"A lot of my job was keeping the press away from the set. Most productions are closed but on rare occasions the producer will allow some press members on the set to interview the principals.

"The film used Chestnut Hill, Vet Stadium, and the Jersey Shore — Island State Park, home of the Wyeth family, and the governor's summer house — and Seaside Heights.

"The production was headquartered at the Holiday Inn at City Line Avenue. There were condos near there where some people stayed. When we moved to Island Beach State Park, they stayed at the Windjammer Hotel [in Seaside Heights].

"Mark Harmon was a nice guy, he was a little leery of the press. He was going through a custody battle with his sister involving his nephew. [So the production was leery about the upcoming film and the custody battle]. But Mark was great. [Wife] Pam Dawber came to town a few times and they would go out to dinner.

"We shot a full day [at Veteran's Stadium], early in the afternoon, like 12 noon until one or two in the morning. Nobody was there except real employees who were allowed there. The producers allowed me to take my mom on the set. She was a big fan of Mark Harmon's. She took a picture with him. To this day, she has the photo in her apartment.

"People don't realize that Jodie Foster and Mark Harmon never worked together. In the film, Jodie Foster is friends with Mark Harmon's character when he's 12 or 13 and later when he's 17 or 18. She was in flashbacks and here at different times.

"Jonathan Silverman was a trip. He was a huge baseball fan so he was happy to be in the production. He had a great sense of humor. I remember I took him on tour. He was like the spokesman for the movie. I took him to all the radio stations and he handled the disc jockeys — you know they could be wise guys — like a pro.

"We had the premiere at the AMC Old City Theater, which is now the Ritz East, in August 1988. All of the festivities were at the Sheraton Society Hill. Mark Harmon was a humble meat-and-potatoes guy. He told me he was going to walk himself from the Sheraton to the AMC Old City. The manager at the theater was so nervous, he wanted everything in line. His name was Anthony.

"We had each celebrity come out of the limousine and Mark Harmon, being the star, would exit from the last limousine. I jumped into the limo because Mark told me so. So here we had this person come out and so-and-so comes out and the director comes out and Mark was supposed to be in the final limousine. So the theater manager tells the press that Mark is about to come out of the limousine so the photogrpahers can get their cameras ready. Lo and behold, who comes out of the limo but me! Needless to say, Anthony's face dropped. And lo and behold, Mark is coming around the other way from the hotel. The press runs over to him. I thought Anthony was going to cry.

"The movie didn't do as well as we hoped. Clark de Leon couldn't understand why either. He wrote a column about it in *The Inquirer*. It was a sweet and touching movie that deserved a better reception."

Stone Reader (2003)

Ever since he was a teenager, Mark Moskowitz had thought about a book he read called *The Stones of Summer*, and its author, Dow Mossman. But after a handful of sterling reviews, the book, along with its author, seemed to disappear off the face of the Earth. Now, decades later, Moskowitz is a successful filmmaker of political commercials. He decides to try to purchase copies of the book and track down Mossman through various literary contacts, critics, and authors. It's an interesting premise, but this film only sticks to it half the time. The other half concentrates of Moskowitz's life, his love for books, his home (his wife won't allow her face to be photographed for some reason), and how important it is for him to succeed in his quest. Unfortunately, the latter stuff is interesting for a few minutes and not half or more of a documentary that clocks in at over two hours. Moskowitz is to be commended for making a pro-literature film that is intelligent and often thoughtful, but if he dropped all the personal jazz, it may have been more effective and compelling.

> " ... but if he dropped all the personal jazz, it may have been more effective and compelling. "

Local Moments:

Moskowitz lives in a cool house located in Chester Springs, PA, which we see a lot of. He has an impressive library of books.

Rating:

Strut! (2001)

Local Moments:

This film is all Philly, all the time, in both its archival footage and newly shot Mummers pageantry. Most of it is on Broad Street, but director Raab and associate Robert Downey, Jr., take us all around the city, to the Port Richmond clubhouses and Kensington headquarters of several Mummers organizations.

Rating:

This is a big wet kiss to the Mummers Parade with a box of yummy chocolates thrown in for the city of Philadelphia. This sweet, loving, working-class documentary from Philly producer Max Raab ("Rittenhouse Square") offers a heartfelt primer on the world of the Mummers, rich in history, tradition, and wry (or is it "rye"?) humor. Through archival footage, we see early Mummers highlights, learn how the parade evolved, and discover nuggets such as in the late 1800s, the parade consisted almost entirely of string and sax players, and longshoremen from Europe became the first breed of Mummers. We get the lowdown on the string bands, the fancies, and the comics though anecdotes and freshly shot footage. We follow Pete Ciarrochi of Chickie's and Pete's as he gets made up to be a Japanese geisha girl for a routine, then see him demonstrate the finer points of doing the Mummer's Strut. We're taken to Two Street, where winners and losers convene. And we go behind the scenes at practices, where an entire year's worth of work and expenses close to $100,000 per team lay on the line for bragging rights and a purse of $7000, and to a church where a priest blesses a troop of feathered friends before they go into battle, shunning the freezing temperatures and hangovers, to bring home the big prize, complete with bragging rights.

> "**We get the lowdown on the string bands, the fancies and the comics through anecdotes and freshly shot footage.**"

Sweet Love, Bitter (1967)

A moody and depressing look at the lives of jazz performers and their friends

in the smoky nightclubs, "Sweet Love, Bitter" is loosely based on the life of the great Charlie Parker, whose real-life exploits are chronicled in Clint Eastwood's excellent biopic "Bird." In fact, the environs of "Sweet Love, Bitter" make one believe Eastwood saw the film before he shot "Bird," as the films are strikingly similar in many ways (as is Bertrand Tavernier's "'Round Midnight" with Dexter Gordon). Here, comedian and activist Dick Gregory is drug-addicted sax player Richie "Eagle" Stokes, whose addiction gets in the way of his musicianship while friends black (Robert Hooks) and white (Don Murray) try to set him straight before he self-destructs. Like the aforementioned films, "Sweet Love, Bitter" has some expert playing on the soundtrack — Mal Waldron does the honors here — and the seedy atmosphere is perfect, but the film plays like one long, mournful sax solo.

> " ... the seedy atmosphere is perfect, but the film plays like one long, mournful sax solo. "

Local Moments:

Some interiors were shot at Louis W. Kellman Studios in Center City where "Diver Dan" and several educational films were filmed ... Filming was split between Philly and New York, but some downtown jazz clubs were used for locations as well as some streets in downtown Philly.

Rating:

Taps (1981)

Local Moments:

The film was shot almost entirely at Valley Forge Military Academy and College.

Rating:

Bunker Hill Military Academy, where boys are sent to be turned into real men, is having its problems. Seems that some real estate developers plan to turn the place into a condo development, and it doesn't sit well with the cadets, especially the head cadet, Brian Morleand (Timothy Hutton, hot off his Oscar for Best Supporting Actor in "Ordinary People"). A fight ensues at an end-of-year celebration between cadets and townies, but when General Bache (George C. Scott channeling a subdued version of George S. Patton) attempts to break up the fracas, his gun goes off triggering a series of unfortunate events that leads to the cadets taking over the facility and keeping it away from any and all outside forces. Directed by Harold Becker ("Sea of Love," "Fallen") with writing contributions from Robert Mark Kamen ("The Karate Kid") and Daryl Ponicsan ("The Last Detail"), "Taps" is riveting stuff that holds up surprisingly well 25 years after its release. It offers some compelling questions in regard to the military and responsibility, and features a top-notch supporting cast that includes Sean Penn as Hutton's ally, caught between his friends and doing the right thing, and an 18-year-old Tom Cruise playing a young cadet so gung-ho that jumping up and down on Oprah's couch would seem somewhat reserved in comparison to his behavior here.

> " ... riveting stuff that holds up surprisingly well 25 years after its release. "

Trading Places (1983)

Dan Aykroyd and Eddie Murphy happily scam veteran wheeler-dealers in the hit comedy "Trading Places."
© Paramount/The Kobal Collection

A modern retelling of Mark Twain's "The Prince and the Pauper," John Landis'"Trading Places" is an uneven but often hysterical social comedy that offers its creative team in solid alignment at the appropriate time. Hot off of "48 Hours," Eddie Murphy plays a street hustler who has no mercy when it comes to panhandling — he'll even act as if he has no legs if it means grubbing some extra nickels from pedestrians. Dan Aykroyd plays a snobby, pampered stockbroker who works for a Philly firm headed by the Duke Brothers (Don Ameche and Ralph Bellamy). Aykroyd's employers make a $1 bet on which is more important: environment or breeding. So, Aykroyd is suddenly left penniless, and homeless and soon loses his fiancée, while Murphy is given all the luxuries Aykroyd was afforded as well as his job. Along for the ride is hooker Jamie Lee Curtis, who proves she has more than just a heart of gold by comforting Aykroyd in his time of need. How both men will react to the radical changes, however, is what the Dukes want to see and where the audience finds the laughs. Both actors soar in comic situations here, with Murphy at the height of streetwise sass as the slickster suddenly living high on the hog and Aykroyd empathetic as the poor shlub who loses everything, while Ameche and Bellamy capture old-school Philadelphia coots with relish. Unfortunately, the final 20 minutes or so of the film involving gorillas, Jim Belushi, Al Franken, and Tom Davis trains is frantic and unfunny. For most of its running time, however, "Trading Places" works as a bracingly funny social comedy about greed just when it was needed — a few years into Ronald Reagan's first term.

Local Moments:

"Legless" Eddie Murphy pans for cash in Rittenhouse Square … Fidelity Bank at Broad and Sansom doubles as the bank owned by the Duke Brothers … Dan Aykroyd's comfy home is at 2014 Delancey Street … Curtis Institute of Music plays the Heritage Club, the Union League-type place where the wealthy hang out … Independence Hall, Broad Street, and the Rosenbach Museum and Library on Delancey Street also get screen time.

Rating:

Philly Filmmakers Tackle "Russell-Mania"

It started at New York University's prestigious film school. Jonathan Yudis and Mike Davis, two Philadelphia guys with mutual friends, caught a few Russ Meyer movies during down time. They were both hooked from the start and couldn't get enough of the sexploitation (but not XXX-rated) films that featured women with large boobs, a comic book sensibility, staccato editing, and double entendres galore.

After time working on different projects following college — Yudis worked in animation, directing stuff like a "Ren and Stimpy" special, parts of Disney's "Pocahontas II," and a film about "The Burning Man Festival" while Davis optioned a screenplay — the two decided to collaborate on a movie that brought them back to their college days.

The result of their efforts is "Pervert!," a wild sex romp about a young man who comes to his father's desert home for the summer and discovers that Dad is getting psychotic, has a randy, huge-breasted girlfriend (played by adult star Mary Carey) who loves to get naked, and a killer is loose terrorizing the area. Oh, did we mention artwork made of different cuts of meat that is his father's passion?

"Pervert!" was shot on the cheap in tough conditions. And there's one weird coincidence that truly makes it the closest thing to Russ Meyer you could get without Meyer's involvement.

"We went out to the desert to look for a location for filming," says Davis. "We came across this house that looked perfect. When we inquired about using it as the main location for the movie, the people told us it was used by another filmmaker a few times years ago. It turns out that Russ Meyer used the place for some of his movies!"

After "Pervert!" received good response at film festivals (including the local First Glance Film Festival) and midnight screenings in Los Angeles and other cities, the film snagged a DVD deal. Now, Yudis — who calls legendary animator Ralph Bakshi his father-in-law — and Davis are looking forward to making other movies for their Stag Films production banner.

In fact, the company has another kooky idea in the works right now: A vampire biker movie.

You kind of get the sense that Ben Franklin would have dug these guys, don't you?

Train Ride (2000)

"Train Ride" is much more complex and provocative than it seems at first glance. The film begins with a bang — literally — as the head of an African-American man is targeted in the scope of a shotgun. We never know until the final scene who this is or why it's happening, but we're quickly introduced to Will (Wood Harris of "The Wire"), a senior at an all-black college who lets us in on his story — which may be the same story as the person being lined up for the shooting. Will is a slick operator who sweet-talks his two friends (Russell Hornsby and Thomas Braxton, Jr.) into partaking in some nasty hanky-panky — that is, having relations with freshman Katrina (rapper MC Lyte) after they drop a date rape drug in her drink. The action, of course, comes with complications for all involved, especially since the calculating Will has a strong desire to videotape the proceedings and two of Katrina's girlfriends leave Will's apartment before the deed is carried out. Powerfully acted, sharply written and well directed (by Rel Dowdell, who now teaches screenwriting at Boston University), "Train Ride" is definitely worth seeking out, as it tackles some serious issues in an up-front and stimulating fashion that demands to be taken seriously.

> **" ... it tackles some serious issues in an up-front and stimulating fashion ... "**

Local Moments:

Most of the exteriors were shot at Cheney University.

Rating:

Trick Baby (1972)

Even though its often been placed in the "blaxploitation" category, this surprisingly sturdy con artist tale is anything but. Yes, it features a predominately all-black cast and indeed, it takes place throughout the seedier African-American section of Philly. But it's more an urban take on "The Sting" than anything else, and to pigeonhole it as blaxploitation (even though it was made a few years before the cycle started) would be a disservice. Based on the story by former pimp Iceberg Slim, the story centers on the exploits of Johnny "Folk" O'Brien (Kiel Martin) , a con from Philly who is the son of a black prostitute mother and white john, and hates his derisive nickname "Trick Baby." O'Brien's partner is "Blue" Howard (Met Stuart), a veteran schemer from the old school. The two pull off a series of dupes, but really set their sights on a big haul. That comes in a real estate scam in which O'Brien tries to pull in some racist

> **"But it's more an urban take on 'The Sting' than anything else …"**

white businessmen on an investment fraud. Complicating matters is a crooked cop (Dallas Edwards Hayes) who's been played by the duo and is out to get back at them just as they're going in for the big score with the businessmen. "Trick Baby" is a swiftly paced affair that's smartly conceived, well acted, and offers a travelogue of some Philly's roughest neighborhoods during the early 1970s. There are also some fascinating racial elements to the film sure to peak interest. Witness, for example, how all of the white characters are fearful of the blacks and how Johnny plays into their fear, then sucks them into his swindle. At the same time, however, Johnny is hypocritical about his heritage, hating the "Trick Baby" name his enemies call him, but using his black roots to get in good with the brothers. It's stuff like this that make "Trick Baby" a volatile time-capsule well worth unearthing.

The Trouble With Angels
(1966)

A surprise hit with family audiences, this endearing comedy stars Rosalind Russell as the Reverend Mother at the St. Francis Academy for Girls, a Catholic school on the outskirts of Philadelphia. Disney regular Hayley Mills tries to change her routine a bit as the determined Mary Clancy, who joins forces with Rachel Devery (June Harding) to cause all sorts of innocuous trouble around the school for the Reverend Mother and her nuns. The illicit activities they pull include puffing cigars that leads to a visit from the fire department, adding bubble bath to the sugar bowls, touring the nun's private quarters, and switching their names to confuse the bus driver. As expected, mastermind Mary has a showdown with the Reverend Mother and a battle of wills turns into an understanding that nuns are, in reality, good people who do good things. Oddly enough, the film was helmed by Ida Lupino, the actress who made her mark as a director of many TV shows and such film noirs "The Bigamist" and "The Hitch-Hiker." In addition, there are some odd casting choices here, including famous stripper Gypsy Rose Lee, European sex siren Camilla Sparv, and an unbilled bit by Jim Hutton as the principal of a progressive Catholic school. The film's success led to the 1968 sequel "Where Angels Go, Trouble Follows," which tried to update the kids-versus-nuns formula for the swinging sixties, minus Ms. Mills.

> "**As expected, mastermind Mary has a showdown with the Reverend Mother ...**"

Local Moments:

St. Mary's Home for Children in Ambler doubled for St. Francis Academy, but much of the film was shot in New Mexico of all places.

Rating:

Twelve Monkeys (1996)

The City of Brotherly Love is presented as a grungy,

dangerous place in this science fiction outing by Terry Gilliam. Inspired by Chris Marker's 1962 French photomontage movie "La Jetee," "Twelve Monkeys" is a challenging effort centering on James Cole (Bruce Willis), a futuristic criminal who is propelled into the past in order to find a deadly virus so scientists in the future can devise a vaccine before it wipes out all mankind. Using a time machine, Cole is hurled back to 1990 — rather than the intended 1996 — and placed in a Maryland mental hospital where only Dr. Kathryn Railey (Madeleine Stowe) and kooky animal activist Jeffrey Goines (an Oscar-nominated Brad Pitt) believe his story of mass annihilation. Cole then uses time travel again to head forward to his projected 1996 time, where he encounters Railey again, and attempts to find the virus. Complex, thought-provoking, and unsettling, "Twelve Monkeys" has the stamp of filmmaker Gilliam all over it, mixing high and low-tech design, elliptical plotting (adapted from "La Jetee" by "Unforgiven" writers Janet Peoples and David Webb Peoples, who also coscripted "Blade Runner"), characters who may or may not be insane, an irreverent sense of humor, a nihilistic view of the world, and references to other films (especially Hitchcock). Boasting admirable acting turns by the constantly brutalized Willis and the continually crazed Pitt, "Twelve Monkeys" is one of the "Brazil" director's best films. If the movie appears confusing at times, bear with it: "Twelve Monkeys" rewards patience and gets richer and more focused upon multiple viewings.

> " … rewards patience and gets richer and more focused upon multiple viewings. "

Kevin Bacon:
Jack of all Movie Trades

Kevin Bacon has been working steadily in films since he was a green 20-year-old making his big screen debut in the classic comedy "Animal House" in 1978. The son of the late city planner Edmond Bacon, Kevin's early roles in the horror hit "Friday the 13th" and Barry Levinson's acclaimed "Diner" paved the way to key roles in such diverse films as "Footloose," "Tremors," "Flatliners," "JFK," "A Few Good Men," "Wild Things," "Apollo 13," "Mystic River," and the Philadelphia-set "The Woodsman." Bacon has also gone behind the camera, directing wife Kyra Sedgwick in two offbeat projects, the cable movie "Losing Chase" and 2006's "Loverboy." And, of course, there's that "Six Degrees of Kevin Bacon" game that people have been talking about for years.

Q. How does it feel to be back in Philadelphia, where you were born and lived until the age of 17?

A. It's very vibrant with restaurants and shops and people on the street all the time. It was a pretty tough place to grow up, just with gangs and the street life downtown. As hard as my father worked, there were people in the 1960s and into the 1970s who were splitting, going to the suburbs and living and coming to town to work.

Q. When you were making such early films as "Animal House" and "Friday the 13th," did you have any idea where they would lead?

A. At that point, I wasn't thinking about it. I was just thinking about trying to make a living as an actor. The first movie, "Animal House," was so overwhelming. People are touching me and putting makeup on me and moving me around and changing lenses and all that crazy s**t. You say, "This is so big and so complicated." The second movie you say, "I know what that guy is doing. He puts a little piece

on the light because it causes some diffusion. It's less harsh." Then you learn something else and you learn something else.

Q. You've directed two features now. Was this transition difficult?

A. After spending your life on movie sets, I think directing is a natural extension. I never thought when I grew up that I wanted to be the leader of the ship, I want to be the guy. I was more into being the character than another character than another character and put on these different hats. One thing people have asked me is if I appreciate how hard it is to be a director, and I said, "No, I've always known that." You have to be an idiot to walk on a movie set and not see how much a responsibility it is and how much pressure a director feels.

> **"So much about making the movie is th experience of it ..."**

Q. Did you have any idea that some of these films, like "Animal House" or "Diner", would be hits that have become iconic in some way?

A. Well, no. I can feel like, "Wow, this felt good" or "This scene went well." Starting with "Footloose," I started to get a sense of how a film was built. I certainly didn't know "Animal House" was going to be a smash, or "Diner" would be come a seminal movie for people. So, no. Plus the other thing is I'm not very likely to think ahead. The second we wrap, I'm onto the next thing. I'm not thinking of that movie. It's different when you're a director cause once you wrap, the work is just beginning with editing and postproduction.

Q. Do you ever pop in a DVD and show your kids your old movies?

A. I don't go back looking at them. I may see them at the premiere or before at a screening just to get a sense of the movie. But I don't look at them. So much about making the movie is the experience of it, not the actual movie. I remember my wife being nine months pregnant, in the desert, making "Tremors." It's just like that's my memory — that we were in this beautiful, spiritual place but there was this excitement and terror about bringing a child into this world. Somebody on the radio [show I was on] this morning was playing some dialogue and I thought it was "Tremors" and it turned out to be "Apollo 13." It took me a while to realize it.

Q. How does it feel having a game named after you that scores of people have played?

A. I just kind of started hearing about it. People came up to me and said it's a drinking game and my cousin invented a game about you. Eventually, it came up on Jon Stewart's show and Howard Stern started talking about it. I met the guys who came up with it a long time ago. I have something I'm still working on. Without going into too much detail, I'm trying to take the subject and mold it into something that's on a charity base. While it's just a silly game, as an idea of connecting us and the rest of the world and the idea of six degrees of separation, it's a beautiful idea. Somebody came up to me recently with the best six degrees I've ever seen. He gave me an incredibly detailed and historically accurate evaluation and connected me to John Wilkes Booth [who assassinated Abraham Lincoln]. He was a stage actor.

Q. We've linked you to famous screen dog Rin Tin Tin.

A. Woof!

(For the record: Rin Tin Tin was in "The Lightning Warrior" with Pat O'Malley. Pat O'Malley was in "Apache Rifles" with L.Q. Jones. L.Q. Jones was in "The Mask Of Zorro" with Anthony Hopkins Anthony Hopkins was in "Nixon" with Ed Harris And Ed Harris was in "Apollo 13" with … KEVIN BACON.)

The Sixth Sense (1999)

Patient Haley Joel Osment walks with psychiatrist Bruce Willis in 1999's "The Sixth Sense."
© Hollywood Pictures/The Kobal Collection

It may have had something to do with the trick ending, but more than likely it was many other elements that made "The Sixth Sense" the sleeper hit of 1999. Superb acting, eerie atmospherics, a thought-provoking premise, and a mysterious new talent behind the camera certainly had some effect on the film's box-office success and subsequent award recognition. Bruce Willis is the child psychologist haunted by the mishandling of a client (Donnie Wahlberg) who committed suicide. His new patient is young Haley Joel Osment, a wide-eyed eight-year-old who claims he can see dead people all over the place, much to the distress of mother Toni Collette. Willis, hoping to sort out his own inner turmoil that includes a breakup with his wife (Olivia Williams), takes Osment's case in hopes of curing him of his anguish while figuring out his own problems as well. Then there's that ending that had the public buzzing and, in many cases, sent them back to the theater again to trace the trajectory of the plot from beginning to end. The genuinely creepy premise is played very seriously, filmed in a methodical, spellbinding style by the "newcomer," a guy based in the Philly burbs with the enigmatic name of M. Night Shyamalan. The film is bolstered by a commanding, subtle turn by Willis, a lights-out kid performance by Osment, and expert supporting work by Collette and others. Unlike most Hollywood efforts, "The Sixth Sense" gets better as it goes along, and rewards audiences with more food for thought in multiple viewings. It's an art film for people who have no interest in art films that delivers a stunning payoff, a real rarity for the movies these days.

Local Moments:

Locations include Striped Bass on Walnut Street, Blue Bell, PA, and Bryn Mawr is the site of the deceased little girl's home … Saint Augustine's Catholic church at 4th and Vine is showcased as is the flower-strewn Saint Alban's Place at 23rd Street. Also used were the Undine Barge Club on Boathouse Row, the Stoddart Fleischer Middle School (13th and Green Streets), and Head House Square.

Rating:

Two Bits (1995)

Local Moments:

Filmed almost entirely in South Philly, the film features: the 600 block of Durfor Street … the 2300 block of South Eighth Street … Saint Gabriel's Church, 29th and Dickenson Streets … the Alcorn Elementary School at 32nd and Tasker … President's Catering Hall at 2308 Snyder Avenue stands in for the La Paloma Theater. Good casting, because form 1936 to 1975, it was called the catering hall was the President Theater.

Rating:

There was lots of talk about this film

when it was being shot in and around the Italian Market, but it seemed to have disappeared for some time. What sounded like a possible Oscar contender for the fall of 1994 featuring a major Hollywood actor turned into a barely released film for February, 2005. So, what happened? "Two Bits" offers Al Pacino in a change-of-pace character role, playing a loquacious 76-year-old with health problems who lives with his daughter (Mary Elizabeth Mastrantonio) and grandson (Jerry Barone) in a South Philly row home during the summer of 1933. A new movie theater called La Paloma

> " … offers Al Pacino in a change-of-pace character role … "

is opening nearby, and Barrone really wants to go check it out, but he needs 25 cents for admission. He tries to do odd jobs in the struggling neighborhood, but has no luck raising the needed funds. So, Pacino, who promised him two bits when he died, strikes a deal: If his grandson will apologize to a woman he wronged years ago, he'll get his movie money. Directed by James Foley ("Glengary Glen Ross," "At Close Range") and written by Philly native Joseph Stefano ("Psycho"), "Two Bits" offers a loving look back in time to a South Philly that used to be. But beyond the film's nostalgia, gloppy sentiment runs amuck in the film. Pacino, with heavy makeup that makes him look a bit like Marlon Brando in "The Godfather," manages to be quietly annoying, spouting little words of wisdom to his grandson. And part of the film plays like an anticlimactic death watch: You know Pacino's going to die from the get-go, so you feel weird rooting for the kid to accomplish his task and getting the promised money. It's good to see Foley and Pacino do something a little more heartfelt than some of their other work, but here they add something so sweet it would make a Termini's pastry taste sour in comparison.

Unbreakable (2000)

This is probably not a popular opinion, but M. Night Shyamalan's follow-up to "The Sixth Sense" is almost the movie his smash sleeper is. The filmmaker once again calls on Bruce Willis for the lead. This time he's playing David Dunn, a security guard at Franklin Field who finds himself the only survivor of a train crash on his way home from New York. Dunn is contacted by Elijah Price (Samuel Jackson), a handicapped man who dresses flamboyantly and walks with a cane. Price attempts to tell him that Dunn is, in fact, "unbreakable," a real-life superhero with special powers who is indestructible. Why Price has such an interest in Dunn's life isn't revealed until the film's surprise finale. "Unbreakable" disappointed many fans of "The Sixth Sense," who may have found it slow paced, couldn't get into the interplay between Dunn and Price, or had problems with the film's trick ending. But the movie's deliberate pace helps heighten its tension, and the relationship between Willis and Jackson's characters is constantly evolving until the final moment, when the truth about both characters is revealed in a way that's true to the superhero theme of the film. The biggest minuses are that Willis's family life with wife (Robin Wright Penn) and son (Spencer Treat Clark) is not fully explored, and Shyamalan's Philly locations are disappointingly limited here. If you didn't get "Unbreakable" the first time around, we suggest you give it another shot. You may not see dead people, but you may see one of the most intriguing, misunderstood films of the last several years.

> "**But the movie's deliberate pace helps heighten its tension ...**"

Local Moments:

Manayunk is where Dunn and family live, and where much of the action takes place ... Franklin Field, where Willis works, is featured in one extended sequence that also boasts M. Night's cameo ... Manayunk's Pretzel Park at Cotton and Cresson Streets is featured ... Many of the interiors were filmed on soundstages constructed at the Civic Center in University City.

Rating:

In M. Night Shyamalan's "Unbreakable," security guard Bruce Willis discovers he may have superhero pow● this picture, Bruce films a scene inside of 30th Sreet Station.
© Touchstone/The Kobal Collection/Masi, Frank

I Was a Roger Corman Star
(For Two Incredibly Low-Budget Movies)

Cliff Henderson, a South Jersey resident who works for the video division of First Look Pictures, has had roles in two ultra low-budget Roger Corman films. He fondly recalls working on the film's produced by the legendary thrifty producer.

"In the first one, 'Caged Heat 3000', which just might be the single worst movie ever churned out of ANY of Roger Corman's various companies, I originally was Journalist #1. I had one line — 'Is that supposed to be happening??' and I worked a total of six hours initially.

"The way my one line turned into a five-minute opening scene was because I got along very well with the director, a guy named Aaron Osborne, and he ended up calling me a few months later to ask me if I'd be interested in coming out for some reshoots. Being the neophyte I am, at first I thought that I'd screwed something up and we were redoing the scene. Turned out he had written a new scene that centered on my character, the journalist, who was referred to in the script as 'Cliff Henderson, the future's answer to Geraldo Rivera.' It had my character on an intergalactic shuttle heading out to the orbiting women's prison in preparation for an expose on the lurid goings-on behind bars there. Interesting note — all the shots of spacecraft doing anything in this flick were lifted from Corman's 1980 low-budget 'Star Wars' imitation called 'Battle Beyond the Stars.' starring Richard Thomas, George Peppard, John Saxon, Robert Vaughn, and a fairly young Sybil Danning. And believe me when I tell you 'Caged Heat 3000' wasn't the only Corman production to use footage from that movie.

"Anyway, I accepted the offer and headed out full of vim and vigor. They said a car would be there to pick me up at the airport, and there was: A beat up '79 Pinto driven by one of the production assistants. When we got to the set, which was an abandoned bank in downtown L.A., I had one brief conversation with Aaron regarding the name of my character. I told him I wasn't comfortable with using my real name, but had a possible alternative: Vas Deferans (think back to Health class in high school). He paused for a second, cocked his head to the side like a dog hearing a high-pitched noise, and said 'I like it!'

"In the end the entire scene he wrote for me, which was basically an expository news report, wasn't used. What was used was the ad-libbing that I did for what I thought was throwaway footage. My inspiration for how I conducted myself was pompous Ted Baxter of the old 'The Mary Tyler Moore Show.' It came out pretty funny, according to the friends and very few family members I actually showed it to (there is a gang-rape during the opening credits!), but I cringe at the thought of having to explain this to my kids someday.

"The second flick I appeared in was a remake of Corman's 1980 drive-in hit 'Humanoids from the Deep,' this one starring Robert Carradine and Emma Samms. In this one I play a soldier, and again only have a single line 'I think we're just about set here, Sir.' The cool part is that the scene that I'm in goes on for a few minutes and I can be seen in the background anxiously fiddling with nonexistent control dials on fake radio equipment in preparation for an assault on the titular creatures who have come from the sea looking for human women to mate with.

"One night I was down here in my basement office working and my wife called down to ask the name of the second movie I'd done for Roger. When I replied, she kind of squealed back 'Oooh, it's on cable right now!!!' She called me up a little while later and we both watched her clean-shaven, VERY square-faced husband-to-be on the TV screen, and we both got lots of laughs.

"I'm now officially three degrees away from Kevin Bacon. I was in 'Humanoids' with Emma Samms, Emma was in 'Only The Lonely' with John Candy, and John Candy was in 'JFK' with Kevin Bacon. Kind of gives you goose-bumps, no?"

Up Close & Personal
(1996)

Former KYW newswoman Jessica Savitch's true-life story

was deemed too dark by Hollywood standards, so the studio (Disney) decided to cobble together pieces from Jessica's life and add them to a more upbeat tale. The result was this glossy behind-the-headlines saga, featuring Michelle Pfeiffer and Robert Redford at their most movie star-iest. Pfeiffer is Tally Atwater, a newscaster wannabe, hired as an assistant to a Miami station by veteran newsman Warren Justice (Redford). He tries to help her make her way into the dog-eat-dog world of the nightly news, and she eventually makes it as an anchor in Philadelphia, then heads on to a national broadcast gig. Meanwhile, Justice, a veteran who covered the big wars and the big stories, follows her to Philly, and they become romantically involved while both crusade to cover the top newsworthy events of the day. Noted husband-and-wife writers Joan Didion and John Gregory Dunne were enlisted to adapt *Golden Girl*, Alanna Nash's no-holds-barred bio of the troubled Savitch to the screen. But after scores of rewrites and heartache, the writers found their edgier work turned into this slick "A Star is Born"-like confection helmed by Jon Avnet ("Fried Green Tomatoes"). In the meantime, cable TV produced the grittier "Golden Girl: The Jessica Savitch Story," a year before, starring Sela Ward.

> **"The result was this glossy behind-the-headlines saga ..."**

NOTE: John Gregory Dunne chronicled the painstaking writing, rewriting, and production of "Up Close and Personal in his superb 1997 book, *Monster: Living off of the Big Screen*.

Local Moments:

Holmesburg Prison is featured as the site where Tally gets to report the big story of a prison riot that garners her national attention ... Former WCAU reporter Andrew Glassman makes an appearance ... Tally works for the Philadelphia station WFIL, which, of course, was Channel 6's name before it became WPVI and the monicker of the popular radio station in the 1960s ... South Philly crooner Fabian plays himself in a cameo, while local thespians Tony Luke, Jr., Sal Mazzotta, and Johnnie Hobbs, Jr., get work.

Rating:

The Village (2004)

Local Moments:

The actual village was situated in a Chadds Ford field off Cossart Road in the Brandywine Valley … Shyamalan reportedly was inspired by artist Andrew Wyeth"s paintings in his designs for the film.

Rating:

M. Night Shyamalan delivers a cropper

with this tale of fear running rampant in a late 19th century village. Set in Covington, PA., a tiny village of about 60 people who act like they're about to perform in a production of Arthur Miller's "The Crucible," the film shows us that Covington's inhabitants are fearful of mysterious, man-eating beasts who live on the outskirts of their settlement, leave animal carcasses all around, and are attracted to the color red. So, nobody in Covington can wear the color, and all must listen closely to the laws concocted by the town's Board of Elders, who include William Hurt, Sigourney Weaver, and Brendan Gleason. Although they forbid anyone from leaving the area, Joaquin Phoenix, Weaver's brooding, near-silent son, challenges the Elders by venturing out of their boundaries to seek

> " … this is the filmmaker's slowest moving and most exasperating film to date … "

medical help. But an incident leads Dallas Bryce Howard, the blind, tomboyish daughter of Hurt, and Phoenix's romantic interest, to take the journey instead. It's a premise that's none too original, but you'd hope that Shyamalan's trademark intensity could refresh the idea. Unfortunately, it doesn't, for this is the filmmaker's slowest moving and most exasperating film to date — at least until "Lady in the Water." In works like "The Sixth Sense," "Unbreakable," and "Signs," Shyamalan seemed content taking an artful (some would say "artsy") approach to tackling a genre film, but here he really believes he's making an art film, and it cracks under its own self-importance and pretentiousness. While the film is exceedingly well shot (by Coen Brothers regular Roger Deakins) and eerily scored (by James Newton Howard), it's got a frustrating script filled with long-winded dialogue spoken in Puritanical argot puzzles and leaves more questions than answers with its trick ending. Then there's Oscar-winning Adrien Brody as a village idiot character, annoyingly mugging his way through the film. Reminiscent in many ways of Christophe Gans' highly entertaining 2001 genre-splicer "Brotherhood of the Wolf," "The Village" has intense and even scary moments. And except for Brody's "what was Night thinking?" performance, it's well acted. Still, it has the goods to lull you to sleep — or at least into a trancelike state. As for the ending, it's reminiscent of at least a classic "Twilight Zone" episodes or two and the novel *Running Out of Time*. If only Rod Serling were around to rewrite Shyamalan's script.

Where Angels Go, Trouble Follows (1968)

Hayley Mills and June Harding, the two stars of 1966's popular "The Trouble with Angels," sat out the sequel, allowing Barbara Hunter, a costar the first time around, to pair with a very young Susan Saint James as the featured students of the Philadelphia-area St. Francis Academy. Here the teenage girls and their cohorts are heading on a cross-country bus trip to Santa Barbara, California, for an "Interfaith/Integrated Youth Rally." Joining them on the trip are the stern, old-fashioned Mother Superior (Rosalind Russell) and the young, hipper Sister George (Stella Stevens at the prime of her beauty).

> **" Surprisingly, the film is not totally frivolous ... "**

Of course the trip is rife with incident, including a run-in with bikers, a car wash that goes out-of-control , and an unexpected stay in Hollywood during a battle between cowboys and Indians in a western movie shoot. The film entertains in a "groovy as you can get" 1960s way. Surprisingly, the film is not totally frivolous: It acknowledges the times with a war protest scene and hints at traditional Catholic Church struggles with the ever-changing ideals of the tumultuous decade. On hand for this trip are Milton Berle, Robert Taylor, Van Johnson, and Arthur Godfrey in cameos, while Boyce & Hart supply the bubblegum-coated theme song.

Local Moments:

A nice aerial shot of City Hall at night opens up the film, preceded by an opening credit sequence in which a motorcade, paddy wagons and 1960s-style red Philly cop cars speed down west Market Street, past scores of now-defunct stores, then into the City Hall courtyard … Sylvester Stallone wasn't first with the Art Museum steps: An anti-war demonstration early in the film takes place atop the steps, and we're offered a nice panoramic view of Logan Square and beyond … The nuns and company stop at Dorney Park in Allentown, PA, where we're offered shots of the roller coaster and the Pirate's Cove ride … Saint Mary's Home for Children in Ambler is back doubling as the Saint Francis Academy for Girls.

Rating:

Wide Awake (1998)

Local Moments:

Locations included Bryn Mawr College's Taylor Hall and the Waldron Mercer Academy in Lower Merion, the director's alma mater.

Rating:

M. Night Shyamalan's second film was sorely mistreated by the powers-that-be at Miramax Pictures, where it was fiddled with by in-house editors and moved around the schedule several times before being released. It was issued with no fanfare. But in light of his smash "The Sixth Sense," "Wide Awake" is a very interesting film indeed, showcasing some of the same themes and ideas that fueled the director's eerie 1999 thriller. The experience also led the filmmaker to insist on calling his own shots. "Wide Awake" centers on 10-year-old Joshua Beal (Joseph Cross), a fifth-grader at a Catholic school in the Philly area. Joshua has been so affected by the death of his beloved grandfather (Robert Loggia) that he wants to know how he's doing on the other side and if, in fact, there is a God watching over him. So, Joshua begins his quest to find the truth about

> " ... his screenplay is sharp and observant ... "

a supreme being's existence by questioning such people as Father Peter (Dan Lauria) and Sister Terry (Rosie O'Donnell), a hip nun who uses sports analogies to teach. Meanwhile, his doctor parents (Denis Leary and Dana Delaney) seem very worried about his determination to seek proof of God's existence. "Wide Awake" is heartfelt and mysterious at the same time, and has a light touch when dealing with pretty big issues involving faith, religion, and coming-of-age. Though the straightforward direction doesn't really hint much at the filmmaking technique Shyamalan shows in his next effort, his screenplay is sharp and observant, with some insightful and funny lines (Joshua's friend Dave notes: "We go to Catholic school. God's like our homework.") But why the film was treated so coolly by its distributor remains the biggest mystery of all. There's certainly nothing to be ashamed of here.

Winter Kills (1979)

A loopy political comedy with extremely dark overtones, "Winter Kills" is based on the book by Richard Condon, the author of "The Manchurian Candidate" and "Prizzi's Honor." Consider this question: What if JFK was shot in Philadelphia? That's the basic premise behind the film that boasts a bizarre sense of humor and a wicked satiric spin. In this case, the president's half-brother, Nick Kegan (Jeff Bridges), hears a dying man confess that he was the second shooter in the death of the American leader years ago. Kegan investigates the confession and enters a web of conspiracies involving a lobbyist, a millionaire, a mobster, a computer expert, and his own father, played by John Huston doing his most perverse Joseph Kennedy impersonation. "Winter Kills" veers all over the place, and includes one of the most eclectic casts ever assembled in movie history: Richard Boone, Anthony Perkins, Toshiro Mifune, Elizabeth Taylor, Thomas Millan, Belinda Bauer, Eli Wallach, Ralph Meeker, and Dorothy Malone. Writer-adapter William Richert's navigation of the material is shaky and his pacing falters at times, but it's never less than interesting, especially when the paranoia factor is turned up a few notches. Perhaps the film's shaky production history has something to do with its shifting tone — it was shut down three times because money ran out and took a few years to complete. Richert raised the needed cash by making a movie called "The American Success Company" in Germany with some of the same cast members. When "Winter Kills" was finally ready for release, Richert claims Avco-Embassy, its distributor, dumped it because they had close contacts in the defense industry. Sounds like a conspiracy to us.

> **"What if JFK was shot in Philadelphia?"**

Local Moments:

City Hall and Market Street get screen time ... There is also a bizarre scene shot at Lombardi's Bread shop on 9th Street.

Rating:

Witness (1985)

A superior police drama with fish-out-of-water elements that often click wonderfully, Peter Weir's film features Kelly McGillis as Rachel Lapp, an Amish woman whose son, Samuel (Lukas Haas), witnesses a murder in the bathroom of the 30th Street Station. Cynical, world-weary cop John Book (Harrison Ford)is called on the case, and soon discovers that Detective James McFee (Danny Glover) is involved in the killing and cover-up. In order to protect the woman and her son, Book heads back to their Lancaster area farm, where he tries to blend in with the Amish and eventually falls for Rachel. The film has the basics of a solid crime story, but the top-notch cast, Weir's eye for detail, the romance between Book and Rachel, and the culture clash between untrustworthy big-city folks and the peaceful Amish push "Witness" beyond an average genre outing. Several scenes stick out as being memorable, including the moving use of Sam Cook's "Wonderful World (Don't Know Much)" for Ford and McGillis' romantic liaison, and the bravura barn-raising sequence which would have made John Ford proud. While the procedural police stuff has an urgency and polish to it when it isn't simply conventional, it's the Amish element that helps make "Witness" shine.

> " … it's the Amish element that helps make 'Witness' shine. "

> **Rachel Lapp (Kelly McGillis):** You said we'd be safe in Philadelphia!

The Woodsman (2004)

Can you feel sorry for a pedophile?

That's the tricky question encountered in "The Woodsman," producer Lee Daniels' controversial follow-up to his controversial, Oscar-winning "Monster's Ball." Directed by newcomer Nicole Kassell and adapted by her and Steven Fechter from his play, the film stars Kevin Bacon as Walter, a man fresh out of prison after serving 12 years for molesting a young girl. Thanks to family ties, he's been able to get a job at a lumberyard and has an apartment that's suspiciously (and unbelievably) close to an elementary school. Walter gets romantically involved with Vickie (Bacon's real-life wife Kyra Sedgwick),

> **"Fine acting down the line helps her endeavor ..."**

a tough coworker at the lumberyard with her own troubled past. At the same time, however, Walter battles his urges to go back and commit crimes similar to what put him prison. The notion that Walter will follow through on his impulses makes the film a very difficult watch at times. Director Cassell has her work cut out for her, not only making a pedophile the main character in a film, but for asking audiences to sympathize with him. Fine acting down the line helps her endeavor, including supporting work from Mos Def (as a cop who checks in on Walter), David Allen Grier (as Walter's boss), and rapper Eve (as a nosy secretary). All would have gone for naught, however, if Bacon and Sedgwick weren't up for the task. Here they both do some of their finest work together, nuanced, intense, and, most importantly, vulnerable. Damn all for tackling such a creepy subject; Kudos all around for pulling it off.

Local Moments:

Walter's apartment is located near 9th and Federal in South Philly, near Capitolo Playground ... Walter rides the SEPTA bus to and from work each day ... A sequence of the film was shot in the Willow Grove Mall. Its antique carousel appears at the end of the sequence ... The offices of the lumberyard are actually at the Navy Yard in South Philadelphia ... Because of a recommendation by Bacon, local Eve got the role as the lumberyard secretary. Reportedly, the role was written for a 45-year-old white woman ... Local songstress Patti LaBelle sings "My Eye is on the Sparrow" for the closing credits.

Rating:

Worth Winning (1989)

Local Moments:

The film takes off at the Atlantic City Race Track … Taylor lives near Head House Square, so there are several scenes of the area and Old City … The Merriam Theater box office is featured in a scene … Local comic legend David Brenner hosts a charity auction near the end of the film and cracks a Phillies joke.

Rating:

In this lightweight romantic farce,

Mark Harmon plays Taylor Worth, a handsome and irresistible Philadelphia Channel 5 weatherman who has loved and left legions of women over the years. Worth's psychiatrist pal Ned (Mark Blum) comes up with a bet: If Taylor can get engaged to three women (and videotape the proposals), he gets the Picasso painting Ned's wife has inherited. The three targets turn out to be Erin (Maria Holvoe), a striking blonde receptionist for the Eagles; Eleanor (Lesley Ann Warren), a sexually frustrated housewife; and Veronica (Madeleine Stowe), a no-nonsense concert pianist. As Taylor, Harmon turns on the blue-eyed charm, and the three women he seeks are surprisingly three-dimensional, as well as fetching in their individual ways. But can the viewer excuse Harmon's dirty rotten scoundrel tactics, seducing then abandoning the ladies? If so, audience members will find a breezy little rom-com. If not, "Worth Winning" is a loser.

Head House Square, seen in "Worth Winning," and other films.
© Sally Lindsay

NOTE: Any similarities to the actions of Taylor Worth and a once-prominent Philly weatherman are purely coincidental — we think.

> **" … But can the viewer excuse Harmon's dirty, rotten scoundrel tactics … ?"**

Lee Daniels: West Philly Power Player

The logo of Lee Daniels Entertainment has a Philadelphia skyline on it. This represents how the producer of "Monster's Ball" and "The Woodsman" and the producer-direcror of "Shadowboxer" feels about his Philly heritage. Born and raised in West Philly, Daniels made his mark at an early age, first as an entrepreneur in the health field, then in entertainment management. This opened the door to become a producer, and he knocked it out of the park with his first project: 2001's low-budget "Monster's Ball," about a black woman who gets romantically involved with a prison guard who executed her husband, brought Halle Berry a historical Academy Award for Best Actress and the film brought in $35 million at the box office. He followed with two Philly-lensed efforts: 2003's "The Woodsman," starring Kevin Bacon as a pedophile recently released from prison, and 2006's "Shadowboxer," a wild crime saga with British actress Helen Mirren as a dying hit woman and Cuba Gooding, Jr., as her loving stepson accomplice.

Q. "Shadowboxer," which was shot entirely in this area and showcases some great Philadelphia locations, seems larger than life and offers moments of fairly explicit sex, excessive drug use, hints of child abuse, seedy characters, and extreme violence. You're no stranger to pushing the envelope, but why did you choose this story to make your directing debut?

A. Every piece of this struck on a personal nerve. It's about killers — my uncle killed people, but he was a great guy. And it wasn't just him. I knew other people in my youth in West Philly who had done that, too. And these people had crosses in their homes. I was physically abused by my dad, he beat me and stuff. So that was very personal to me. My sister was a recovering crack addict and she was obese, and yet she was able to get many good-looking white men. So all of these people were understood and close to my heart. The script was not the same at one time — all the characters were written white, so I sort of intermingled characters in my world into the script's world. This is my vision. If I hired another director, they would not have done what I have done with the character choices.

Q. With "Monster's Ball"'s success you obviously made new friends at the Hollywood studios, yet you continue to work independently, tackling controversial subjects. How do you think Hollywood views you?

A. They can't figure me out in the studio world. How does this n****r get his money? How does he pull it together and what happens? It's just independent filmmaking. I don't have to answer to suits and the actors have fun with it. The actors toll up their sleeves for 10% of what they [usually] make and it's our playground. It's fun, it's work, it's all on the page and it's risky. It may be a flop and we may end up as a joke. On all of our sets we have a party. One, it's about the love on the set. And two, it's courageous. I feel good saying that. It's courageous work.

Q. Your production offices are now based in Harlem, but you used to live and operate in Philadelphia. What was it like running a movie company from Philly?

A. The great part of living in Philly is that if they are racist and they let you know. They are in your face! Philadelphians are ugly honest. Everybody helped me, though — I've never had a bad experience here. I get deals. With Tennessee (where Daniels is making a new movie), I'm nervous. I don't know if I can get what I need. With Rendell, I was part of that tax deal. I was in his office when it was signed. The stores here ... the unions here ... they are my dogs!

> **"I was physically abused by my dad, he beat me and stuff. So that was very personal to me."**

The Young Philadelphians

(1959)

A glossy soap opera that keeps getting better as it goes along, "The Young Philadelphians" shows us that the barriers between the blue bloods and working class in the City of Brotherly Love was often made of iron. The movie seems quite complicated on paper, with loads of characters and overtly dramatic turns of events, but it

> **" ... it all plays out nicely under the assured direction of veteran director Vincent Sherman ... "**

all plays out nicely under the assured direction of veteran helmsman Vincent Sherman ("The Adventures of Don Juan," "Old Acquaintance"). Hot off his electrifying turn in "Cat on a Hot Tin Roof," a strapping Paul Newman plays Anthony Lawrence, born to a socially conscious mother (Diane Brewster) and wealthy father (Adam West), who mysteriously dies in a car accident before he's born. Lawrence is an aspiring lawyer paying for his education at Princeton by working construction for a family friend, Mike Flanagan (Brian Keith with a brogue and heavy makeup). He meets and falls in love with lovely Joan Dickenson (Barbara Rush), the daughter of powerful Main Line attorney Gilbert Dickenson (John Williams). After Lawrence is shanghaied by father Dickenson into an agreement to work for his law firm, he loses Joan to a Main Line suitor (Anthony Eisley), which makes him more determined than ever to prove himself an effective lawyer and his own person. Along the way he becomes a hot-shot tax attorney, learns an amazing secret about his past, and has to defend old pal Chet Gwynn (the Oscar-nominated Robert Vaughn), a depressed, one-armed Korean war veteran, who has been charged with murder. With all of these convoluted predicaments — and even more we haven't mentioned — "The Young Philadelphians" resembles the Douglas Sirk-helmed glossy soap operas of the era like "Written on the Wind" and "Magnificent Obsession." But "The Young Philadelphians" is anything but glossy. Shot in black and white, it's dark and noirish in style and content — it shows us how hidden deals, clandestine family arrangements, and manipulative characters can affect the well being of its young and innocent protagonists who live under Billy Penn's hat.

Local Moments:

Although most of the film was shot in L.A., on soundstages, and at Will Rogers State Park, the film has a nice Philly flavor ... Newman's character does undergrad work at Princeton, but attends law school at the University of Pennsylvania ... There are a few mentions of Rittenhouse House Square, but for some reason, they are linked to the Main Line ... Brian Keith's scrappy construction boss Flanagan hangs out on the "South Side," but his home turf is modeled after an old Two Street bar ... The "blue bloods" hang out at "The Cricket Club" ... The law firm Newman winds up working for is Wharton, Biddle & Clayton, clicking with at least two famous Philly names. And the name of "Jerome Shestack,": a prominent Philadelphia lawyer (and husband of TV newscaster Marciarose Shestack) is recognizable on the building's directory.

Rating:

More Philly Films

We'd be remiss to leave out the following unique movies shot and/or set in and around the area.

The 4-D Man (1959)

From the people who gave us "The Blob" comes this solid, shot-around-Valley Forge sci-fi foray in which Robert Lansing enters the fourth dimension and gains the ability to pass through objects. Everytime he does the deed, however, he gets nastier and nastier. Lee Meriwether, Miss America 1955 and future "Catwoman" in the "Batman" movie, costars with Patty Duke.

The 24th Day (2004)

The HIV-positive Scott Speedman takes one-night stand James Marsden captive, believing he's responsible for transmitting AIDS to him. The intense interplay between the two comprises most of the film, directed and written by Tony Picccirillo, based on his own play.

Bald (2001)

Vince Mola, best known for his routine as the wacky Philly sports-obsessed "Superphan" on WIP Radio's morning show, directs and stars in this extremely offbeat comic look at an advertising guy (Mola) whose follicle loss has made him depressed and taken him into a midlife crisis even though he's far from 50-years-old. A parade of local personalities, including Angelo Cataldi, Joe Conklin, and chicken wing-eating champion "El Wingador," make cameos in this video feature shot at WIP's old studios near 5th and Callowhill, Bucks County, and other area locales. The film shows that Mola has talent as both a filmmaker and performer, but the movie's checkered distribution history makes it hard to find.

Ben and Me (1953)

Oscar-nominated, Disney-animated version of the prize-winning children's book centering on a rodent who helps Ben Franklin create his greatest inventions.

Best In Show (2000)

Christopher Guest's hilarious look at a dog show featuring a load of goofy canine owners played by the likes of Guest, Eugene Levy, Catherine O'Hara, Parker Posey, and Michael McKean is set in Philly, but the former Spinal Tap member actually shot most of it in Vancouver, British Columbia. You could tell it wasn't here, right?

Black Devil Doll From Hell (1984)

An African-American twist on "Trilogy of Terror" in which a highly religious woman is terrorized by a dummy doll with dreadlocks from hell. Laughably bad and cheaply shot on video.

The Block (1964)

A long-lost film with an interesting local cast that includes Dick Lee, who once owned a popular South Jersey nightclub; James E. Myers, the colorful writer of the song "Rock Around the Clock"; and Red Benson, who had a radio show in Philly in the 1960s, wrote for "Get Smart" and hosted "Name That Tune" in the 1950s. The movie is a sordid affair involving crooked cops, strippers, and blackmail, but we've found it impossible to find.

Blur (2005)

The first half of this locally lensed thriller offers fine direction, a creepy mood, and scares to spare. It centers on artist Adrian Jonas (Salvator Xureb), who has disturbing premonitions before a big art show. The premonitions seem to have inspired him to paint a picture of a devilish figure that creeps him and others around him out. At a party at his home, a series of incidents involving him, his girlfriend, his prank-happy next-door neighbor, and a party guest with psychic powers. Director Nick Briscoe shows real promise in the suspense genre and a real command of the camera in this stylish outing.

Buddy (1997)

The fictionalized story of Massa, the gorilla that was adopted by an eccentric socialite, then given to the Philadelphia Zoo. Rene Russo plays the woman who cares for the simian, and the film is darker than you'd expect for a kid's film.

Centennial Summer (1946)

A musical with tunes by Jerome Kern set in the City of Brotherly Love? You bet, but it's extremely hard to locate. The setting is the 1876 Centennial celebration in Philly and Jeanne Crain and Linda Darnell are sisters vying for the attention of dashing Frenchman Cornel Wilde. Directed by Otto Preminger, the film is Hollywood all the way, but the Philly locale, the premise, and supporting players Dorothy Gish and Water Brennan as Darnell and Crain's parents make it worth a look — if you can find it!

A Chronicle of Corpses (2000)

Andrew Mark Repasky's mix of exploitation and art film landed on a *New York Times* "Ten Best" list." The film is set in the early 19th century and centers on a family on a Philly-based estate with lots of skeletons in their closet. Gorgeously photographed in black and white (by Abe Holtz), the film has an eerie quietness that is unsettling and an oddball sense of humor and heightened dramatics that make it an off-balanced curio.

The Coatroom (2005)

Quirky independedent film plays like "'Clerks' Goes to a Museum" detailing the misadventures of a despondent college flunkee who takes a job at the Art Museum and deals with his own and his coworkers anomie, as well as a student creepily obsessed with Marcel Duchamp's painting "Nude Descending a Staircase."

Diary of a City Priest (2001)

David Morse turns in a quiet and powerful performance as Father John McNamee, a priest at a church in an impoverished North Philadelphia neighborhood, who questions his mission. The film was shot at St. Malachy's, 11th and Master Streets.

Down Liberty Road (1956)

Also known as "Freedom Highway," this obscure road saga tells of a group of people who board a Greyhound bus and cross the U.S., making stops in San Francisco, Chicago, Reno, Gettysburg, and Philadelphia. Historical events are reenacted (on a very small scale), and Tex Ritter, playing himself, gets to sing. Other cast members include Angie Dickenson, Tommy Kirk, and Marshall Thompson. A rarity with a lot of campy charm today.

Edge City (1998)

Partially based on the Eddie Pollack incident in which a Fox Chase teen was beaten to death, Eugene Martin's appropriately edgy inquisition into teen-on-teen violence packs an emotional wallop, dissecting the social components that lead to hostility and, eventually, bloodshed.

Fallout (1995)

Robert Palumbo's edgy drama centering on four businessmen's interactions when they're locked in their building's fallout shelter after there's an explosion in the structure.

Fat Albert (2004)

Hey, hey, hey! Finally, a "Fat Albert" movie, but most was shot in L.A. What would Mushmouth say?

Girls School Screamers (1986)

A group of coeds think they're going to have fun in "an old dark house," but soon terror disrupts their party and they are hunted down by a mysterious creep. John P. Finegan was shooting for something more subtle in "The Haunting" vein, but when he sold it to Troma, the company added gore effects. The location is Belvedere Mansion.

Hairspray (1988)

Dorney Park is the site where John Waters filmed sequences of his retro musical comedy.

Harold & Kumar Go to White Castle (2004)

A stoner farce in which a Korean-American banker and an Indian-American med student go on a wild, incident-filled road trip in search of munchies has a White Castle hamburger stop in Cherry Hill as its destination. But the filmmakers went nowhere near the Jersey locale in reality — most of the film was shot in Ontario, Canada and the White Castle was actually a Swift Burger stand. And another reality check: The film purports Harold & Kumar can't find a White Castle in North Jersey. The place is loaded with them!

Head Trauma (2006)

Lance Weiler, "The Last Broadcast" director, returns to the filmmaking fray with this digital video horror show featuring Vince Mola ("Superphan") as a drifter trying to restore his grandmother's old house and encountering weird visions and demons from his past. Shot in and around Doylestown and Scranton, the film is a genuinely unsettling affair.

Independence (1976)

Made for the Bicentennial celebration (what bicentennial celebration?) and shown at the Independence National Park Visitor's Center at 3rd and Chestnut Streets for years, John Huston's salute to the Declaration of Independence and our Founding Fathers was at least shot in the city — unlike "1776." While it boasts a fine cast — Eli Wallach as Ben Franklin, Pat Hingle as John Adams, Patrick

O'Neal as George Washington — the film is a tough sit, talky and pompous, even at a 30-minute running time.

The King of the Corner (2005)

Peter Reigert makes his directing debut and stars in this study of middle-aged malaise with some funny and heartfelt moments. Reigert is a market research guy with an attractive but disinterested wife (Isabella Rossellini), a rebellious teenage daughter (Ashley Johnson), and an elderly father (Eli Wallach). When Reigert meets up with an old flame (Beverly D'Angelo) while in Philly for business, he must decide whether to pursue an affair with her. Perhaps a rabbi (Eric Bogosian) can help him figure everything out. Some Center City locations in the Washington Square area and near South Street are used here.

A Kiss Before Dying (1991)

Psychotic University of Pennsylvania student Matt Dillon throws wealthy Sean Young off of Billy Penn's hat at City Hall in this so-so thriller, a remake of an earlier Robert Wagner suspenser.

Mafioso: The Father, The Son (2004)

The son of the head of a Philadelphia mob family discovers that some people in the family may have been involved in trying bump off Dad. All hell breaks loose in this very serious drama spiked with violence and many local locations, including South Philly, the old China Castle Restaurant on Race Street, Atlantic City, and Bellmawr, New Jersey, plus local talent like Tony Luke, Jr., Leo Rossi, Sal Mazotta, and playwright Louis Lippa.

Money for Nothing (1993)

Pittsburgh locations stand in for real-life Philly locales in the bittersweet saga of the legendary Joey Coyle (John Cusack), the dockworker who decides to keep the $1.2 million that fell out of an armored car. James Gandolfini, Philip Seymour Hoffman, Debi Mazar, and Michael Rapaport comprise the outstanding supporting cast.

Outside the Wall (1950)

A stark, now-forgotten crime drama with Richard Basehart as a young ex-con trying to go straight who just can't stay out of trouble with crooks, guns, and women. Eastern State Penitentiary, City Hall, and the now-closed Philadelphia General Hospital on 34th Street are among the locations prominent in the film's early proceedings.

Perils Of Pauline (1914)

Anyone familiar with this classic old serial with Pearl White (or even the "Dudley Dooright" cartoon that spoofed it) recalls the scene in which the heroine is tied to the train tacks and rescued at the last minute. Believe it or not, the scenes were shot on a trestle used by the New Hope-Ivyland Railroad in Bucks County.

The Philadelphia Experiment (1984)

Another Philly-related film that helped launch Michael Pare's acting career, this science-fiction opus tells the supposedly true saga of a Navy ship that put under an electromagnetic field in a Navy experiment at the Philadelphia shipyard in 1943. The story tells us that the experiment intended to make the ship invisible, but when things go awry, crew members Pare and Bobby DiCicco get hurled into the future. South Carolina, however, stood in for the Philadelphia ship sequences in this popular outing.

Postcards from Paradise Park (2000)
Local advertising guy Curt Crane directs this movie about a local advertising executive who loses everything in a short span of time, then lands in a New Jersey trailer park populated by weirdos.

Prison Song (2001)
What was intended as an all-out musical drama is now a drama with some musical moments as we follow the trajectory of Q-Tip, a kid with a talent for photography and art, who can't get a break in the system and winds up in a Philadelphia prison. Coproduced by Robert de Niro, the film offers a interesting cast that includes Mary J. Blige, Harold Perrineau, and Elvis Costello and direction by Darnell Martin ("Oz").

Return To Paradise (1998)
Eastern State Penitentiary was used for prison sequences in this exotic true-life drama in which Vince Vaughn and David Conrad must decide whether to return to Malaysia and turn themselves into authorities to save friend Joaquin Phoenix who is being held on drug charges.

Saint Christopher (The Good Thief) (2002)
A thief just out of the slammer for breaking and entering finds difficulty going straight, especially when he's recruited to pull off one last job. R.T. Herwig's film is a gritty little character study that grows on you.

The Scar of Shame (1927)
An all-black silent "race film" shot in Philadelphia and centering on a woman saved from an abusive relationship with her father when a music student marries her. But one of her father's friends tries to break up their marriage, which leads to a series of other complications. Produced by the Colored Film Corporation of Philadelphia, the film offers an interesting view of the race relations among African-Americans.

The Short Films Of David Lynch
The director of "Blue Velvet" and creator of "Twin Peaks" has always said that Philadelphia has had a huge influence on him, and in this DVD compilation the proof is in the pudding. Here Lynch's earliest works — a few made when he was a student at the Pennsylvania Academy of Fine Arts — have been collected, and, man, are they weird! The Philly-connected shorts include 1966's "Six Men Getting Sick" (which is pretty much what it is), 1968's "The Alphabet" and 1970's "The Grandmother." You can see the seeds beginning to sprout in these artful and unsettling projects. Listen to the audio commentary and catch Lynch's reminiscences of his Philly days.

State Property 2 (2005)

Local rap star Beanie Siegel is a gangsta trying to keep things In check as rival hoods try to encroach his Philly turf. Rap impresario Damon Dash directs and costars in this sequel to the hit 2002 film that's loaded with gunplay and sex, and features bits by Mariah Carey, Bernard Hopkins, and Ol' Dirty Bastard.

Surrender Dorothy (1998)

This startling directorial debut by Kevin DiNovis is just your basic "shy guy turns drug-addicted male friend into a female sex slave" story. An uncompromising look at a very bizarre relationship, the film offers a glimpse at a young former Penn student named Elizabeth Banks.

Uncle Scam (1981)

If you thought the ABSCAM scandal of 1978 was a riot — and who didn't? — wait until you see (if you can find it) this supposed political satire made three years later, based on the incident. The names have been changed, but the comedy is pretty lame. Local character actor Tom McCarthy has a key role and Joan Rivers and Pat Copper show up for cameos. At its world premiere at the Orleans Theater, local promotions maven Stanley Green wore Arab garb.

Viral Assassins (2000)

Troma released this title, and, true to form, it looks like it was shot for $1.25 with amateur actors. But it is a serious affair, a tale of a futuristic society where a virus threatens to kill everybody, and anyone carrying the disease is killed by government-sanctioned hitmen.

Waiting (2001)

A waiter at an Italian restaurant in South Philly finds his life spinning out of control as his girlfriend dumps him, his parents want him to move out of his home, and his acting career has him entertaining at kids' parties. Funny stuff from local director Patrick Hasson, plus a cast that includes Will Kennan ("Trick"), Kerry Kenney ("Reno 911"), porn star Ron Jeremy, and local character actor Steve Lippe.

The Watermelon Woman (1997)

Writer-director Cheryl Dunye plays a variation on herself, an African-American lesbian worker at a video store (TLA to be precise) who becomes obsessed with a a actress in an old film who was also an African-American lesbian with Philly connections. The gritty film is thought-provoking and ambitious. It also features locally based Camille Paglia playing herself in a small part.

> **Ghostbusters (1984)**
> **Dr Ray Stantz (Dan Aykroyd):**
> Symmetrical book stacking. Just like the Philadelphia mass turbulence of 1947.

Shore Things

The sun, the
sand, the surf
— roll 'em!

Atlantic City (1944)

This tune-filled, live-act-packed tale tells the fictionalized story of how Atlantic City became the nation's playground. It's set in 1915, when impresario Brad Taylor (Stanley Brown) decides that the city's sun, beach, and boardwalk are just what the public wants, and decides that a beauty pageant may add some more luster and publicity to the area. Meanwhile, he has an interest in singer Marilyn Whitaker (Constance Moore), but she has her sights set on Broadway. Can Taylor do enough to make A.C. a showplace pronto before Whitaker heads to the Big Apple? Along with appearances by mustachioed funnyman Jerry Colonna, Paul Whiteman and his Orchestra, Louie Armstrong, Dorothy Dandridge, and several popular nightclub acts of the time, we get shots of the boardwalk, push chairs, Lucy the Elephant, several classic hotels, and musical numbers based on such tunes as "By the Beautiful Sea." In all, this is an enjoyable time capsule of a bygone era.

Atlantic City (1981)

The city of Atlantic City and the film's primary characters are wonderfully captured in transitional times in Louis Malle's acclaimed drama. The older hotels are being imploded, replaced by condominiums and casinos. Meanwhile, aging small-potatoes gangster and numbers runner Burt Lancaster seeks one major score in a cocaine deal, and going along for the ride is seafood restaurant worker/croupier wannabe Susan Sarandon, married to a sleazy hood (Robert Joy). Lancaster, in love with the good old days, also falls in love with Sarandon, who routinely undresses in front of her window as the old man looks on. The relationship marks a turn towards new directions for both people concerned, but is it doomed from the start? The film opens with the demolition of the huge Traymore Hotel, and includes scenes shot at Resorts, near Lucy the Elephant, and around the ill-fated buildings in the residential areas of the city.

Atlantic City Jackpot (1975)

Obscure crime drama with Atlantic City background concerns a street hustler who takes an immoral businessman's kids and babysitter girlfriend hostage, then tries to cut a deal with him. Laurence Luckenbill, Regina Baff, Danny De Vito, and George Hearn star in this film codirected by local guy Chuck Workman, best known for his film clip wonders that show annually on the Academy Award show.

Beaches (1988)

Prime chick flick soap opera has soon-to-be-friends Bette Midler and Barbara Hershey meeting each other in Atlantic City.

Blades (1989)

"'Jaws' Goes Golf" may be the best way to describe this enjoyable but a tad too laid-back spoof from producer John P. Finegan ("Girls' School Screamers") in which a killer lawn mower terrorizes the members of a Wildwood course, chewing off their legs and leaving the greens a crimson mass. The movie's salutes to Steven Spielberg's classic are sometimes sharp and often silly, but Jeremy Whelan does well as the grizzled pro trying to track down the killer a la Robert Shaw. The film was shot primarily at "Billy Pflaumer's Beer World" in the Villas, which most recently was known as "Ponderlodge Golf Club."

The Cohens And Kellys Of Atlantic City (1929)

The first entry in a five-part series finds Jewish businessmen battling Irish businessmen in marketing bathing suits at "America's Playground."

Cold Hearts (1999)

It's a little bit of "The Lost Boys" crossed with "Near Dark," set in and around Ocean City. A vampiress and her posse of female bloodsuckers are threatened by her ex-boyfriend and his creepy crew. To the rescue comes a new goth in town. Directed by sometime disc jockey and Philly guy Robert Masciantonio, the movie shows promise with its eerie atmosphere and quirky characters, all done on a low-budget.

The Color Of Money (1986)

In Martin Scorsese's 25-years-later sequel to "The Hustler," the climactic showdown in a Nine-Ball Tournament between Paul Newman's "Fast" Eddie Felson and Tom Cruise's Vincent Lauria takes place in Resort's International.

Convention Girl (1935)

Thanks to some interesting Atlantic City sights and sounds, this creaky comedy-drama is worth a look. There's a convention for men who make "electric washers" in Atlantic City, and it's the job of Rose Hobart to keep the fellows entertained. This means providing female chaperones for the out-of-towners, who take them to Boardwalk animal exhibitions and to The Steel Pier to see acrobats and the famous diving horse show. Meanwhile, Ms. Hobart has to decide whether she likes gambler Weldon Heyburn or older, richer soap mogul Herbert Rawlinson.

Delivering Milo (2001)

Unusual fantasy tale from Nick Castle ("The Boy Who Could Fly") about a child about to be born, reincarnated from a dead man, who can't decide whether he wants to exist on Earth. An angel played by Albert Finney helps him with his decision, and takes him to Atlantic City's Tropicana Resort and Casino because he's obsessed with cards and gets to meet his new mother.

Desperately Seeking Susan (1985)

Susan Seidelman's hip screwball comedy that helped make Madonna a movie star (briefly at least) is set mostly in and around East Greenwich Village and North Jersey (Fort Lee to be exact), but includes sequences shot and set in Atlantic City.

Duane Hopwood (2005)

A low-key, elegiac tale of a life on the skids, this low-budget independent production serves up "Friends" star David Schwimmer as the title character, an Atlantic City casino worker who finds his life dissipating because of alcoholism, but isn't quite sure what to do about it. Trouble begins when he's pulled over by a cop for a DUI while his daughter sleeps in the back seat of his car. This begins the chain of events that will come close to ruining him, from his ex-wife Janeane Garofalo moving away with his daughters, to losing his license and then his job. AA meetings, companionship from aspiring comic pal Judah Friedlander, and a tentative relationship with new girlfriend Susan Lynch are parts of the support system Schwimmer uses to get back on his feet. Caesar's Palace and Bally's were the casinos used in the quick, low-budget, super 16 mm shoot, while homes in Brigantine in the winter served as the dreary neighborhood for Hopwood and friends.

The Godfather, Part III (1990)

The Trop served as the location where Michael Corleone (Al Pacino) gets together with all of the veteran Dons, but guns go via helicopters at the rooftop gathering, and Michael, Vincent Corleone (Andy Garcia), and Al Neri (Richard Bright) narrowly skidaddle by limo out the Palozza Casino parking lot. The hotel/casino is actually the Trump Castle (now the Trump Marina) in Brigantine, but the lavish interiors in the Atlantic City sequence were actually shot at Rome's famous Cinecitta Studios.

Gunshy (1998)

Quirky crime comedy with "CSI" star William Petersen as an alcoholic New York writer who meets small-time mob operator Michael Wincott in Atlantic City. The two learn about each other's interests — Petersen teaches Wincott about his love for great books, Wincott shows Petersen how to collect on debts. Complicating matters is the fact that Petersen falls for Wincott's girlfriend, a nurse played by Diane Lane. Worth a look!

Going Home (1971)

Partially filmed in Wildwood, this intense drama stars Robert Mitchum as a man out of prison after serving time for killing his wife who attempts to reconcile with son Jan-Michael Vincent, who witnessed his mother being murdered. The film didn't fare well at the box office, but got some nice reviews and Mitchum reportedly held court with some local journalists between scenes and glasses of booze around the set.

The King of Marvin Gardens (1972)

Jack Nicholson's second collaboration with director Bob Rafelson ("Five Easy Pieces") is one of the most underrated films of the 1970s. Jack is a Philly disc jockey who helps his Atlantic City-based hustler brother Bruce Dern get out of prison, then tries to reconnect with Dern as he tries to raise financing for a hotel in Hawaii. Featuring Ellen Burstyn as an aging beauty queen, the film serves up a powerful but downbeat dual character studies set against the fading resort. Irene's Gift Shop, Central Pier, Lucy the Elephant, Convention Hall, the Boardwalk auction houses, and the crumbling but still dignified hotels on the Boardwalk offer an unforgettable backdrop of pre-casino A.C., while the city's dreamers and losers make memorable impressions in the forefront of this powerful story.

The Lemon Sisters (1990)

Diane Keaton, Carol Kane, and Kathryn Grody are three childhood friends who used to sing together that contemplate their lives against the backdrop of their hometown, a rapidly changing Atlantic City in this sensitive female bonding tale. Bally's Park Place, the Harlem Club, and various Boardwalk locations were used as the backdrop that really was where the three actresses spent their summers as kids.

Looking For an Echo (1999)

Overlooked musical drama with Armand Assante as a former doo-wop singer dealing with his three children and a midlife crisis as he makes a living as a bartender. Members of his former group called Vinnie and the Dreamers take him to New York and try to get his creative juices flowing again. Some shooting was done at the Trump Taj Mahal and the director was Martin Davidson of "Eddie and the Cruisers" fame.

Oceans Eleven (2001)

The highly enjoyable reworking of "The Rat Pack" original boasts a high-powered cast led by George Clooney, Brad Pitt, Julia Roberts, Matt Damon, Eliott Gould, Don Cheadle, and Carl Reiner try to outwit casino boss Andy Garcia in Vegas. Before the plan goes into action, however, Bernie Mac is recruited for the team, right out of the baccarat pit of Trump Plaza Hotel and Casino.

Owning Mahowny (2003)

This alarming true-life drama shows the dark side of Atlantic City, circa 1980s. Philip Seymour Hoffman plays Dan Mahowny, a milquetoast Canadian bank official who uses funds from his place of employment to fuel his heavy gambling addiction. This fascinating, downbeat film features a bravura performance by Hoffman, but its casino sequences aren't quite convincing since they were shot in the Great White North.

Penn & Teller Get Killed (1989)

The feature vehicle for the "bad boys of magic" hocus-pocused out of theaters quickly, but remains a darkly humorous curio. Penn, the tall, loud one, says he wishes someone would target him for murder on a TV show. While in Atlantic City for a show, the comic duo find that someone is, in fact, trying to kill Penn, but the audience is never quite sure if the murder attempts or assassins are real. Directed by Philly legend Arthur Penn ("Bonnie and Clyde"), this film offers a grand guignol sense-of-humor and eccentric plotting but what did you expect from the mischievous musicians?

The Pick-Up Artist (1987)

Picking up girls and gambling were (and still may be) two of writer-director James Toback's passions, so the premise of this uneven but interesting edgy romantic comedy should come as no surprise. School teacher Robert Downey, Jr., is an incessant skirt chaser smitten with museum guide Molly Ringwald. She heads to the casinos to win money for father Dennis Hopper who owes mobster Harvey Keitel big bucks. Atlantic City gets some screen time in Toback's obsessive saga, produced by Warren Beatty.

Rounders (1998)

Mike (Matt Damon) plays poker at the Trump Taj Mahal. Oddly enough, he mentioned he could get to Atlantic City in two hours via the New Jersey Turnpike. We all know that the Turnpike takes you nowhere near Atlantic City, and if he took the Turnpike from New York City, there's no way he'd do it in two hours.

Snake Eyes (1998)

This uneven suspenser from Brian De Palma stars a frantic Nicolas Cage as a crooked Atlantic City cop who tries to get to the bottom of a shooting of a government official at an Atlantic City boxing match. The hyperactive Cage has no less than an audience of 14,000 onlookers as potential culprits. Among them are Navy Commander and close friend Gary Sinise, who was supposed to protect the victim; boxing champ Stan Shaw, who seems to have taken a fall in the match; and Carla Gugino, a mysterious woman in a blonde wig who spoke to the fallen politico before he was shot. Conspiracy, paranoia, and a 13-minute opening salute to Hitchcock make this prime De Palma territory, but its plot machinations stretch credibility while the film just wears you down. Some Atlantic City locales are used, but most of the interiors were filmed in Montreal, with the boxing and arena scenes staged at the Montreal Forum, closed shortly before filming. Reportedly, De Palma wanted to shoot in Convention Hall, but it was tied up with Miss America stuff.

Sour Grapes (1998)

Fans of "Seinfeld" and "Curb Your Enthusiam" may want to check out this dark, cynical comedy written and directed by Larry David. Released on a limited basis in theaters, the film centers on cousins Craig Bierko, a shoe designer, and Steven Weber, a neurosurgeon, who head down to A.C. for some R&R with respective gal pals Robyn Peterman and Karen Sillas. With all but a quarter left to his name, Bierko asks Weber to loan him two quarters for the Trump slot machine — and hits over $400,000. Weber thinks he deserves half the take for his loan; Bierko doesn't believe he should part with any of the cash. The fighting spirals into all sorts of other areas, and other characters are soon affected by it, including Bierko's doting Jewish mother, a TV star with medical problems, and a homeless man (Orlando Jones). The kvetch factor is up high, but what did you expect when Larry David's involved?

Tattoo (1981)

There must be something about the Jersey shore and Bruce Dern that gets him going. In the Atlantic City-based "The King of Marvin Gardens," he was Jack Nicholson's sibling — wackier than Jack — a wheeler-dealer loser with big dreams. And in this controversial film, he's just plain psycho, a Philly-based tattoo artist obsessed with model Maud Adams. He kidnaps her after they meet on a photo shoot and takes her to his late father's abandoned Ocean City home, where he holds her captive. To show his love, he drugs her and inks a huge tattoo across her body. Must be something in the ocean air.

Three Little Girls in Blue (1946)

Three sisters from Red Bank, New Jersey head to Atlantic City in 1905 to snag rich hubbys. The men they meet turn out to be not as well-off as they claim, leading to some funny and tune-filled moments. The siblings are played by June Haver, Vera Ellen, and Vivan Blaine; the men are George Montgomery, Frank Lattimore, and Charles Smith. If the story sounds familiar, it may be because it's the same one as "Moon Over Miami" or "How to Marry a Millionaire." But this film works just fine, and scores points for its spirited cast and bouncy musical numbers, which include "On the Boardwalk in Atlantic City."

Touched (1983)

Following the smash success of 1980's "Airplane!," Robert Hays wanted to stretch his acting chops by appearing in this serious drama in which he plays an escapee from a mental hospital who gets a job on the Wildwood Boardwalk and gets involved with emotionally troubled Kathleen Beller. North Wildwood's Morey's Pier serves as the backdrop for this sensitive saga.

True Love (1989)

The first film of Annabella Sciorra and director Nancy Savoca ("Dogfight," "Household Saints") is an insightful, funny comedy about the impending wedding between Sciorra and Ron Eldard, two Italian kids from the Bronx. But before the big day, a number of things go awry, Eldard develops cold feet, the wedding plans are questioned, and there's a bummer of a bachelor party in Atlantic City.

Wise Guys (1986)

Uneven mob comedy from director Brian De Palma and writer George Gallo ("Midnight Run") starring Danny De Vito and Joe Piscopo as low-level gophers for the Newark mob who get into big trouble when they don't place the right bet on a horse race leading to a $100,000 miss for their boss. To correct the problem, each one gets the assignment to rub the other one out. Unfortunately, hilarity rarely ensues. Lots of location work in Resort's International, however, will help hold interest, along with a terrifically surly supporting cast that includes Harvey Keitel, Lou Albano, Ray Sharkey, and Dan Hedaya.

Delaware Namesbook

Valerie Bertinelli

(Wilmington b. 1960)

The cute, dimpled TV-favorite's father was a GM executive who moved with her family to L.A. when she was in her young teens, and soon began taking acting classes. After minor TV work, she got a big break in Norman Lear's "One Day at a Time," playing even-keeled sister to rebellious MacKenzie Phillps, daughters of divorced Bonnie Franklin. The show ran from 1975 to 1984, and helped bring the actress assignments in scores of TV movies. She married guitarist Eddie Van Halen in 1981 (and divorced him in 2005).

Rex Carlton

(b. 1915, d. 1968)

A writer and producer of low-budgets films like "Guilty Bystander," "The Brain That Wouldn't Die," "Nightmare in Wax," and "Hell's Bloody Devils," Carlton committed suicide when he fell into serious financial trouble.

Yvette Freeman

(Wilmington b. 1957)

Best known as Nurse Haleh Adams on "ER" for its entire run, this University of Delaware graduate has also appeared in "Sisters," "Hanging with Mr. Cooper," and "Boston Public." Film roles have included "Switch," "Dead Again," and "Angus."

Patrick Kerr

(Wilmington b. 1956)

The man who played nerdy Trekkie Noel Shempsky in "Frasier" has also been seen in the features "Jeffrey," "Ed", and "Domino" and regularly on such TV entries as "The Drew Carey Show," "Curb Your Enthusiasm," and "3rd Rock from the Sun" as Irving.

George Maguire

(Wilmington b. 1946)

This character actor and acting teacher specializes in authority figures. Roles include "The Game," "Fight Club," and the Will Smith starrer "The Pursuit of Happiness."

Bernie McInerney

(Wilmington b. 1936)

Popular character actor has done time on soaps ("The Edge of Night," One Life to Life," and "As the World Turns") as well as in films "Trading Places," "The Natural," "The American President," and "Duane Hopwood," and TV ("Spenser for Hire," "Law & Order").

Joey Perillo

(Wilmington b. 1952)

This local comedian has had lots of work in movies, including small roles in "Philadelphia," "Wide Awake," "Unbreakable," and "The Manchurian Candidate" (2004).

Judge Reinhold

(Wilmington b. 1957)

After a few years in small roles in TV series like "Wonder Woman" and films like "Running Scared" (1980) and "Stripes," Reinhold garnered attention for his key supporting role as teenager Jennifer Jason Leigh's brother who has a serious thing for Phoebe Cates in "Fast Times at Ridgemont High." Two years later, Reinhold was overshadowed by Gismo and the rest of the "Gremlins," but won a new following in "Beverly Hills Cop," playing a befuddled L.A. cop hired to help Eddie Murphy's Axel Foley find a killer. High profile roles in "Head Office," "Off Beat," "Ruthless People," "Visa Versa" and other projects were designed to make Reinhold a leading man specializing in light comedies, but he appeared better suited for his solid character work. He has performed steadily in films (including three installments of "The Santa Clause") and TV, where he has done extensive voice work.

Cynthia Rothrock

(Wilmington b. 1957)

A world champion martial artist with five black belts in Korean and Chinese disciplines and a five-time champion kickboxing and weapons expert, Rothrock parlayed her abilities into screen stardom, and became a viable star in many action films. She started on screen overseas, playing opposite Sammo Hung and Yuen Biao in "Millionaire's Express" and with Biao and Corey Yuen in "Righting Wrongs" (both 1986), Rothrock brought her act to the States for a series of video hits in the early 1990s that includes "China O'Brien," "Rage and Honor," and "Tiger Claws." She currently teaches martial arts in Studio City, California, and frequently runs exursions to the Far East for martial arts enthusiasts.

Elisabeth Shue

(Wilmington b. 1963)

While attending college at Wellesley, Shue began acting in commercials for such products as Burger King and Hellman's Mayonnaise. She landed two key roles in 1982, playing Ralph Macchio's girlfriend in "The Karate Kid" and the daughter of Craig T. Nelson and Cindy Pickett in the TV series "Call to Glory." A series of high-profile roles followed, playing leads in "Link" and "Adventures in Babysitting," opposite Tom Cruise in "Cocktail," and appearing in the final two installments of "Back to the Future." She was nominated for an Academy Award for her portrayal of a prostitute in 1995's acclaimed "Leaving Las Vegas" and has appeared in big studio films ("The Saint," "The Hollow Man"), and smaller, independent productions like "Leo" and "Mysterious Skin." Her younger brother is soccer player-actor-activist Andrew Shue.

Susan Stroman

(Wilmington b. 1952)

She's won scores of awards for directing and/or choreographing such stage productions as "Crazy for You," "Steel Pier," "Contact," "The Music Man," "The Frogs" and "The Producers," which she brought to the big screen in 2005 with Broadway cast members Nathan Lane and Matthew Broderick. She was married to the late stage director Michael Ockrent.

Estelle Taylor

(Wilmington b. 1891, d. 1958)

She made her way to New York as a teenager and got a job as a chorus girl on Broadway before breaking into silent films with "The Golden Shower" in 1919 and playing Miriam, Moses's sister in Cecil B. DeMille's 1923 silent version of "The Ten Commandments." She also appeared with John Barrymore and Myrna Loy in "Don Juan" (1926). Her sound films include "Liliom," "Cimarron ," and "The Southerner." Taylor's second husband was boxer Jack Dempsey, with whom she had a headlines-capturing divorce in 1930 after five years of marriage. After a fan approached her for her autograph one day, she noticed Dempsey's name scrawled on the top of the paper. She wrote: "This is the last time that son-of-a-bitch is on top me. Estelle Taylor."

Sean Patrick Thomas

(Wilmington b. 1970)

A graduate of Brandywine High School, Thomas had small roles in such films as "Courage Under Fire" and "Conspiracy Theory" before getting attention for his dancing and acting abilities in the surprise 2001 hit "Save the Last Dance." Other film roles have included "Halloween Resurrection," two "Barbershop" films, and "The Fountain," and he's been a regular on "The District," playing Detective Temple Page.

Herta Ware

(Wilmington b. 1917, d. 2005)

The granddaughter of socialists and labor activists, Ware grew up in apolitical climate which she carried into her personal life. In New York she met actor Will Geer her Broadway debut "Let Freedom Ring," and the couple married in 1934. They would stay wed for 20 years while both performed in theater and Geer became a popular supporting actor. In 1951, Geer was blacklisted when he refused to testify in from of the House Un-American Activities Committee, and didn't work in films or TV for five years. During that time, he and Hare built an experimental theater in Topanga Canyon, California, that showcased the couple's interest in acting and botany. With the blacklist over, Geer got steady work, and eventually landed the part of Grandpa Walton on "The Waltons" in 1972. The couple, however, divorced in 1954, but remained friends. Ware went on to have her own successful career in TV (she was Captain Picard's mother in "Star Trek: The Next Generation") and movies, appearing in such films as "2010," "Cocoon," "Soap Dish," and "Practical Magic." She's the mother of actress-director Ellen Geer.

Kathleen Widdoes

(Wilmington b. 1939)

On the small screen she's had regular spots on the soaps "Another World," "Ryan's Hope," and "As the World Turns," and "Oz." And in the movies, Widdoes has had key roles in "The Group," "Petulia," and "Courage Under Fire."

New Jersey Namesbook

James L. Avery Sr.
(Atlantic City b. 1948)
He was Will Smith's uncle, attorney Phillip Banks, on "The Fresh Prince of Bel-Air." He's also been on ""Soul Food," "That '70s Show," and "The Closer" as a medical examiner.

Priscilla Barnes
(Fort Dix b. 1955)
A former Penthouse Pet under the name of Joanne Witty, she got into the spotlight as a regular on "Three's Company," playing "Terri Alden." Since then, she's done lots of TV and B pictures (including "The Devil's Rejects") and appeared as the three-nippled fortune teller in Kevin Smith's "Mall Rats."

Adam Bernstein
(Princeton b. 1960)
Prolific writer-director-producer whose work includes extensive TV work ("Oz," "The Upright Citizen's Brigade," "Scrubs," "Rescue Me") and features ("It's Pat" and the quirky Ohio-based gangster film "Six Ways to Sunday.") He's married to actress Jessica Hecht.

Betty Bronson
(Trenton b. 1906, d. 1971)
She was the screen's first Peter Pan, handpicked by author J.M. Barrie to play the character for Paramount's 1924 silent film version of the story. An expert at pantomime, Bronson tried to follow up the film's fairy tale success in 1925's "A Kiss for Cinderella," but the same magic wasn't there. She also played Mary in the silent "Ben-Hur: A Tale of Christ," and appeared opposite Al Jolson in the talkie "The Singing Fool" in 1928. She soon retired, but later did character roles, mostly in TV shows during the 1960s.

Roscoe Lee Browne
(Woodbury b. 1925)
An African-American actor with a commanding presence and distinctive voice, Browne is best known for his work in the theater ("The Ballad of the Sad Café," a Tony nominee for "Two Trains Running"), his movie roles ("Topaz," "Logan's Run," "The Cowboys"), his extensive TV roles (from "Mannix" to "Will & Grace"), and voice work (he narrated both "Babe" movies and has supplied the voices for scores of animated characters).

Rosalind Cash

(Atlantic City b. 1938, d. 1995)

A graduate of Atlantic City High School, the versatile actress — often in dreadlocks — usually played the independent "sister" in several early 1970s movies, including "Klute," "The Omega Man," "The New Centurions," "Melinda," and "Hickey and Boggs." In 1985, she was nominated for an Emmy for the PBS presentation of James Baldwin's "Go Tell It on the Mountain" and appeared in "The Adventures of Buckaroo Banzai." She also was a fixture on a a variety of TV shows, including "thirtysomething," "A Different World," and "Roc."

Joanna Cassidy

(Haddonfield b.1945)

Throughout the 1980s, Cassidy appeared in key roles in major films, playing the replicant Zhora in "Blade Runner," the radio reporter in "Under Fire," and Dolores, Bob Hoskins' girlfriend in "Who Framed Roger Rabbit?" She's mixed steady TV stints on such shows as "Buffalo Bill," "Diagnosis Murder," "Six Feet Under" and "Boston Legal" with parts in such films as "The Package," "Club Paradise," and "Larry the Cable Guy: Health Inspector."

Michael Cristofer

(Trenton b. 1945)

He won the Pulitzer and Tony for his 1977 play "The Shadow Box" about the final days of terminally ill patients. His screenplays include "Falling in Love" and high-profiled adaptations of the best-sellers "The Witches of Eastwick" and "The Bonfire of the Vanities." He's also scripted and directed "Gia" for HBO starring Angelina Jolie as drug-addicted Philly model Gia Carangi, and "Original Sin," the 2001 erotic drama with Jolie and Antonio Banderas.

Joe Dante

(Morristown b. 1946)

Movie buff Dante was a reviewer for the Philly-based trade publication *Film Journal* and put together a clips-filled program called "Son of Movie Orgy" for college campuses in the 1970s. He eventually moved to L.A. to take a job editing trailers for Roger Corman's New World Pictures. Along with pals Jon Davison and Alan Arkush, he collaborated on the spoof "Hollywood Boulevard," which was filmed for $60,000 in ten days. Its success led to "Piranha" for Corman, then "The Howling," both showcasing Dante's penchant for mixing horror, inside jokes, and humor. He collaborated with Steven Spielberg on two "Gremlins" films, "Twilight Zone: The Movie," "Innerspace," "Small Soldiers," and a few episodes of "Amazing Stories." Other films include "Explorers," "Matinee," "Looney Tunes: Back in Action," and the acclaimed "Homecoming" installment of the "Master of Horror" series. Dante has often used the same actors in supporting parts, including Kevin McCarthy, Robert Picardo, Dick Miller, William Schallert, and his mentor Corman.

Jon Davison

(Haddonfield b. 1949)

Along with Joe Dante, Davison was a local boy who got his start behind-the-scenes working for Roger Corman. After working as a producer and second unit director on such films as "Piranha" and "Grand Theft Auto," Davison went to Paramount for the smash hit "Airplane!" and the controversial "White Dog." He also produced the first two "RoboCop" films, as well as "Top Secret!" with the same crew who made "Airplane!" Other credits include two "Starship Troopers" films and "The 9th Day," the cloning thriller with Arnold Schwarzenegger.

Al Dempster

(Atlantic City b. 1911, d. 2001)
Longtime Disney Studio background artist who worked on such classics as "Fantasia," Peter Pan," "Sleeping Beauty," "The Jungle Book," and "Mary Poppins." He's also credited with illustrating several Golden Book adaptations of Disney films.

Kirsten Dunst

(Point Pleasant b. 1982)
A child model and actress who worked for Woody Allen in "Stardust Memories" and "New York Stories," and played Tom Hanks and Kim Cattrall's daughter in "The Bonfire of the Vanities," Dunst's breakthrough came as the grief-stricken Claudia in 1994's "Interview with a Vampire." Key roles in "Little Women," Jumanji," and "Wag the Dog" followed, and critical acclaim came with 1999's "The Virgin Suicides," directed by Sofia Coppola. She would work again with her in 2006's "Marie Antoinette." Audience favorites like "Bring It On" and the "Spider-Man" films, have given her opportunities to work in high-profile studio films ("Mona Lisa Smile," "Elizabethtown") and independent productions ("Eternal Sunshine of the Spotless Mind," "Levity") alike.

Calista Flockhart

(Freeport, Illinois b.1964)
The svelte "Ally McBeal" star and Harrison Ford paramour moved to the Medford area with her family — mother was a school teacher and father a Kraft Foods executive — when she was 11 years old. She was a cheerleader at Shawnee High School and attended Rutgers where she received a BFA in theatre, then did the regional theater route around the country. After roles in the soap opera "The Guiding Light," TV movies, and a small part in "Quiz Show," she snagged the lead in 1997's quirky series "Ally McBeal," playing the young Boston lawyer with a hyperactive imagination. The David E. Kelley show lasted until 2002. Flockhart's latest TV assignment is opposite Sally Field and Rachel Griffiths in "Brothers & Sisters."

John Forsythe

(Penn's Grove b. 1918)
The debonair actor with the long and varied career moved to New York with his family when he was young, and soon began acting in radio soap operas. After fighting in World War II, he was one of the pioneers of the Acting Studio, and went on to act in many TV dramas and films in the 1950s. He's best known for his roles as the star of the sitcom "Bachelor Father," his role as "Blake Carrington" on "Dynasty" and "The Colbys," and the voice of Charles "Charlie" Townsend in both the "Charlie's Angels" TV series and movies.

Preston Foster

(Ocean City b. 1900, d. 1970)
Strapping leading man and character actor served in the U.S. Coast Guard during WWII, then made a splash on Broadway before heading to Hollywood. Credits include "I Am a Fugitive from a Chain Gang," "Geronimo," "North West Mounted Police," "The Harvey Girls," "Guadalcanal Diary," "My Friend Flicka," and "I Shot Jesse James." Later in his career, he appeared in many TV shows and the 1964 sci-fi cult item "The Time Travelers."

Roxanne Hart

(Trenton b. 1952)
Married to local guy Phillip Casnoff, this red-haired actress has had success in theater (nominated for a 1983 Tony in "Assassins"), movies ("The Verdict," "Once Around," "Art School Confidential"), and TV ("Dream On," "Chicago Hope," "Oz").

Jessica Hecht

(Princeton b. 1965)

She was the ex-wife of Miles (Paul Giamatti) in "Sideways" and a perennial performer on TV as a regular on "The Single Guy," the short-lived Joan Cusack series "What About Joan?," and Ross' ex-wife's lesbian lover on "Friends." Additional film work includes "Kicking and Screaming" (1995), "The Grey Zone," "The Forgotten," and "Stay." She's married to producer-director Adam Bernstein.

Brian Herzlinger

(Marlton b. 1971)

This South Jersey native who once worked at the AMC Marlton movie theater drew attention for his feature debut, "My Date with Drew," in which he gives himself 30 days to land a date with dream girl Drew Barrymore. The film was shot on a home video camera (which was returned to the store within 30 days) and got a major national release. Herzlinger has also appeared on "The Tonight show with Jay Leno" covering such events as the Academy Awards.

Debra Hill

(Haddonfield b. 1950, d. 2005)

Born in New Jersey and raised in Philadelphia, Hill went to Los Angeles where she hooked up with director John Carpenter on "Assault on Precinct 13" and took jobs as production assistant and second unit director. She collaborated with Carpenter on the screenplay for "Halloween," which she produced. The low-budget shocker became a smash hit, making almost $50 million on a $350,000 budget and spawned several sequels, some of which she produced. She also produced "The Fog," "Escape from New York" and "Escape from L.A." with Carpenter. Other production credits include "The Dead Zone," "Cue," "Adventures in Babysitting," "The Fisher King," and a series of films for Showtime based on American-International Pictures fare like "Dragstrip Girl" and "Girls in Prison." She died of cancer in 2005, after she had begun production on "World Trade Center." As a homage to her hometown, she named the city in "Halloween" Haddonfield, but it was based in Illinois.

Hugh Holub

(Trenton b. 1952)

Bald, wearing glasses, usually with a mustache — Holub has been a busy character actor, usually playing teachers, doctors, accountants, or pharmacists in such TV series as "Charmed," "Melrose Place," and "The Practice."

Richard Kind

(Trenton b. 1956)

Barbra Streisand's cousin and one of George Clooney's best friends, Kind has carved a niche for himself, playing the hyperactive chatterbox coworker or relative who's essentially a nice guy but tends to get annoying after a while. He was Helen Hunt and Paul Reiser's gynecologist friend in "Mad About You" and a loudmouthed mayoral press secretary on "Spin City." Film roles include "Quicksand" and "The Big Empty." He's also supplied voices for "A Bug's Life," "Garfield," "Cars," and "The Wild."

Zalman King

(Trenton b. 1942)

It's hard to believe that the man that gave us erotic potboilers like "9 ½ Weeks," "Wild Orchid," and the "Red Shoe Diaries" series started out as a curly-haired young actor in such TV shows as "Gunsmoke," "Bonanza," and "The Man from U.N.C.L.E." in the 1960s. He graduated to leading man in his own series ("The Young Lawyers") and played the counterculture anti-hero type in 1971's "The Ski Bum." In the 1980s, he became a writer and producer, working with Alan Rudolph on "Roadie" and "Endangered Species," then shifted gears into erotic stuff, often collaborating with his screenwriter wife Patricia Louisiana Knop on films and cable series.

Henry Levin
(Trenton b. 1909, d. 1980)

A steady workhorse director who could deliver in almost every genre, Levin gave us such pictures as "Jolson Sings Again" (1949) with Larry Parks in the lead; "The President's Lady" (1953) with Charlton Heston as Andrew Jackson and Susan Hayward as wife Rachel; "Mister Scoutmaster" (1953) starring Clifton Webb as a crotchety TV star who becomes scout leader to bond with the youngsters; "April Love" (1957) and "Journey to the Center of the Earth" (1959), both with Pat Boone; "Where the Boys Are" (1960); "Genghis Khan" (1965) ; two Dean Martin-Matt Helm films, "Murderer's Row" 1966) and "The Silencers" (1967); and the Fred Williamson blaxploitation yarn "That Man Bolt" (1973).

Judith Light
(Trenton b. 1949)

This versatile, blonde actress attended St. Mary's Hall in Burlington and Carnegie-Mellon, then did lots of regional theater and stage work before winning awards for a six-year run on the soap opera "One Life to Live," where she met actor husband Richard Desiderio. Acclaimed work in TV movies "The Ryan White Story" and "Defense of the Married Man" took her to "Who's the Boss," the hit sitcom in which she played the business-minded owner of the home where Tony Danza works as housekeeper. Other credits include several TV movies and the part of Judge Elizabeth Donnelly on "Law & Order: Special Victims Unit."

Ernie Kovacs
(Trenton b. 1919, d. 1962)

Smoking a cigar and with his trademark mustache, Ernie Kovacs was a pioneering television talent and a welcome presence in supporting movie roles. He started on TV in Philly, hosting a shows from 1950 to 1952 called "This Is Ernie" and "Ernie in Kovacsland" on Philly's NBC then-affiliate WPTZ. In these shows and in "The Ernie Kovacs Show," which ran on NBC in 1953, Kovacs proved to be a master of the ad-lib, a masterful comedian adept at playing different characters, and an innovator of the medium, using classical music for his spoofing and experimenting with chroma-key effects, blackouts, and continuous gags throughout his shows. Between his TV work, which included hosting and serving as a panelist on several game shows, Kovacs appeared in three movies with close friend Jack Lemmon ("Operation Mad Ball," "Bell, Book and Candle," and "It Happend to Jane"), as well as "Wake Me When It's Over," "North to Alaska," and "Sail a Crooked Ship." He was set to play Melville Crump in "It's a Mad, Mad, Mad, Mad World" when he died in a car accident in 1962. Second wife Edie Adams kept her role as Monica Clump in the film, while Sid Caesar replaced Kovacs. Jeff Goldblum played Kovacs in a 1984 TV movie.

Michael Landon
(Forest Hills, NY b.1936, d. 1991)

Eugene Morris Orowitz was born in New York, but raised in Collingwood, and graduated from Collingswood High School. A champion javelin thrower, he attended UCLA on an athletic scholarship, but dropped out of school after an injury prevented him from participating in javelin throwing. At the urging of a friend, he went to an audition at Warner Brothers, and did so well, they sent him to acting school. After getting jobs performing in several TV series and live television dramas, Landon landed the lead in the low-budget "I Was a Teenage Werewolf" in 1957. The film became a hit, and brought the actor more formidable TV parts, and eventually movie roles in "High School Confidential" and "God's Little Acre" (both 1958). But it was his part as Little Joe, the youngest member of the Cartwright family on the long-running hit series "Bonanza", that sent him into the national spotlight. Following its 14 year run, Landon produced and starred in two hit series with huge followings and sentimental value, "Little House on the Prairie" and "Highway to Heaven." He also wrote and directed several episodes of the two shows, as well as several TV movies. He died of pancreatic cancer at the age of 55.

Ali Lauter
(Cherry Hill b. 1976)
This attractive blonde with a strong following was a teenage model who got attention for her role in 1999's surprise hit "Varsity Blues," playing Paul Walker's sleep-around cheerleader girlfriend. Other roles include the first two "Final Destination" movies, "House on Haunted Hill," "Jay and Silent Bob Strike Back," and the direct-to-video favorite "3-Way."

Amy Locane
(Trenton b. 1971)
A graduate of the Christian high school Vila Victoria Academy in Ewing, Locane began modeling at an early age and appeared in many commercials during her adolescence. At the age of 13, she was cast as a regular on TV's 1984 series "Spencer," then took high-profile roles opposite "Beastie Boy" Adam Horvitz in "Lost Angels" and Johnny Depp in "Cry-Baby." She became a regular on "Melrose Place," playing Sandy Louise Harling. She's also had key roles in such films as "School Ties", "Airheads", "Blue Sky," Carried Away" (playing Dennis Hopper's young lover), and "Secretary," as Maggie Gyllenhaal's sister.

Heather McComb
(Barneget b. 1977)
She was in TV ads when she was a toddler and played Zoe in Francis Coppola's "Life with Zoe" segment of 1989's "New York Stories." Most of her work has been in TV, including regular roles on such shows as "Profiler" and "Party of Five," as well as guest shots on "Chicago Hope" and several "CSI" variations. She's married to James Van Der Beek.

Kelly Jo Minter
(North Trenton b. 1966)
She's had key supporting roles in "Mask, "Summer School," and "Cat Chaser," and several horror efforts like "The Lost Boys," "A Nightmare on Elm Street 5: The Dream Child," "Popcorn," and "The People Under the Stairs."

Michael E. Knight
(Princeton b. 1959)
He played Prince Edward in the 1982 telemovie "The Royal Romance of Charles and Diana" and had a "Date with an Angel" in a 1987 flop with Emannuelle Beart. He is probably best known for his work in soap operas playing Tad Martin in "One Life to Live" and Tad Garner in "All My Children."

Bebe Neuwirth
(Princeton b. 1958)
She's best known as Lilith, wife and ex of Frasier Crane on TV's "Cheers" and "Frasier," but has had an impressive career in the theater. A graduate of Princeton High School and Julliard, she first gained attention in Broadway's "A Chorus Line," won Tony Awards for "Sweet Charity" and "Chicago," and appeared in "Damn Yankees" and "Kiss of the Spider Woman." Film roles include "Say Anything,"

"Green Card," "Bugsy," "Malice," "Jumanji," "Summer of Sam," "Liberty Heights," and "Tadpole."

Carl Anthony Paine
(North Trenton b. 1969)

He was Walter "Cockroach" Bailey on "The Cosby Show," Cole Brown on "Martin," and has had guest spots on "George Lopez," "NYPD Blue," and the short-lived ABC 2006 series "The Evidence."

Paul Robeson
(Princeton b. 1898, d. 1976)

A true Renaissance man, Robeson was the son of a Presbyterian minister who was once a slave and a mother who came from a well-connected Philadelphia family. He went to Rutgers, then Columbia Law School and became an attorney before turning his attention to sports and show business. He played professional football (and was inducted into the NFL Hall of Fame) in the early 1920s, and made waves in the theater soon after, performing in "The Emperor Jones" (he would repeat the role later on screen) and Eugene O'Neill's "All God's Chillun Got Wings." In London, he became a sensation for singing "Ol' Man River," as Joe in "Show Boat," and would later sing the Jerome Kern-penned song in the 1936 film version. As the first black Othello with a white supporting cast, he topped Broadway records at the time with 300 performances. Other screen credits include "Sanders of the River," "Song of Freedom," "Jericho," and "King Solomon's Mines," but he renounced Hollywood for its racial politics, refusing most of the parts offered to him. Senator Joseph McCarthy led the charge against Robeson's political views and had his passport revoked, despite Robeson's stance against fascism and his efforts entertaining Allied troops during World War II. After several years, the passport was given back, allowing him to travel, but McCarthy's efforts to label him a Communist stuck. Robeson experienced severe depression over the ordeal, was hospitalized several times, and had trouble finding work. He died in seclusion in Philadelphia in 1976.

Amy Robinson
(Trenton b. 1948)

She started as an actress, playing Teresa, Harvey Keitel's love interest in Martin Scorsese's 1973 breakthrough film "Mean Streets." After some TV work, Robinson became a producer, forming a company with actor Griffin Dunne and producing independent-minded films that were distributed by the studios like Joan Micklin Silver's "Chilly Scenes of Winter," John Sayles' "Baby It's You" (which she also wrote and set in her Trenton hometown), and Martin Scorsese's "After Hours." Robinson's other producing credits include "Running on Empty," "Once Around," "White Palace," "For the Love of the Game," "From Hell," "Twelve and Holding," and "The Great New Wonderful."

Leo Rossi
(Trenton b. 1947)

A busy character actor who also produces and writes on occasion, Rossi played Bonnie Bedelia's husband in "Heart Like a Wheel," a detective in "Black Widow," one of the men who rapes Jodie Foster in "The Accused," cop Robert Loggia's partner in "Relentless," and Carlo in "Analyze This." He's also had major roles in Philly-themed films "Mafioso: The Father, the Son" and "10th & Wolf," both of which he helped produce.

Bryan Singer
(New York City, NY b.1965)

Raised in the Trenton area, Singer went to West Windsor-Plainsboro High School, then attended the School of Visual Arts in New York.

1993's "Public Access" was his first film, a bizarre tale of a drifter who starts his own public access TV show. It shared the Grand Jury Prize at the Sundance Film Festival, but got spotty distribution. Singer followed with 1995's tricky thriller "The Usual Suspects," a movie that garnered acclaim, a healthy following, and Oscars for screenwriter Christopher McQuarrie and supporting actor Kevin Spacey. 1998's "Apt Pupil," an adaptation of a Stephen King story, was mired in problems and controversy, but Singer's two "X-Men" films, based on the Marvel comic books, were hits with audiences and critics. He also helmed 2006's well-received "Superman Returns" and produces the TV show "House."

Michael Showalter

(Princeton b. 1970)
The son of two college professors, Showalter was a member of "The State," a comedy troupe with a show on MTV from 1993 to 1995, that featured frequent contributors David Wain and Michael Ian Black. The three would join forces for the 2001 feature "Wet, Hot American Summer" and the 2005 Comedy Central show "Stella." Showalter has also been featured in such films as "Signs" and "Kissing Jessica Steen," and directed and starred in 2005's "The Baxter," a throwback to 1940s screwball comedies.

Steven Spielberg

(Cincinnati, Ohio b. 1946)
The most successful director in film history spent some formative years in Haddonfield before his family moved on to Scottsdale, Arizona. You know the credits.

Jon Stewart

(New York City, NY b. 1962)
Though born in New York, Stewart — born Jonathan Liebowitz — was raised in Lawrenceville and attended Lawrence High School, graduating in 1980. People tend to forget the host of the popular "The Daily Show" since 1999 has acted in many films. including "The Faculty," "Playing By Heart," and "Death to Smoochy."

Jon Tenney

(Princeton b. 1961)
Tall, dark, and handsome ex-husband of Teri Hatcher has starred in such TV series as "The Division" and "The Closer," playing star Kyra Sedgwick's FBI agent romantic interest. Film roles include "Watch It," "Tombstone," "The Phantom," "You Can Count On Me," and Joe Dante's "Masters of Horror" installment, "Homecoming."

Rich Wilkes

(Princeton b. 1966)
Screenwriter of "Airheads," "The Jerky Boys" and "XXX."

Bruce Willis

(Idar-Oberstein, West Germany b. 1955)
Though born on a military base in West Germany, Willis grew up in Penn's Grove and attended Montclair State University and the Stella Adler Conservatory. After uncredited bit parts in such films as 1980's "The First Deadly Sin" and 1982's "The Verdict," Willis beat out 300 actors and snagged the lead role of David Addison opposite Cybil Shepherd in the ABC's comic detective series "Moonlighting" in 1985. With the show winning a big following for its onscreen and offscreen bickering between the two leads, Willis began cranking out films that showed he was adept at comedy, drama, and action — in the case of 1988's "Die Hard" and its sequels, Willis

showed he could handle all three in one role. Starring in films of great success and big disappointment, and mixing mega-budget spectacles with small independent projects, the former New York City bartender has proven to be one of Hollywood's most versatile performers.

Albert Zugsmith

(Atlantic City b. 1910, d.1993)

The producer of many exploitation pictures and B movies like "High School Confidential," "The Beat Generation," and "Sex Kittens Go to College," the colorful Zugsmith also produced bona fide classics such as "The Incredible Shrinking Man," "Touch of Evil," and the Douglas Sirk dramas "Written on the Wind" and "The Tarnished Angels" for Universal Pictures in the 1950s. He also produced Russ Meyer's ill-fated version of "Fanny Hill" in 1964 and low-budget westerns featuring Rory Calhoun.

The Sixth Sense (1990)
Stanley Cunningham (Bruce Willis):
Philadelphia is one of the oldest cities in this country. A lot of generations have lived here and died here. Almost any place you go in this city has a history and a story behind it. Even this school and the grounds it sits on. Can anyone guess what this building was used for a hundred years ago, before you went to this school, before I went to this school? Yes, Cole?

Pennsylvania Namesbook

Shari Albert

(Philadelphia)

This graduate of the Philadelphia High School of the Performing Arts has been a regular in Edward Burns' films, performing in "The Brothers McMullen," "No Looking Back, and "The Groomsmen."

Steven Austin

(Philadelphia b. 1959)

A devotee of director Stanley Kubrick, this former student of Philadelphia College of Art helmed two action films in the early 1990s, "Expert Weapon" and "American Streetfighter," then an award-winning short, " A Moment of Silence," in 2000. His recent work includes a documentary on special effects master Willis O'Brien.

Frankie Avalon

(Philadelphia b. 1939)

South Philly crooner with big hits ("Why," "Venus," "I'll Wait For You") who became a bona fide box-office draw in beach party movies (opposite Disney fave Annette Funicello), and, later 1960s comedies like "Dr. Goldfoot and the Bikini Machine" and the all-star fiasco "Skidoo."

Val Avery

(Philadelphia, b. 1924)

Steady working character actor can be seen in "The Pope of Greenwich Village," "Brubaker," and "Cobra."

Henny Backus

(Philadelphia b. 1911, d. 2004)

She played opposite hubby Jim Backus, aka Thurston Howell III and Mr. Magoo, in "Hello Down There" and "The Love Boat."

Kevin Bacon

(Philadelphia, b. 1956)

Son of city planner Edmund Bacon, he made his debut in "Animal House," flirted with idoldom starring in "Footloose," and has given strong performances in juicy roles in "Diner," "Murder in the First," "JFK," "Apollo 13," "Sleepers," "Wild Things," "Stir of Echoes," "The Woodsman," and "Loverboy," which he directed, and which features wife Kyra Sedgwick.

Carroll Baker

(Johnstown b. 1931)

The former "Miss Florida Fruit and Vegetables 1949" later became a blonde bombshell after drawing heat and attention as the teenage virgin desired by Karl Malden and Eli Wallach in Elia Kazan's "Baby Doll," based on a Tennessee Williams screenplay. After appearing in steamy roles in such efforts as "The Carpetbaggers" and "Harlow," she moved to Europe, working there for most of the late 1960s and 1970s, mostly in low-budget horror films, erotic thrillers, and westerns. She returned to the States for 1977's "Andy Warhol's Bad" and other films.

John L. Balderston

(Philadelphia b. 1889, d. 1954)

Prolific screenwriter who penned scripts for original Universal horror classics "Dracula," "Frankenstein," "The Mummy," and "The Bride of Frankenstein," as well as "The Last of the Mohicans" (1936) and "The Prisoner of Zenda" (1952).

Mabel Ballin

(Philadelphia b. 1887, d. 1958)

Silent-screen star who played opposite Tom Mix in "Riders of the Purple Sage" (1925), and worked for her director husband Hugo Ballin in "Vanity Fair" (1923) and "Code of the West" (1927).

George Bancroft

(Philadelphia, b. 1882, d. 1956)

Busy character actor played Mac Keefer in "Angels with Dirty Faces" and Marshal Curly Wilcox in "Stagecoach" (1939).

Chuck Barris

(Philadelphia b. 1943)

Started as songwriter penning hit "Palisades Park," then became a TV producer of "The Dating Game," "The Newlywed Game," and "The Gong Show," which he also hosted. He later revealed he was also a hitman for the CIA, and chronicles his experiences in the book and movie "Confessions of a Dangerous Mind."

Ethel Barrymore

(Philadelphia b. 1879, d. 1959)

Sister of John and Lionel, she was born Ethel Mae Blythe and made her stage debut at age 15. She made several silent films, and appeared with her siblings in "Rasputin and the Empress" in 1932. Other key roles include "None but the Lonely Heart", for which she won the Oscar for Best Supporting Actress, "The Paradine Case," "The Farmer's Daughter," and "Portrait of Jennie." Later in her career, she appeared in many live TV dramas.

John Barrymore

(Philadelphia b. 1882, d. 1942)

Brother of Ethel and Lionel, the man who was nicknamed "The Great Profile" was born John Sidney Blythe and was expelled from a school in Georgetown, reportedly for attending a bordello. Barrymore delivered powerful performances on Broadway and in silent and sound films such as "Don Juan" (1926), "Dr. Jekyll and Mr. Hyde" (1930), "Svengali" (1931), and "Dinner at Eight" (1933). He showed his chops for comedy in Howard Hawks' classic screwball classic "Twentieth Century" (1934, playing an egomaniacal producer who tries to win back Carole Lombard, an actress he turned into a star, while aboard a train.) The grandfather of Drew Barrymore, he married four times, and all of his wives were actresses.

Lionel Barrymore

(Philadelphia b. 1878, d. 1954)

Sibling of Ethel and John, Lionel became a Broadway sensation in his twenties in such plays as "Peter Ibbetson" and "the Jest," then made a mark in the movies, as an actor first, then as a director (he was nominated for an Oscar for 1929's "Madame X"). Along with parts in many silent films, his talkie credits include an Academy Award-winning turn as an alcoholic physician in 1931's "A Free Soul," "Mark of the Vampire," "Captains Courageous," "It's a Wonderful Life" (as Mr. Potter) "Duel in the Sun," and "Key Largo." In his latter roles, Barrymore was confined to a wheel chair because of hip problems. He was also a composer and the inventor of the boom microphone.

Toni Basil

(Philadelphia b. 1949)

She started as a choreographer who worked with Elvis in "Viva Las Vegas" and The Monkees in "Head," then became a character actress in such films as "Five Easy Pieces" and "Easy Rider" (playing a hooker in the New Orleans brothel sequence). She also choreographed rock stars (David Bowie for tours during his "Thin White Duke" era and the "Beast of Burden" video with Mick Jagger and Bette Midler). She may be best known, however, for her song and music video for the MTV favorite "Mickey," based on her experiences as a cheerleader at Las Vegas High School.

Maria Bello

(Norristown b. 1967)

Sassy, risk-taking Villanova grad caught attention on TV's ER" and "Coyote Ugly," then segued into acclaimed roles in "The Cooler," "The History of Violence," "Thank You for Smoking," and "World Trade Center."

Henry Bean

(Philadelphia b. 1945)

He scripted such sharp crime thrillers as "Deep Cover" with Laurence Fishburne and Jeff Goldblum and "Internal Affairs" with Richard Gere, then made his directorial debut with "The Believer," a film about a neo-Nazi who is also a Jew. Although the film won the Grand Prize at the Sundance Film Festival, it had trouble getting distribution because of its controversial nature. Bean, who attended Yale, is married to screenwriter Leora Barish, who wrote the script for "Desperately Seeking Susan" and collaborated with Bean on "Basic Instinct II."

David Berenbaum

(Philadelphia b. 1970)

Within weeks in 2003, Berenbaum was a hot Hollywood commodity with two family-flavored hit comedies in release: "The Haunted Mansion" with Eddie Murphy, and "Elf," starring Will Farrell. The brother of editor Michael Berenbaum, his latest writing projects include "Zoom" with Tim Allen and the fantasy "The Spiderwick Chronicles," based on a book series by Holly Black.

Michael Berenbaum

(Philadelphia b. 1962)

A graduate of George Washington High School (and NYU Film School), Berenbaum was an assistant editor on many films by the Coen Brothers before he became the chief editor on such works as "Before Night Falls," "Hollywoodland," and several episodes of "Sex in the City" and "Desperate Housewives." Brother of David Berenbaum.

Marki Bey

(Philadelphia b. 1946)

African-American actress with exotic looks appeared as voodoo goddess "Suger Hill" and drive-in standards "The Roommates" and Class of '74" (aka Gabriella) in the 1970s. Also did a stint on "Starsky & Hutch" as Officer Minnie Kaplan.

Herbert J. Biberman

(Philadelphia b. 1900, d. 1971)

A director and screenwriter ("Meet Nero Wolfe," "The Master Race"), he was blacklisted in the 1950s by Joseph McCarhty and became known one of the Hollywood Ten. During the period, he joined other blacklisted filmmakers and actors, writing and directing "Salt of the Earth" about striking New Mexico mine workers.

Joey Bishop

(The Bronx b. 1918)

Although he was born in New York, he's been closely associated with Philly because he moved to South Philly as a youngster. He started in vaudeville, then moved on to TV, where he starred in his own sitcom and hosted his own talk show in the 1960s with Regis Philbin as his sidekick. Bishop was also a member of the famed "Rat Pack" appearing in such films as "Oceans 11" (1960) and "Sergeants 3" with Sinatra, Martin, Davis, and Lawford. Other film roles include "The Naked and the Dead," "Onionhead," "The Delta Force," and "Betsy's Wedding."

Marie Blake

(Philadelphia b. 1896, d. 1978)

The sister of Jeanette MacDonald was best known as Blossom Rock, who played Grandmama Addams on hit 60s show "The Addams Family."

Eleanor Boardman

(Philadelphia b. 1898, d. 1991)

A graduate of the Academy of the Fine Arts, Boardman became a model, posing as one of the "Kodak Girls," then signing a contact with Goldwyn Pictures as an actress. She attracted the attention of leading silent film director King Vidor, who married her, then cast her in such films as "Three Wise Fools," "Proud Flesh," and the classic "The Crowd."

Donald Bogle

(Philadelphia b. 1944)

Author and historian specializing in African-Americans in the movies, he has written such books as *Black Sugar: Eighty Years of American's Black Female Superstars* and *Toms, Coons, Mulattos, Mammies and Bucks.*

David Boreanaz

(Buffalo b. 1969)

Raised in Philly, the son of Channel 6 weatherman Dave Roberts made his mark in "Buffy the Vampire Slayer" and its spinoff "Angels" then appeared in the crime series "Bones." He's married to former Playboy Playmate Jamie Bergman, star of "Son of a Beach."

Peter Boyle

(Philadelphia b. 1935)

Son of TV kid's show host Peter Boyle (Sr.), this popular La Salle graduate drew raves for his lead performance as the bigoted, working class "Joe" in 1970, then scored in supporting parts in 1970s faves "The Candidate," "Crazy Joe," "Young Frankenstein," "Taxi Driver," and "The Friends of Eddie Coyle." After years of solid work, he struck gold (and seven Emmy nominations) as Ray Romano's cantankerous father on "Everybody Loves Raymond."

Andy Breckman

(Philadelphia b. 1955)

A longtime writer for "Saturday Night Live," he's also had his hand in scripts for "Moving," "I.Q.," "Rat Race," and the TV series "Monk."

Richard Brooks

(Philadelphia b. 1912, d. 1992)

West Philly High and Temple University graduate Brooks started out as a sports reporter and journalist, then became the screenwriter of such film noir greats as "Brute Force" and "Crossfire," as well as "Key Largo" and "Storm Warning." He moved into directing, and adapted and directed such films as "The Blackboard Jungle," "The Brothers Karamazov," "Cat on a Hot Tin Roof," "Elmer Gantry" (for which he won the Oscar), "Lord Jim," "The Professionals," "In Cold Blood," "The Happy Ending" (with wife Jean Simmons), "Looking for Mr. Goodbar," "Bite the Bullet," and the gambling film "Fever Pitch."

Garrett Brown

A Philly-based inventor (and occasional voiceover talent), Brown conceived (and holds the patent for) the SteadiCam, the revolutionary camera that stabilizes while following moving objects and people. It was first used on such films as "Bound for Glory" and "Rocky," and later utilized in "Return of the Jedi," "The Shining," and "Altered States." The Oscar-winning Brown's other inventions include Skycam, a suspended flying camera system; SuperFlyCam, a flying camera system (used in "The Brothers Grimm"); and MobyCam, a submarine tracking system first used during the 1992 Olympics. His latest creation is MoleCam, which offers mole's eye, low-angle views.

Andrew Bryniarski

(Philadelphia b. 1969)

Who is this masked man? A graduate of North Penn high in Lansdale, he's best known as Leatherface in the recent "Texas Chainsaw Massacre" movies.

Michael Callan

(Philadelphia b. 1935)

The son of parents who owned a sandwich and pizza shop called "Dante's" in Northeast Philly, Callan appeared as Riff in the original production of "West Side Story" on Broadway, then scored in Hollywood with roles in "Mysterious Island," "The Interns," and, later, "Cat Ballou." He's also appeared in loads of TV shows, and starred in "Occasional Wife" opposite real-life future wife Patricia Harty.

Wilt Chamberlain

(Philadelphia b. 1936, d. 1999)

Overbrook High grad and NBA superstar appeared on screen as "Bombata" opposite another behemoth, Arnold Schwarzenegger, in "Conan the Destroyer" and made a couple appearances on "Rowan & Martin's Laugh-In." Very interesting.

Philip Casnoff

(Philadelphia b. 1953)

Best known for playing the lead the 1992 "Sinatra" miniseries, Casnoff also counts "ER," "North and South," "Oz," and "Law & Order" among his credits. He's married to Trenton-born Roxanne Hart.

Dennis Christopher

(Philadelphia b. 1955)

A graduate of Monsignor Bonner in Drexel Hill, Christopher is best recognized as Dave Stoller, the kid obsessed with bicycles and Italian words in "Breaking Away." He's also the psycho who takes on the persona of different screen monsters and villains in "Fade to Black."

Imogene Coca

(Philadelphia b. 1908, d. 2001)

Best known as a cast member of Sid Caesar's "Your Show of Shows", Coca was one of TV's foremost female personalities throughout the 1950s. She later appeared as a cavewoman in the 1966 sitcom "It's About Time," made frequent appearances on Carol Burnett's TV shows, and won over a new generation of fans as Aunt Edna in "National Lampoon's Vacation."

Mae Clark

(Philadelphia b. 1907, d. 1992)

1931 was a big year for this former musical stage actress, as she appeared in "Frankenstein," "The Front Page," and "Waterloo Bridge," as well as the woman who gets the grapefruit pressed into her face by James Cagney in "Public Enemy." She went on to make a few more films with Cagney, and became a reliable supporting actress in such efforts as "The Great Caruso," "Singin' in the Rain," and "The Catered Affair."

Lauren Cohan

(Philadelphia b. 1982)

Dark-haired Philly-born, British-educated beauty starred opposite Heath Ledger in 2005's "Casanova," then went for something completely different as the babe in "Van Wilder 2: Rise of the Taj."

Michael Constantine

(Reading b. 1927)

He was the father with the Windex in "My Big Fat Greek Wedding," but counts hours of TV work on his resume, including his gig as Principal Seymour Kaufman on the beloved 1960s show "Room 222."

Bill Cosby

(Philadelphia b. 1937)

"The Cos" is a North Philly native who made good — real good. He quit high school in 10th grade, later enlisted in the Navy, then got his diploma via correspondence school. He attended Temple University on an athletic scholarship, and was on the school's football team. Carl Reiner helped discover him, and appearances on "The Ed Sullivan Show" led to his Emmy-winning role in "I Spy" in 1964 with Robert Culp. Hit comedy records followed as did movie roles, a production company and the animated series "Fat Albert and the Cosby Kids," featuring characters from his childhood that he spoke about in his stage act. Cosby met with great success as a TV pitchman (for Jell-O and other products) and in TV, starring (and producing) several series, the most popular of which was "The Cosby Show," which ran from 1984 to 1992. Over the last ten years, Cosby's life has had its share of heartache (his son Ennis was killed near San Diego in 1997), scandal (he's been the target of sexual harassment suits), and controversy (in public forums he's criticized blacks for their use of language, violence, and poor parenting).

Alexander Courage

(Philadelphia b. 1919)

Best known for composing the "Star Trek" theme, he also gave us music for "Lost in Space," "Daniel Boone," and "Judd for the Defense."

David Crane

(Philadelphia b. 1957)

The son of veteran Philly weathercaster Gene Crane attended Brandeis and met partner Marta Kauffman (along with her future husband, composer Michael Skloff), while producing shows in New York. They worked on a musical version of "Arthur," then won awards for "Personals." Crane and Kauffman moved to TV, producing the HBO series "Dream On," as well as "The Powers That Be," "Veronica's Closet," and "Jessie" with Christina Applegate. In 1994, NBC debuted their "Friends," a smash, that ran for 10 years. "The Class," a 2006 show produced by Crane, focuses on a group of twentysomethings reevaluating their lives after attending a reunion of their third grade class.

Broderick Crawford

(Philadelphia b. 1911, d. 1986)

The gruff man many remember as Chief Dan Mathews on the 1950s TV series "Highway Patrol" won an Academy Award for Best Actor playing power-mad politico Willie Stark, the thinly veiled version of Louisiana's Huey Long, in 1949's "All the King's Men." He also won kudos as the cantankerous tycoon opposite ditsy Judy Holliday in 1950's "Born Yesterday." 10-4.

Laird Creger

(Philadelphia b. 1914, d. 1944)

Best known for roles in the noir "I Wake Up Screaming," as Captain Harry Morgan in the swashbuckler "The Black Swan," and as the creepy Slade in "The Lodger," this portly actor died at the age of 30 after attempting a crash diet to lose 100 pounds.

Morton Da Costa

(Philadelphia b. 1914, d. 1989)

An actor-turned-director, Da Costa is best known for bringing two of his Broadway successes to the big screen: "Auntie Mame" with Rosalind Russell and "The Music Man" with Robert Preston.

Lee Daniels

(Philadelphia b. 1959)

The West Philly native and Radnor High School grad was a young success in the medical field who jumped ship to talent manager and casting director for the Prince films "Purple Rain" and "Under the Cherry Moon." Scratching an itch to produce films, he produced "Monster's Ball," a huge hit and Oscar winner for Halle Berry. The follow-up was "The Woodsman," starring Kevin Bacon as a pedophile, and his first movie as a director, "Shadowboxer," stars Helen Mirren and Cuba Gooding, Jr. He's made a habit of casting musicians in his challenging films, including Sean Combs, Mos Def, Eve, Macy Gray, and (in upcoming projects) Mariah Carey and Lenny Kravitz.

Blythe Danner

(Philadelphia b. 1943)

A graduate of the Wood School in Newtown, Danner made a name for herself on stage, winning a Tony for "Butterflies Are Free," before scoring in such films as "1776" (as Martha Jefferson), "Lovin' Molly," "The Great Santini" "Mr. and Mrs. Bridge," "Meet the Parents" and "Meet the Fockers" as well as TV series like "The X Files" and "Huff." Her husband was the late TV director Bruce Paltrow; her daughter is Gwyneth Paltrow.

Mason Daring

(Philadelphia b. 1949)

Versatile composer specializing in independent projects whose work with director John Sayles stretches back to the filmmaker's first effort, 1980's "Return of the Secaucus 7" through 2005's "Silver City."

James Darren

(Philadelphia b. 1936)

He was a singer with a few hits ("Her Royal Majesty") who made a smooth transition to acting, appearing in "Gidget" movies, "The Guns of Navarone," and starring in popular TV series "The Time Tunnel" and "T.J. Hooker." The father of former CNN anchor Jim Moret, Darren has also directed episodes of "Melrose Place," "Walker: Texas Ranger," and "Beverly Hills 90210."

Bruce Davison

(Philadelphia b. 1946)

Amidst counterculture favorites like "Last Summer," "The Strawberry Statement," and (the hard-to-find) "Been Down so Long It Looks Like Up to Me," Davison scored a big hit at age 25 in "Willard," in which he played a rat's troubled best friend. He's been seen regularly on TV and screen since the late 1960s, in such films as "Short Eyes," "Crimes of Passion," "Short Cuts," and the first two "X-Men" movies and on TV in numerous series as a regular and guest star.

Joe DeRita

(Philadelphia b. 1909, d.1993)

The chubby "third stooge" or "The Last Stooge," "Curly-Joe" replaced the "Curly" and "Shemp" Howard and Joe Besser in the act with Moe Howard and Larry Fine. The burlesque veteran and one-time child actor is best known for his clowning in such features as "Snow White and the Three Stooges," "Three Stooges in Orbit," and "The Three Stooges Meet Hercules."

Richard Deacon

(Philadelphia b. 1921, d. 1984)

Fondly remembered as Mel Cooley, the producer on "The Dick Van Dyke Show," the bespectacled, bald actor's resume includes scores of TV and film appearances. He had roles in several Disney films, a starring part on the Desi Arnaz-produced "The Mothers-in-Law," recurring roles as Dr. Klingner on "The Beverly Hillbillies" and as Fred Rutherford in "Leave It to Beaver," and multiple appearances on "Love, American Style."

Emile De Antonio

(Scranton b. 1920, d. 1989)

Leftist, politically, committed documentary filmmaker behind "Point of Order" (1964), about the Army-Joseph McCarthy hearings of 1954; "Rush to Judgment" (1967), based on Mark Lane's book about the Kennedy assassination conspiracy; "Milhouse" (1971), a scathing assault on Richard Nixon; "Underground" (1976), centering on the 60s radical group The Weather Underground; and "In the King of Prussia" (1982), about the "Plowshares Eight," led by Daniel and Phillip Berrigan, who broke into a weapons plant in King of Prussia to protest war.

John de Lancie

(Philadelphia b. 1948)

Known to sci-fi fans as "Q" on various incarnations of "Star Trek" and recognized as Eugene Bradford on the soap opera "Days of Our Lives," this son of a Philadelphia Orchestra oboist has also appeared in "Stargate SG-1", "Charmed," and many other TV shows,

Kim Delaney

(Philadelphia b. 1960)

 A former teen model and soap opera star, Delaney worked regularly on TV drama throughout the mid 1980s and the 1990s. Regular stints in "NYPD Blue" and "CSI: Miami" led to a short-lived starring role in the Steve Bochco-produced "Philly," followed by a recurring role on "The O.C.," a role in the miniseries "Nightmares and Dreamscapes: From the Stories of Stephen King," and a DUI charge in 2002. She's been married to actors Charles Grant and Joe Cortese.

Annie De Salvo

(Philadelphia b. 1949)

She was Woody Allen's sister in "Stardust Memories," the hooker in "Arthur," and Gina Grossett in TV's "WiseGuy." She's also the director of the 2000 chick flick "The Amati Girls" starring Mercedes Ruehl, Cloris Leachman, and Sean Young.

Roy Del Ruth

(Philadelphia b. 1895, d. 1961)

He was a gag writer for the silent comedies of Mack Sennett, who later signed with Warner Brothers, where he directed the first version of "The Maltese Falcon" in 1931, starring Ricardo Cortez, Thelma Todd, Bebe Daniels, and Dwight Frye, and "Blonde Crazy" with James Cagney and Joan Blondell. The all-star musicals "Broadway Melody of 1936," "Broadway Melody of 1938," and "Ziegfeld Follies" followed, along with such varied works as "The Babe Ruth Story" with William Bendix as the " Sultan of Swat" and "The Alligator People" with Lon Chaney, Jr.

Brian De Palma

(Newark b. 1940)

Although he was born in New Jersey, De Palma moved to Philly with his surgeon father and the rest of his family when he was young, and attended Friend's Central School. He went to Columbia to study physics, but switched his attention to film and studied at Sarah Lawrence College. After working on several shorts, he helmed his first feature, "Murder A La Mode," in 1968, then made three films starring a young Robert De Niro: "Greetings," "The Wedding Party," and "Hi, Mom!" His interests in voyeurism and tweaking movie conventions were apparent in earliest efforts as was his attention-getting visual style. In 1973's "Sisters," however, a psychological shocker about conjoined twins, De Palma's infatuation with Alfred Hitchcock surfaced and would influence almost all of his subsequent works, including "Carrie," "Obsession," "Dressed to Kill," and "Body Double." But De Palma has also shown he's versatile enough to work in different genres, including gangster pictures ("Scarface," "The Untouchables," "Carlito's Way"), war films ("Casualties of War"), comedies ("Wise Guys"), and suspense thrillers without the horror element ("Mission: Impossible, "The Black

Dahlia"). Among his films shot locally are "Blow Out," "Dressed to Kill," and "Snake Eyes." Formerly married to producer Gale Ann Hurd and actress Nancy Allen, De Palma also directed the "Dancing in the Dark" video for Bruce Springsteen.

Caleb Deschanel
(Philadelphia b. 1944)
Five-time Oscar nominated cinematographer counts "The Black Stallion," "The Right Stuff," "The Natural," "The Patriot," "National Treasure," and "The Passion of the Christ" among his achievements. He's also directed "The Escape Artist," "Crusoe," and several episodes of "Twin Peaks." Actresses Zooey and Emily also call him "Dad."

Steve E. De Souza
(Philadelphia b. 1947)
He was raised in Northeast Philadelphia and Levittown, and at a young age, wrote and directed the now-lost "Arnold's Wrecking Co.," a 1973 propot precursor to "Up in Smoke." He had freelance writing gigs and moved to L.A. where he won big on a quiz show. In the same week, he was hired to work as a staff writer on a TV show and contributed scripts for "Gemini Man," "The Six Million Dollar Man," and "The Bionic Woman." His first screen credit was on Walter Hill's hit "48 Hours," which showed he could mix humor with action and led to led to writing "The Running Man," "Die Hard," "Ricochet," "The Flintstones" and sequels to "Die Hard," "48 Hours," and "Beverly Hills Cop." He's also directed "Street Fighter" and episode of "Tales from the Crypt." He's also penned scripts for several projects in development, including "Sgt. Rock" and a new version of "The Phantom."

Heather Donohue
(Upper Darby b. 1974)
She was the star of the 1999 horror sensation "The Blair Witch Project," the film with the greatest cost ($22,000) to gross ($240 million) in history. Since then, the University of the Arts grad has been in the Freddie Prinze, Jr., vehicle "Boys and Girls" and episodes of "It's always Sunny in Philadelphia," "Taken," and "Without a Trace."

Paul Douglas
(Philadelphia b. 1907, d. 1959)
Popular off-beat leading man from the late 1940s and 1950s is best remembered for 1951's "Angels in the Outfield" in which he played the troublemaking coach of the Pittsburgh Pirates whose slumping team gets some heavenly help from the spirits of late baseball greats. Douglas also appeared in many live TV broadcasts and in such films as "It Happens Every Spring" (as a baseball catcher), "Panic in the Streets," "Clash by Night," and "The Gamma People."

Ja'net Du Bois
(Philadelphia b. 1945)
She sang the theme to "The Jeffersons" and appeared as the nosy neighbor Willona Woods and as Grandma on "The Wayans Bros." Film work includes "I'm Gonna Git You Sucka" and "Charlie's Angels: Full Throttle."

Harry Elfont
(Philadelphia b. 1968)
Screenwriter-director-partner to fellow Philly native Deborah Kaplan, both of whom have collaborated as directors-writers on "Josie and the Pussycats" and "Can't Hardly Wait," and scriptors on "A Very Brady Sequel" and "Surviving Christmas."

Cy Endfield

(Scranton b. 1914, d. 1995)

A one-time magician who was blacklisted during the McCarthy era because of his ties to communism, Endfield moved to England to work, and helmed such adventure films as "Mysterious Island," "Zulu," and "Sands of the Kalahari," as well as the 1969 biopic misfire "DeSade" with Keir Dullea.

Fabian

(Philadelphia b. 1943)

A South Philly crooner and "American Bandstand" favorite with such hit singles as "Tiger," "Turn Me Loose," and "Hound Dog Man," which inspired his acting debut in a 1959 movie of the same name directed by Don Siegel ("Dirty Harry"). After some TV work and roles in "North to Alaska," "The Longest Day," and "Five Weeks in a Balloon," Fabian (who was sometimes credited with his real last name of Forte) starred in a series of American-International Pictures projects, including "Marijane," "The Wild Racers," and "The Devil's 8."

Peter Farrelly

(Phoenixville b. 1956)

Master of rude, crude, and lewd filmmaking, along with younger brother Bobby (who was not born in the area), the Farrellys have scored such hits as "Dumb and Dumber," "There's Something About Mary," and "Shallow Hal."

Norman Fell

(Philadelphia b. 1924, d. 1998)

A Temple University graduate (class of '47) best known for his portrayal of landlords: First, in "The Graduate," he's the boarding house owner causing trouble for Dustin Hoffman; then, he's Mr. Roper on "Three's Company and its spinoff, "The Ropers." Fell, who claimed his craggy demeanor and big nose helped him get most of his roles, can also be seen "Ocean's Eleven" (1960), "It's a Mad, Mad, Mad, Mad World," and "Catch-22."

Wilhelmenia Fernandez

(Philadelphia b. 1949)

An opera star who has performed "Carmen," "Aida," and "La Boheme" around the world and won accolades for "Carman Jones" at the Old Vic, she's was the enchanting opera star Cynthia Hawkins in 1981's arresting, high-style thriller "Diva."

Tina Fey

(Upper Darby b. 1970)

She honed her skills at Second City in Chicago, then nailed a spot on "Saturday Night Live" in 1995, and went on to become their first female head writer. Scripting the Lindsay Lohan-Rachel McAdams 2004 hit "Mean Girls" helped broaden her career options, proving the diminutive, bespectacled Fey a versatile talent. She left "SNL" in 2006 with several films in the pipeline and as an executive producer writer-star of the NBC show "30 Rock," about the people who work on a late-night comedy sketch show.

W.C. Fields

(Philadelphia b. 1880, d. 1946)

"Went to Philadelphia the other day. Couldn't get in — it was closed." The line is attributed to William Claude Dunkenfield, better known as acerbic funnyman W.C. Fields. He rarely had a good word to say about the city, dogs, or children. A huge drinker, he worked at a Norristown amusement park, juggled in Atlantic City, and was part of the famed Ziegfeld Follies from 1915 through 1921. He moved into silent films in 1915, making his first film at the age of 36, and worked with the legendary D.W. Griffith in "Sally of the Sawdust" ten years later. He signed a contract with Lasky Famous Players, which later merged with Paramount, and made silents, shorts, and talkies such as "If I Had a Million," "It's a Gift," "The Bank Dick," "My Little Chickadee," "Never Give a Sucker an Even Break," and "Poppy."

Larry Fine

(Philadelphia b. 1902, d. 1975)

Born Louis Feinberg in the area of Third and South Streets, "the Stooge in the middle" started playing violin at an early age, then boxed and sang for a living. After a stint in vaudeville, he joined Ted Healey and Moe Howard in 1925 in the act that eventually became The Three Stooges. He went on to star as the Brillo-haired straight man who often bore the brunt of his fellow comics' physical monkey business in 200 shorts and a handful of features.

Linda Fiorentino

(Philadelphia b. 1960)

A mystery woman even when she was appearing in such acclaimed films as "The Last Seduction," "Men in Black," and "Jade," this South Philly native and Rosemont College grad has apparently gone underground, taking an early retirement from the entertainment world or at least a long sabbatical. If you love Linda, check out "Acting on Impulse," a dandy little spoof of B movies in which she plays a manipulative scream queen.

Paul Fishbein

(Philadelphia b. 1959)

A Temple University graduate, Fishbein is best known as the publisher of several magazines including *Adult Video News*, a publication that covers the adult movie industry. He produced "The Money Shot," a miniseries that ran on the Internet that satirized the porn world, and is a frequent guest on "The Howard Stern Show."

Meg Foster

(Reading b. 1948)

"The Girl with Eerie Catlike Eyes" was a favorite in 1970s TV ("The F.B.I.," Hawaii Five-O) and 1980s films ("Carny," "The Emerald Forrest," "They Live"). She was also the original Cagney in "Cagney & Lacey," replaced by Sharon Gless after a few episodes. Ex-wife of actor Stephen McHattie.

Jonathan Frakes

(Bethlehem b. 1952)

Best known for his association with "Star Trek," this graduate of Penn State and Harvard played Commander William Riker on "Star Trek: The Next Generation," after steady TV work on soaps and in such series as "The Waltons," "Quincy M.E.," and "Falcoln Crest." He went on to helm episodes of several "Star Trek" incarnations, as well as the features "Star Trek: First Contact" and "Star Trek: Insurrection." Other directing assignments include episodes of "Rosewell," "Clockstoppers," and "Thunderbirds," which also featured his wife, actress Genie Francis.

Milton Frome

(Philadelphia b. 1912, d. 1989)

A vaudeville veteran, Frome excelled at second banana and nervous nelly types throughout his busy career. He was often used in comedies on TV and the movies, and shared TV and the screen with Milton Berle, Jack Benny, Jerry Lewis, Dick Van Dyke, Bob Hope, Superman (George Reeves), and Batman (Adam West). He may best be remembered as movie studio mogul Lawrence Chapman in "The Beverly Hillbillies."

Martin Gabel

(Philadelphia b. 1912, d. 1986)

A graduate of Lehigh University, Gabel started on radio with Orson Welles' famous "Mercury Theatre," then made a name for himself on stage, winning accolades in such plays as "Life With Father," "Julius Caesar" (as Cassius) "Will Success Spoil Rock Hunter?" and "Big Fish, Little Fish," for which he won the Tony Award for Best Featured Actor in a Play. Long married to frequent quiz show associate Arlene Francis, Gabel can be seen on screen in "Deadline USA," "Marnie," "Divorce American Style," and "The First Deadly Sin."

Megan Gallagher

(Reading b. 1960)

A regular on the acclaimed but short-lived Dabney Coleman show "The Slap Maxwell Story," this actress, at home in comedy or drama, was also Gary Shandling's second ex-wife in "The Larry Sanders Show"; played Wayloo Marie Holmes in the first two seasons of "China Beach"; played Lance Henricksen's wife in two seasons of "Millenium" from "The X-Files" creator Chris Carter; and has also appeared in "Boston Legal," "7th Heaven," and the feature "Mr. and Mrs. Smith." She's married to actor Jeff Yagher.

Alan Gasmer

(Philadelphia b. 1959)

Once labeled "King of the Spec Script," Temple University Communications grad Gasmer has gone from lawyer to working at the William Morris mailroom to Vice President in the motion picture division of the talent agency. Among the clients he's represented are Nicolas Meyer ("Time After Time"), Henry Bean ("The Believer"), and Steven E. deSouza ("Die Hard").

Janet Gaynor

(Philadelphia b. 1906, d.1984)

Born in Philly but raised in San Francisco, Gaynor won the first Academy Award for Best Actress — for three films made in the same year ("Seventh Heaven," "Street Angel," and "Sunrise"). During the late 1920s through the mid 1930s, Gaynor was a huge star. Her most famous role, however, was in 1937's "A Star is Born," playing the part of the wannabe actress later covered in remakes by Judy Garland and Barbra Streisand. At the time of her death, she was working on a stage version of "Harold and Maude," in which she was to play the role Ruth Gordon popularized in the film.

Richard Gere

(Philadelphia b. 1949)

The popular human-rights activist and star of "American Gigolo," "Chicago," and "Shall We Dance?" was born here, but his family moved to Syracuse when he was a child.

Michael Goldberg

(Philadelphia b. 1959)

A Northeast High School who attended Carnegie-Mellon, Goldberg relocated to L.A. where he acted and wrote for an independent theater company, often with writing partner Tommy Swerdlow. His big break came when "Cool Runnings," the true story of the Jamaican bobsled team which he cowrote, became a surprise hit in 1993. Family-oriented fare like "Little Giants," "Bushwacked," and "Snow Dogs" followed. He also cowrote and directed "The Lovemaster" featuring Philly comic Craig Shoemaker.

William Goldenberg

(Philadelphia b. 1959)

One of Hollywood's top editors, this Northeast High School grad has worked on several of Michael Mann's films (including "Heat," "Ali," and "Miami Vice," along with "Pleasantville," "Seabiscuit," and the locally shot "National Treasure."

Benny Golson

(Philadelphia b. 1929)

Jazz saxophone great and composer, Golson has supplied music for such TV shows as ""M*A*S*H," "Mannix," "Mission: Impossible," and "It Takes a Thief."

Dexter Gordon

(Philadelphia b. 1923, d. 1990)

This jazz saxophone master played a variation on himself and Charlie Parker in Bertrand Tavernier's acclaimed "'Round Midnight" For his efforts, he was nominated for an Academy Award. Sadly, he died a few years after the widespread recognition he received for his performance.

Lance Gordon

(Delaware County b. 1958)

Played the imposing cretin Mars in Wes Craven's original "The Hills Have Eyes" (1977) and its 1985 sequel.

Bruce Graham

(Philadelphia)

One of Philly's most visible playwrights, he's written "Belmont Ave. Social Club" and "The Champagne Charlie Stakes." He's also scripted such films as "Dunston Checks In," the animated "Anastasia," the Abbie Hoffman biopic "Steal This Movie!" and the TV films "Hunt for the Unicorn Killer" about Philly fugitive Ira Einhorn, and "Tiger Cruise" for the Disney Channel.

Ronny Graham

(Philadelphia b. 1919, d. 1999)

The writer-actor was a frequent collaborator with Mel Brooks, appearing in and/or coscripting "History of the World, Part I," "Spaceballs," "To Be or Not to Be," "Robin Hood: Men in Tights," and "Life Stinks." He also cowrote Richard Lester's underrated 1984 comic chase film "Finders Keepers," starring Michael O'Keefe, Beverly D'Angelo, Lou Gossett, Jr., and Jim Carrey.

Seth Green

(Philadelphia b. 1974)

The diminutive, red-headed Overbrook Park native seems to be constantly in-demand, whether it be for TV appearances ("That 70's Show," "Buffy the Vampire Slayer"), voice work ("Robot Chicken," "Family Guy"), or key supporting roles in popular films (he's Scott Evil in the "Austin Powers" series and Lyle, the computer expert in "The Italian Job" films.)

Bill Gunn

(Philadelphia b. 1934, d. 1989)

An actor, writer, and director, Gunn's best-known work is 1973's "Ganja & Hess," a mystical vampire movie with an African-American cast. Because it was more complex and headier than most horror films of the era, the movie was unceremoniously re-edited and distributed under a number of titles upon its release. Gunn also scripted two interesting but under-appreciated films of the early 1970s: Hal Ashby's "The Landlord" with Beau Bridges, and Jan Kadar's "The Angel Levine," starring Zero Mosel and Harry Belafonte.

Grayson Hall

(Philadelphia b. 1923, d. 1985)

Best known as Dr. Julia Hoffman on the horror soap opera "Dark Shadows," she was also nominated for an Oscar for Best Supporting Actress for her role as jealous Judith Fellowes in "The Night of the Iguana." Other appearances include "End of the Road," "That Darn Cat!," and the TV movie "Gargoyles."

Veronica Hamel

(Philadelphia b. 1943)

The brunette actress began modeling right after graduating from Temple University, and eventually passed on an offer to star in Aaron Spelling's "Charlie's Angels" — the role went to Jaclyn Smith instead. Hamel did take a lead role in "Hill Street Blues," playing Joyce Davenport, girlfriend (and later wife) of police captain Frank Furillo (Daniel J. Travanti). The actress's subsequent roles are in many TV movies, a pair of disaster films ("Beyond the Poseidon Adventure" and "When Time Ran Out") and 1991's made-for-TV "Here Comes the Munsters," in which she played Yvonne De Carlo's part of Lily.

Lois Hamilton

(Philadelphia b. 1942, d. 1999)

After a stint as a top model for the Ford Agency in the late 1970s, this Temple University grad had significant supporting roles in "The Electric Horseman," "The Cannonball Run" (as Roger Moore's girlfriend), "Stripes" (as John Laroquette's girlfriend) and "Summer Rental," as well as spots on TV shows "Three's Company," "The Ropers," and "Hunter." A sculptress, painter, and pilot who also studied at the University of Florence, Hamilton became addicted to painkillers after a 1999 auto accident and took her own life by overdosing on sleeping pills in Rio de Janeiro.

Jack H. Harris

(Philadelphia)

A former usher and child vaudeville collaborator with Cliff "Ukelele Ike" Edwards (the voice of Jiminy Cricket), Harris joined forces with Valley Forge Film Studios in 1958 to produce "The Blob," a low-budget sci-fi film about an icky mass from outer space. A smash, the film led Harris to other low-budget horror and sci-fi outings like "The 4-D Man," "Dinosaurus," "Equinox," and the early John Carpenter effort "Dark Star." He was also involved in the goo-in-cheek 1972 sequel "Beware! The Blob" and the 1988 reworking of "The Blob." Another remake of the film is planned for the future.

Julius Harris

(Philadelphia b. 1923, d. 2004)

This erudite African-American actor appeared in such black exploitation films as "Hell Up in Harlem," "Superfly," and "Shaft's Big Score." He also costarred in "The Taking of Pelham One Two Three," and "Live and Let Die," appeared in many sitcoms, and drew raves for his portrayal of Idi Amin Dada in the TV movie "Victory at Entebbe."

Mel Harris

(Bethlehem b. 1957)

Caught the public's attention as Hope Steadman on "thirtysomething," and appeared in Brian De Palma's "Raising Cain," the indy film "Suture," and a bevy of TV shows like "Stargate SG-1" and "JAG."

Sherman Hemsley

(Philadelphia b. 1938)

The former postal worker got a break playing Gitlow in the hit 1970 Broadway staging of "Purlie," then appeared as loquacious, wealthy dry cleaning mogul George Jefferson on "All in the Family." The popular character got his own series, "movin' on up" to "The Jeffersons" in 1975. Later, Hemsley starred in the Philly-based "Amen," in which he played the minister of a North Philly church.

Marshall Hershovitz

(Philadelphia b. 1952)

Along with Edward Zwick, he produced "thirtysomething," (the ABC drama) as well as "My So-Called Life" and "Once and Again." The partnership has continued with Hershovitz producing and coscripting such Zwick-helmed films as "The Last Samurai" and the upcoming "The Blood Diamond." His own directorial credits include "Jack the Bear," and "Dangerous Beauty."

Kevin Hooks

(Philadelphia b. 1958)

As a child performer, this son of actor Robert Hooks gained enthusiastic notices at the age of seven for his role of the kid who befriended a cat in the award-winning CBS Children's Hour production called "J.T." After appearing in the films "Sounder," "Aaron Loves Angela," and "A Hero Ain't Nothing But a Sandwich" and the TV series "The White Shadow," Hooks became a prolific director, mixing TV assignments ("ER," "Lost," "24") with action-oriented feature films ("Passenger 54," "Fled," "Black Dog").

Monica Horan

(Upper Darby b. 1963)

For several years, she was MacDougall, the on-again, off-again girlfriend of Brad Garrett's Robert on "Everybody Loves Raymond." Eventually she married him on the show. In real life, she's married to Phil Rosenthal, creator and writer of "Everyone Loves Raymond." They both attended Hofstra University.

Dom Irrera

(Philadelphia b. 1947)

South Philly-born and bred, this streetwise comic is a regular on sitcoms and talk shows and can be seen in such films as "Hollywood Shuffle" and "The Big Lebowski."

Tamara Jenkins

(Philadelphia b. 1962)

She started as a performance artist who made short films and was the recipient of a grant from the Guggenheim Foundation. Then Jenkins drew attention for her feature film debut, 1998's "The Slums of New York," a darkly comic look at a nomadic Jewish family, starring Alan Arkin, Natasha Lyonne, and Marisa Tomei. Her newest film, "The Savages," stars Philip Seymour Hoffman and Laura Linney.

Clark Johnson

(Philadelphia b. 1954)

A regular on "Homicide: Life on the Streets" as Detective Mildrick Lewis, Johnson appeared in scores of TV dramas and action series, before breaking through as director. His directing credits include "Homicide," "Third Watch," "West Wing," and "The Shield," while his feature slate includes "S.W.A.T." and "The Sentinel."

James Karen

(Wilkes-Barre b. 1923)

Best known locally for his long-running stint as the spokesperson for Pathmark, this dependable character actor (and serious movie buff) can play it straight or for comedy, as evidenced in his roles in such films as "The China Syndrome," "Poltergeist," "Jagged Edge," "Return of the Living Dead," and "Superman Returns." In addition, he's been on such TV shows as "Lou Grant," "The Practice," and "Coach."

Ross Katz

(Philadelphia b. 1971)

On WYSP Radio in the late 1980s, he was a teenage disc jockey known as Ross Andrews. He worked for Good Machine Films and producer Lindsay Doran, eventually graduating to producing with such efforts as "Trick," "In the Bedroom," and the made-for-HBO "The Laramie Project." Most recently, he's produced two films directed by Sofia Coppola, "Lost in Translation" and "Marie Antoinette."

William Keighley

(Philadelphia b. 1880, d. 1984)

Versatile Broadway veteran became a Warner Brothers contract director for such films as "Bullets or Ballots," "The Prince and the Pauper," "The Fighting 69th," and "The Adventures of Robin Hood," on which he was replaced with Michael Curtiz when the action sequences seemed sluggish to studio executives. Later, he showed he could also do well in screwball comedies ("The Bride Came C.O.D." with James Cagney and Bette Davis), film noir (The Street with No Name"), and farces ("George Washington Slept Here" with Jack Benny and Ann Sheridan, a precursor to "Green Acres").

Grace Kelly

(Philadelphia b. 1929, d. 1982)

The screen princess who became a real-life fairy tale princess, Grace Kelly was Philly royalty before she married Prince Rainier of Monaco in 1956. The daughter of Olympic rower and brickwork mogul John B. Kelly, Sr., and a former model, Grace became a model, then entered show business, first appearing on live TV dramas, and making her debut in the 1951 drama "Fourteen Hours." Over a five year period, before she retired and got married, she appeared in ten films, including "High Noon," "Mogambo," "Dial M for Murder," "Rear Window," "The Country Girl" (for which she won an Oscar), "The Bridges of Toko-Ri," "To Catch a Thief," "High Society," and "The Swan." Just before her death (she had a stroke while driving in Monaco in 1982), she was working on a film called "Rearranged," about the Monaco Garden Group. It was never completed.

Walt Kelly

(Philadelphia b. 1913, d. 1973)

He was best known for drawing the comic strip "Pogo," but he also helped Disney animate portions of "Fantasia" and "Dumbo."

Jamie Kennedy

(Upper Darby b. 1970)

The creative force behind the practical-joke-oriented WB series "The Jamie Kennedy Experiment" has also amassed some unusual credits during his acting and producing career. He cowrote and costarred in the spoof "Malibu's Most Wanted"; stole scenes in the "Scream" films; had key roles in "Bowfinger," and "Three Kings"; and produced the TV series "Living with Fran" and the reality show "The Starlet." OK, we may as well mention "Son of Mask," too.

Irvin Kershner

(Philadelphia b. 1923)

Most Star Wars fans agree that "Episode V: The Empire Strikes Back" is the best of the series. It was directed by Kershner, George Lucas' former film instructor at USC. Kershner's varied career includes helming offbeat 1960s romantic comedies, "A Fine Madness" with Sean Connery and "Loving" with George Segal, along with the terrific 1977 TV movie "Raid on Entebbe" and Connery's return to 007 turf with "Never Say Never Again."

Sidney Kimmel

(Philadelphia b. 1930)

Founder of the Jones Apparel Group, leading philanthropist, and the man for whom the Kimmel Center is named, he's also produced several films over the years, including "9½ Weeks," "Mother," "Town & Country," "Strut" (with former partner Max Raab), "Alpha Dog," "Trust the Man," and "United 93."

Randal Kleiser

(Philadelphia b. 1946)

"Grease" was the word for Kleiser, George Lucas' college roommate, who scored big with the 1978 musical hit after sturdy work directing such made-for-TV films as "The Gathering" and "The Boy In the Plastic Bubble" with Travolta. His work appears divided between family-oriented material like "Honey, I Blew Up the Kids," "White Fang," "Flight of the Navigator," and the misfire "Big Top Pee-Wee," and more provocative fare a la "The Blue Lagoon," "Summer Lovers," "Getting It Right," and "It's My Party."

Jack Klugman

(Philadelphia b. 1922)

Best known for his work as Oscar Madison in TV's "The Odd Couple," and as "Quincy, M.E.," Klugman has also given fine performances in the films "12 Angry Men," "Days of Wine and Roses," and "Goodbye, Columbus." Klugman, who has logged hundreds of hours on network TV and was nominated for a Tony for his supporting role on Broadway in "Gypsy," is a graduate of Carnegie-Mellon University.

Nancy Kulp

(Harrisburg b. 1921, d. 1991)

She had small parts in "Shane" and "Sabrina" and was a regular on "The Bob Cummings Show" before she received her signature role as the befuddled, bird-watching Jane Hathaway on "The Beverly Hillbillies." As a liberal Democratic candidate she ran for Congress in Pennsylvania's 9th District in 1984, but lost; former "Hillbillies" costar Buddy Ebsen, a conservative Republican, actively campaigned against her. Once married, she admitted to being a homosexual later in her life.

Kurupt

(Philadelphia b. 1972)

Born Ricardo Dean but also known as Little Gotti, this rapper-turned-actor is a member of The Dogg Pound and a close pal of Suge Knight. He has been a formidable presence in such films as "Dark Blue," "Hollywood Homicide," and "Johnson Family Vacation." Our favorite film title of his: "I Accidentally Domed Your Son."

Audrey Landers

(Philadelphia b. 1956)

There's more than meets the eye with this blonde bombshell who had a regular gig on "Dallas" as Afton Cooper, and has appeared in hours of TV with and without her sister Judy. She's a graduate of Columbia and Julliard who also lists "Happy Days," "Hotel," and "Fantasy Island" on her resume. Film credits include "A Chorus Line," "Freakshow," and "Circus Camp," a film she made with many family members. She was born Audrey Hamberg.

Judy Landers

(Philadelphia b. 1958)

The bodacious younger sister of Audrey was a big pinup girl in the late 1970s and 1980s appearing as a regular in two popular shows, "B.J. and the Bear" and "Vega$." She's also taken several trips on "The Love Boat" and to "Fantasy Island" and "Night Court." Film credits include "Dr. Alien," "Cub Fed," and Steven Austin's "Expert Weapon." She's married to former baseball relief pitcher Tom Niedenfuer. Her real name is Judy Hamberg.

Mario Lanza

(Philadelphia b. 1921, d. 1959)

Known as "The American Caruso," the South Philly tenor (born Alfred Cocozza) studied singing when he was a child and drew attention in his early 20s for performing at the Berkshire Summer Festival in Tanglewood. Incredible fan adulation followed along with a recording contract and a picture deal with MGM. He was cast in "That Midnight Kiss" in 1949 and "Toast of New Orleans" in 1950 and as "The Great Caruso" in 1951. Lanza was let go from his contract after a squabble with the director of "The Student Prince" in 1952 — the studio would use his voice only and hired Edmund Purdom to play the role in which he was originally cast. Battling his frustrations with show business and weight problems after making "Serenade" for Warner Brothers in 1956, Lanza moved to Italy with his wife and four children, where he made a few low-profile movies before he died from a heart attack at the age of 38. Six months later, wife Betty Hicks, took her own life with a drug overdose in Hollywood. In a way, Lanza's short, tragic life sounds like an epic opera.

Stan Lathan

(Philadelphia b. 1945)

This African-American director-producer has mixed careers in TV and movies successfully for over 40 years. He worked at WCAU in the 1960s, then helmed many episodes of "Sesame Street" in its formative mid 1960s years. He directed hundreds of episodes of sitcoms ("Sanford & Son," "Moesha," and David Chappelle specials) and such features as "Amazing Grace" and 1984's "Beat Street," which many regard as the first hip-hop movie. He's also the father of actress Saana Lathan.

Joseph Lawrence

(Philadelphia b. 1976)

Woh! Best known as Joey Lawrence from the "Gimme a Break" and "Blossom" TV shows when he was a kid, Lawrence's grown-up roles include the movies "Tequila Body Shots" and "Urban Legends: Final Cut." On TV he's been on "American Dreams" and "Half & Half." Brother of Matthew Lawrence.

Matthew Lawrence

(Abington b. 1980)

Joey's younger brother has had some key roles in films like "Mrs. Doubtfire" (playing Robin Williams' son) and TV series like "Brotherly Love" (with his sibling) and "Boy Meets World," in which he starred.

Richard Lester

(Philadelphia b. 1932)

A former producer and director at WCAU TV-10 in the 1950s, Lester moved to England where he worked with "The Goons" (Peter Sellers, Spike Milligan, and Harry Secombe) and in other television enterprises before turning to film with the short "The Running, Jumping, and Standing Still Film" in 1959. He was enlisted to capture the Fab Four at the height of Beatlemania with "A Hard Day's Night" and "Help," and later helmed the 1960s cult favorite "Petulia." Other credits include "The Three Musketeers" and "The Four Musketeers," "Robin and Marian," and "Superman II" and "Superman III." He's been retired since 1991's "Get Back," Paul McCartney's concert film.

Tony Luke, Jr.

(Philadelphia b. 1962)

Local cheesesteak wiz has also acted in films, including "The Evil Within," "Mafioso: The Father, the Son," and "Frankie the Squirrel."

Sidney Lumet

(Philadelphia b. 1924)

The son of Yiddish theater actor Baruch Lumet and dancer Eugenia Wertmus Lumet, he grew up in the theater and appeared in childhood roles in films and on stage. He studied at the Actor's Studio and directed many TV dramas in the late 1940s and 1950s before making his feature debut with "12 Angry Men" in 1957. "The Pawnbroker" and "Fail-Safe" are among his best-received works of the 60s, but it was in the 1970s that Lumet became a Hollywood force — even though he rarely set foot there, preferring New York as the location for such films as "Serpico," "Dog Day Afternoon," and "Network." Other well-received efforts include "Murder on the Orient Express," "Prince of the City," "The Verdict," "Running on Empty," "Q&A" and the recent "Find Me Guilty." As he works into his 80s, Lumet has many films planned for the future. After five Academy Award nominations without a win, he was given an honorary Oscar in 2005.

David Lynch

(Missoula, Montana b. 1946)

Lynch attended the Pennsylvania Academy of the Fine Arts in the late 1960s, and has claimed Philadelphia's creepy ambiance was a huge influence on his work. Most of the shorts featured in the collection "The Short Films of David Lynch" were shot here when he was a student, and he's gone on record saying the city inspired his breakthrough film, 1977's midnight movie classic "Eraserhead." Lynch was courted by Mel Brooks for the acclaimed "The Elephant Man"; had his sci-fi epic "Dune" taken out of his hands and re-edited; was reviled and revered for 1986's "Blue Velvet"; produced the groundbreaking TV series "Twin Peaks" and turned a TV pilot bust "Mulholland Dr." into a critical success and head-scratching audience delight in 2001. His latest experimental film, "Inland Empire," was shot secretly over a two-year period and stars Laura Dern, Jeremy Irons, and Harry Dean Stanton.

Jennifer Chambers Lynch
(Philadelphia b. 1968)
The daughter of David Lynch and Peggy Chambers was born while Dad was attending the Pennsylvania Academy of the Fine Arts. Jennifer's only directing credit so far is "Boxing Helena," the bizarre tale of obsessive love in which doctor Julian Sands amputates former lover Sherilyn Fenn's limbs following an auto accident. The film is noted for its topsy-turvy history: Madonna was originally cast in the lead, then Kim Basinger agreed to play the part, but backed out at the last minute, prompting a lawsuit between her and the producers. Eventually, it was settled out of court, and Fenn took the role.

Charles MacArthur
(Scranton b. 1895, d. 1956)
Writer, actor, producer, and bon vivant, MacArthur is best known as Ben Hecht's collaborator on such stage and screen comedy classics as "The Front Page" (and its remake "His Girl Friday") and "Twentieth Century," "Gunga Din," and "Wuthering Heights. But MacArthur was also an adventurer who joined General Pershing in search of Pancho Villa in Mexico and fought in World War I, and one of Chicago's most popular writers during the Roaring '20s. During the late 1920s and early 1930s, he joined witty friends Dorothy Parker and Robert Benchley at the famed Algonquin Roundtable. MacArthur married "The First Lady of Theater" Helen Hayes; their son is James MacArthur of "Hawaii Five-O" fame.

Stephen Macht
(Philadelphia b. 1942)
Steady working character actor has been in several prominent TV shows since the mid 1970s, including "Knot's Landing," "Hill Street Blues," "Star Trek: Deep Space Nine," and "General Krim."

Joseph L. Mankiewicz
(Wilkes-Barre b. 1909, d. 1993)
He began his career as a translator and writer of titles for Paramout Films overseas, broke through writing screenplays for such films as "Manhattan Melodrama" and "Keys to the Kingdom," then sat in the director's chair the first time for in 1944's "Dragonwyck," leading to a long and storied career as one of Hollywood leading writer-directors. Credits included "The Ghost and Mrs. Muir," "A Letter to Three Wives," the Oscar-winning "All About Eve," "Guys and Dolls," "Cleopatra," and "Sleuth." Brother Herman Mankewicz cowrote "Citizen Kane"; son Tom Mankiewicz helped script the Bond films "Diamonds Are Forever," "Live and Let Die," and "The Man with the Golden Gun."

Abby Mann
(Philadelphia b. 1927)
After serving as writer on such dramatic TV shows as "Studio One," "Playhouse 90," and "Goodyear Television Playhouse," Mann won an Academy Award for "Judgment at Nuremberg," Stanley Kramer's all-star film about the Nazi war trials. Kramer's "Ship of Fools" and "The Detective" with Frank Sinatra followed, as did his TV movie adaptation of the book "The Marcus-Nelson Murders," which introduced Lt. Theo Kojak to the world. The writer has garnered several awards for his real-life TV treatments of "King," "The Atlanta Child Murders," "Murderers Among Us: The Simon Weisenthal Story," "Indictment: The McMartin Trial," and "Whitewash: The Clarence Brandley Story."

Jayne Mansfield

(Bryn Mawr b. 1933, d. 1967)

The platinum blonde screen siren was born Vera Jane Palmer, daughter of a prominent New Jersey lawyer. After his death, her mother remarried and she moved to Dallas, Texas, and attended the University of Texas. She moved to L.A., got a bit part in Jack Webb's "Pete Kelly's Blues," then, after being cast in small roles for her physical attributes and dumb blonde persona and posing for Playboy in 1955, she got a big part playing the same bombshell role in Frank Tashlin's 1956 rock-and-roll infused "The Girl Can't Help It." The crime thriller "The Burglar," shot near her Main Line birthplace, was released, although shot two years earlier, followed by "Kiss Them for Me," opposite Cary Grant, and "Will Success Spoil Rock Hunter?" in a role she originated on Broadway. Because she had trouble shaking the "poor man's Marilyn Monroe" tag and bimbo image the press gave her (her actual IQ was 163), good film roles in studio pictures were in short supply. She starred in a Hercules movie with Mr. Universe hubby Mickey Hargitay, with whom she moved into the fabled 40-room "Pink Palace" mansion in L.A, once owned by Rudy Vallee. She divorced Hargitay and married director Matt Cimber in 1964. But after the death of Monroe, her movie career suffered, and she was relegated to low-budget efforts like "Dog Eat Dog," "The Fat Spy," and "Single Room Furnished," directed by Cimber. She was also offered the role of voluptuous movie star Ginger on "Gilligan's Island," but turned it down. She died at the age of 34 in a 1967 car accident in Louisiana on the way to a nightclub performance. Her daughter Mariska Hargitay is the star of "Law & Order: Special Victims Unit."

Bam Margera

(West Chester b. 1979)

Daredevil Margera first gained notoriety in "Jackass" with Johnny Knoxville, then starred and produced the CKY video series, featuring musician brother Jess and other wacky family members.

Guy Marks

(Philadelphia b. 1923, d. 1987)

A South Philly native, Marks began doing shtick and impersonations as an opening act for Eddie Fisher and Sammy Davis, Jr. He appeared on several TV shows during the 1960s, was a regular on the "Dean Martin Roasts," and costarred as a wisecracking Native-American "Pink Cloud" in the Tim Conway TV western spoof "Rango." He also had a nostalgic novelty hit with "Loving You Has Made Me Bananas" in the early 1970s.

Hugh Marlowe

(Philadelphia b. 1911, d. 1982)

After his work as a radio announcer and stage performer, Marlowe (born Hugh Hipple) became an extremely busy actor from the early 1940s through the mid 1960s. He's best remembered for his leading roles in two 1956 sci-fi favorites: "World Without End," in which he plays an astronaut caught in a time warp while exploring Mars, and "Earth Vs. Flying Saucers," about alien spacecraft that attacks the world, featuring special effects by Ray Harryhausen. He was also seen on TV in "The Virginian," "Perry Mason," and as the lead in "The Adventures of Ellery Queen."

Al Martino
(Philadelphia b. 1927)

Popular crooner who played Sinatra-like Johnny Fontaine in the first two "Godfather" films and played regularly at South Philly restaurant Palumbo's. He also sang the theme song to the 1964 gothic horror yarn "Hush…Hush, Sweet Charlotte."

Elaine May
(Philadelphia b. 1932)

She was one-half of the famed comedy team with Mike Nichols who brought her comic talents to the screen — performing memorably in "Enter Laughing," "A New Leaf," "California Suite," and "Small-Time Crooks" — and on the page, having her hands in writing "Heaven Can Wait," "The Bird Cage," "Primary Colors," and, sans credit, "Reds" and "Tootise." She also directed "The Heartbreak Kid" (featuring her daughter Jeanie Berlin), Philly-based "Mikey and Nicky," and "Ishtar."

Melanie Mayron
(Philadelphia b. 1952)

This actress-director made her big splash as Melissa Steadman on "thirtysomething" after years of steady character work in films like "Car Wash," "Girlfriends," and "Missing." Her directing assignments have included the features "The Baby Sitter's Club" and "Slap Her … She's French" and such TV series as "Ed," "Arliss," and "Dawson's Creek."

Sal Mazzotta
(Philadelphia b. 1964)

Locally-based writer-producer-actor-stunt man with such credits as "The Evil Within," "Mafioso: The Father, the Son," and "Frankie the Squirrel" behind him.

Alex McArthur
(Telford b. 1957)

Most memorable as a vicious serial killer in William Friedkin's long-on-the-shelf courtroom thriller "Rampage" (1991), McArthur has also appeared in "Conspiracy Theory," "Kiss the Girls," and "Out for Blood." He also played Madonna's boyfriend in the music video for "Papa Don't Preach."

Tom McCarthy
(Philadelphia b. 1936)

Philadelphia-based character actor, definitely from the "you'll-see-and-you'll-know-him" category. He often plays working class guys — a cop in "Blow Out," a hostage negotiator in "Up Close and Personal," and a gardener in "Mannequin." He's also appeared in many local theater productions.

Paul McCrane
(Philadelphia b. 1961)

The red-headed actor made his screen debut in "Rocky II" but really got attention for his role as Montgomery, the gay performing arts student in 1980's "Fame." He's worked steadily since then, excelling in edginess, playing the creepy Dr. Romano on "ER" and Graham on "24." He's also directed several hours of dramatic TV.

Jeanette MacDonald
(Philadelphia b. 1903, d. 1965)

Best known for her eight films for MGM with Nelson Eddy, including "The Naughty Marietta," "Rose Marie," and "Maytime," MacDonald was a singing star when she was just a toddler, then made her way to Broadway. There she caught the eye of director Ernst Lubitsch who cast her in 1929's "The Love Parade" and in 1934's "The Merry Widow". Along with the Eddy films, she appeared opposite Clark Gable in

"San Francisco" and with Alan Jones in "The Firefly." In the 1950s, she performed live and appeared in TV productions, including the 1957 "Playhouse 90" production of "Charlie's Aunt" with Art Carney. The Eddy-MacDonald team was the inspiration for the characters "Dudley Dooright" and "Nell" in the Jay Ward cartoons. .

Rob McEllheney
(Philadelphia b. 1977)
Along with friends Charlie Day and Glenn Howerton, McEllheney invested $200 in a pilot for a TV show, shot it on a video camera, edited it on a home computer — and got a series on F/X, costarring Danny De Vito! The show, "It's Always Sunny in Philadelphia," debuted in 2004, and centers on a group of friends who run an Irish bar in Philly. St. Joseph Prep grad McEllheney, who writes and stars in the show, has also appeared in "13 Conversations About One Thing" and "Latter Days."

Kristin Minter
(Miami b. 1965)
Raised in Yardley, this Philadelphia College of the Performing Arts grad started out in a key supporting role in "Home Alone," but her romantic lead in the Vanilla Ice flop "Cool as Ice" didn't help her career. Loads of TV work followed, including a spot on "ER," playing Randi Fronczak for several seasons.

Michael Mislove
(Philadelphia b. 1941)
As a member of the Ace Trucking Company, a popular L.A.-based improv group of the 60s and 70s that included Fred Willard and Bill Saluga, Mislove appeared and helped write parody films "Tunnelvision," "Cracking Up," and "Americathon" in the 1970s.

Katherine Moening
(Philadelphia b. 1976)
She had an attention-getting spot as a cross-dresser on the TV series "Young Americans," then played a transsexual on "Law & Order: Special Victims Unit." Her biggest role to date, however, has been as the rock-starlike womanizing lesbian Shane McCutcheon on the Showtime series "The L Word."

Kelly Monaco
(Philadelphia b. 1976)
Born in Philly but raised in the Poconos, the former Playboy Playmate was a "Baywatch" babe and a soap opera star of "Port Charles" and "One Life to Live." She won TV's "Dancing with the Stars" competition in 2005 in a controversial vote and was later placed in a playoff to defend her title.

Mark Moretti
(Abington b. 1958)
A former graphic designer for Movies Unlimited and comic book artist, Moretti is one of Hollywood's top storyboard artists who has worked on such films as "I, Robot," "Catwoman," the "Underworld" films, "Talladega Nights: The Ballad of Ricky Bobby," and "The Reaping."

Robert Mugge
(Chicago, Ill. b. 1960)
After attending Temple University's graduate film school program, Mugge went on to make a series of enlightening, highly acclaimed musical documentaries, including "Sun Ra: A Joyful Noise," about the experimental Philly jazz performer, "The Gospel According to Al Green," and "Saxophone Colossus," about sax great Sonny Rollins. He also directed 2006's "New Orleans": Music in Exile," centering on the effect Hurricane Katrina had on

the city's music community. Mugge also welcomed controversy with his 1978 doc "Amateur Night at City Hall," about mayor Frank Rizzo.

Matt Mulhern

(Philadelphia b. 1960)

An actor with an impressive resume in TV (a regular on "Major Dad," appearances on "JAG" and "Law and Order: Special Victims Unit"), Mulhern has also directed the independent films "Walking to the Waterline" and the local production "Duane Hopwood" with David Schwimmer.

Alex North

(Chester b. 1910, d. 1991)

A one-time protégé of Aaron Copland and a jazz enthusiast, composer North's film career got a quick start out of the box, scoring applause for his first two assignments in 1951, "Death of a Salesman" and "A Streetcar Named Desire." He often collaborated with director John Huston ("The Misfits," "Prizzi's Honor"), and contributed lyrical work to epics like "Spartacus," "Cleopatra," "Cheyenne Autumn," "Bite the Bullet," and "Shoes of the Fisherman." He also wrote "Unchained Melody" for the film "Unchained," which was later turned into one of the biggest hits of all-time by The Righteous Brothers. Nominated for 15 Academy Awards, he was given an honorary "Lifetime Achievement Award" in 1986.

Patrick J. Nolan

(Philadelphia)

He wrote the script for Michael Mann's award-winning TV movie "The Jericho Mile," starring Peter Strauss as an inmate who channels his anger into becoming a world class runner. Nolan is now a retired professor of literature at Villanova University.

Paul L. Nolan

(Philadelphia b. 1954)

Locally based character actor with appearances in "Ocean's Eleven" "Condition Red," and "Signs."

Edward Norris

(Philadelphia b. 1911, d. 2002)

At home in supporting roles or leading parts, Norris began his show biz career as a double for Buddy Rogers in 1927's Oscar-winning "Wings." He had contracts at both MGM and Fox, appeared in key roles in "Boys' Town," "They Won't Forget," and "The Man from the Alamo," and was married to actresses Ann Sheridan and Sheila Ryan.

J.J. North

(Philadelphia)

Although she's petite, standing at 5 ' 2," this blonde actress starred in "Attack of the 60 Foot Centerfold." She's specialized in exploitation movies, appearing in "Depraved," "Hybrid," and "Bikini Hotel."

Jack O'Halloran

(Philadelphia b. 1943)

This Runnemede-raised former boxer has appeared in several films, usually playing a big galoot. See him as the silent space criminal Non in the first two Christopher Reeve "Superman" movies, as Moose Malloy in "Farewell My Lovely," as a serial killer in Chuck Norris vehicle "The Hero and the Terror," and as The Yeti in "The Flintstones." Reportedly, he was considered for the Jaws role in the James Bond films, but Richard Kiel snagged the part.

Clifford Odets

(Philadelphia b. 1906, d. 1963)

A charter member of Group Theater and a subscriber to the Method-acting style developed by Lee Strasberg and Harold Clurman, Odets was a celebrated playwright who saw many of his works translated for the screen. Among them: "The Big Knife," "Clash by Night," "The Country Girl," and "Golden Boy." He also scripted "The Sweet Smell of Success" and worked on Hitchcock's "Notorious" without a credit. His directing work includes "None But the Lonely Heart" with Cary Grant, and "The Story on Page One" with Rita Hayworth and Anthony Franciosa. Word has it that Odets is the person the Coen Brothers' based John Turturro's "Barton Fink" on.

Ken Olin

(Chicago b. 1954)

The University of Pennsylvania grad had a regular gig on "Hill Street Blues," playing Detective. Harry Garibaldi for a season, but became a recognizable actor with his turn as ad agency head Michael Steadman in "thirtysomething" with local producer Marshall Hershowitz. He went on to star in the short-lived "EZ Streets" and "L.A. Doctors," and has had a hand in producing "Alias" and other series.

Josh Olson

(Philadelphia)

Thanks to his Oscar-nominated work adapting the graphic novel "A History of Violence," Temple University grad Olson has become a writer in demand in Hollywood. Before the David Cronenberg-directed film hit theaters, Olson worked on B movies, shorts ("A Moment of Silence"), and wrote and directed the smart horror spoof "Infected." Among his upcoming projects are "Monster," adapted from a Japanese comic book about a mysterious killer, and "Until Gwen," adapted from a story by Dennis Lehane ("Mystic River").

Cheri Oteri

(Philadelphia b. 1965)

The "Saturday Night Live" performer was raised in Upper Darby and attended Archbishop Pendergast High School. She worked on the show from 1995 to 2000, playing such parts as the perky cheerleader opposite Will Farrell, Barbara Walters, Judge Judy, and a the prescription-needy Collette. Oteri has also appeared in "Dumber and Dumberer," "Southland Tales" and provided the voice of Doreen Nickle in "The Ant Bully."

Stuart Pankin

(Philadelphia b. 1946)

He's been a reliable character actor for almost 30 years, starting with a small role in Paul Mazursky's "Next Stop, Greenwich Village" in 1976, then in such films as the maligned honor student Fudley Laywicker in "The Hollywood Knights" and with Chuck Norris in "An Eye for an Eye." His many TV credits include "Barney Miller," "Matt Houston," "Knot's Landing," "Dharma and Greg," and "Entourage." He also provided the recognizable voice of Earl Sinclair, the father of the "Dinosaurs" series.

Adrian Pasdar

(Pittsfield, Mass. b. 1965)

At the age of two, Pasdar and family moved to Poweltown Village. He later attended Marple-Newton High School, and performed regularly at People's Light and Theater Company in Malvern. After studying acting in New York, Pasdar landed a role in "Top Gun," playing Chipper. He took the lead in the 1987 cult vampire film "Near Dark," and counts TV shows "Judging Amy" and "Desperate Housewives" on his resume. He's married to Natalie Maines of the Dixie Chicks.

Dennis Patrick

(Philadelphia b. 1918, d. 2002)

He was the businessman who joined Peter Boyle's racist in a rumble against hippies in the powerful 1970 generation gap drama "Joe." But Patrick was also one of the busiest actors on both coasts, appearing in over 1500 hours of TV, in a career that spanned over five decades. Name the TV show and he was probably in it, from early live TV dramas to "Gunsmoke," from "Perry Mason" to "Dark Shadows," and from "The Streets of San Francisco" to "Coach." Sadly, he died in a fire to his Hollywood home in 2002.

Scott Patterson

(Philadelphia b. 1958)

Born in Philly and raised in Baltimore and New Jersey, Lauren Graham's romantic interest on "The Gilmore Girls" is also the guy who Julia Louis Dreyfuss' Elaine dubbed "sponge-worthy" on "Seinfeld. He dropped out of Rutgers, became a minor-league baseball player, then decided to shift gears to acting. It was a long haul to stardom and he was living out of his '66 Pontiac at one time. Work in TV series and low-budget films eventually helped him get things together.

Holly Robinson Peete

(Philadelphia b. 1964)

Her father, Matt Robinson, was Gordon on "Sesame Street"; her mother Dolores Robinson is a producer-agent. And Holly's husband is Rodney Peete, former backup quarterback for the Philadelphia Eagles. Holly appeared at a young age on "Sesame Street" and did some TV and movie work ("Howard the Duck") before getting into the spotlight as a regular on the entire four-year run of "21 Jump Street," playing Officer Judy Hoffs. She's also been a cast member on TV shows "Hangin' with Mr. Cooper," "For Your Love," and "Love Inc."

Arthur Penn

(Philadelphia b. 1922)

His father was a Philly watchmaker and Irving Penn, his brother, became a famous photographer. While in the service, he began an acting troupe with fellow soldiers, then headed to New York, where he studied with director Joshua Logan, and began writing and directing live TV productions for "Playhouse 90" and other shows in the 1950s. He broke into films with the 1958 adaptation of "The Left-Handed Gun," Gore Vidal's revisionist look at the outlaw Billy the Kid, played by Paul Newman. The film was coolly received in the U.S., but European audiences took to it. Success on Broadway with "The Miracle Worker," "Two for the Road," "Toys in the Attic," and "All the Way Home" followed. Penn returned to films in 1962 with the "The Miracle Worker," a stunning adaptation of Helen Keller's life story, with Anne Bancroft as teacher Annie Sullivan and Oscar-winning Patty Duke as Keller. The rest of the 1960s were filled with ups and downs: "Mickey One," an experimental effort with Warren Beatty as a nightclub entertainer, didn't win many fans; "The Chase," an all-star racial drama was taken out of Penn's hands; and the director was fired from "The Train," a World War II thriller starring Burt Lancaster. However, Penn reunited with Beatty as producer and star of "Bonnie and Clyde," a film that fizzled at first, but was resurrected by its studio to become a bona fide pop culture phenomena. Penn's other assignments include "Alice's Restaurant," "Little Big Man," "Night Moves," "The Missouri Breaks," and, oddly enough, "Penn and Teller Get Killed."

Rod Perry

(Coatseville b. 1941)

The African-American actor appeared in the TV movie "The Autobiography of Miss Jane Pittman" and blaxploitation films like "The Black Godfather" and "The Black Gestapo," but he's probably best remembered for the role of Sgt. David "Deacon" Kay on the TV series ""S.W.A.T."

Robert Picardo

(Philadelphia b. 1953)

Born in East Falls, this graduate of Penn Charter went to Yale as a premed student before he shifted gears, heading to New York to make it in the theater. He appeared in a production of "Gemini," the South Philly-set comedy, with Danny Aiello, "The Primary English Class" with Diane Keaton, and "The Normal Heart," which brought him accolades and awards. In films, he's worked extensively with area native Joe Dante, in such films as "Innerspace," "Matinee," and "Looney Tunes: Back in Action," and has appeared in many episodes of network TV, including "The Wonder Years" and "Star Trek: Voyager," in which he played the doctor.

Sharon Pinkenson

(Philadelphia)

The executive director of the Greater Philadelphia Film Office since 1992 has production credits on such films as "Kimberly" and "Shadowboxer."

Noam Pitlik

(Philadelphia b. 1932, d. 1999)

He directed scores of sitcoms and appeared in them, too, often playing a authority figure — a rabbi in "The Partridge Family," veteran cop Swanny Swanhauser in "Sanford and Son," a veteran cop in "Police Story." Pitlik also produced "Barney Miller" and the TV version of "9 to 5," starring Rita Moreno, Rachel Dennison, and Valerie Curtin.

Marc Platt

A graduate of University of Pennsylvania where he was member of the glee club, Platt is a former lawyer turned studio executive-turned producer whose credits include "Legally Blonde," "Josie and the Pussycats," "Empire Falls," and the Broadway hit "Wicked."

Jon Polito

(Philadelphia b. 1950)

He's usually bald, sporting a pencil thin mustache and speaking in a gruff voice. He also has made a habit of stealing scenes in a number of film roles and TV series. He's a regular in the Coen Brothers movies (the studio chief in "Barton Fink," hood Johnny Gaspar, in "Miller's Crossing," Da Fino in "The Big Lebowski"), and scored as a regular in the series "Homicide: Life on the Street" as Detective Steve Crosetti. "Seinfeld" fans remember Polito as Silvio in "The Reverse Peephole" episode.

Robert Prosky

(Philadelphia b. 1930)

Born Robert Porzucke, this busy character actor is at home TV and the silver screen. A graduate of Temple University, he's best known for his parts in "The Natural," "Things Change," "Rudy," and "Dead Man Walking," and has had major TV stints on "Hill Street Blues" as Major Stan Jablonski and "The Practice" as Father Patrick.

Paul Provenza

(New York City b. 1957)

He attended University of Pennsylvania and was a member of the Mask and Wig Club before he became a regular stand-up comic at local clubs like The Comedy Factory Outlet and The Comedy Works. He took his comedy national on several talk shows and acted in "Miami Vice," "Northern Exposure" and "The West Wing." With Penn Jillette, he codirected 2005's shot-on-a-shoestring hit "The Aristocrats," featuring scores of comics telling a famous dirty joke.

Joe Pyne

(Chester b. 1924, d. 1970)

The outspoken TV talk show host predated Morton Downey, Jr. and Bill O'Reilly with his cranky, almost abusive demeanor. He also made guest appearances playing himself in the groovy sixties films "The Love-Ins" and "Skidoo."

The Quay Brothers

(Philadelphia b. 1947)

Stephen and Timothy Quay are identical twin brothers who studied illustration in Philly before they moved to England to continue their art studies at London's Royal Academy of Art in the 1960s. They moved into animation, and worked on several commercials and were the creative force behind Peter Gabriel's "Sledgehammer" music video. Their surrealistic features have showcased stop-motion animation, live action, and pixilation, and include "Street of Crocodiles" (1986), "Institute Benjamenta" (1995), and "The Piano Tuner of Earthquakes" (2005).

Joe Queenan

(Philadelphia b. 1950)

Satirist, essayist and movie critic Joe Queenen has written numerous books, including *If You're Talking to Me, Your Career Must Be in Trouble* and *Red Lobster, White Trash and The Blue Lagoon: Joe Queenan's America*. He also directed and starred in 1995's "Twelve Steps to Death," about an abusive therapist who is murdered. He produced the film for $7,000, and the experience is documented in the book *The Unkindest Cut*.

Max L. Raab

The former main man at fashion label J.G. Hook, the Rittenhouse-Square-based Raab dabbled in producing films over the years, producing such 1970s cult faves as "End of the Road," "Walkabout" "A Clockwork Orange" and "Lion's Love." Raab made his directing debut in 2001 with "Strut!," the documentary on The Mummers, and produced and appears in 2004's "Rittenhouse Square," about the famous park.

David Raksin

(Philadelphia b. 1904, d. 2004)

Prolific composer for movies and TV shows, Raksin worked from the 1930s into the late 1980s. Best known for his haunting theme for Otto Preminger's "Laura," he also arranged music with Charlie Chaplin for "Modern Times," composed the scores for the films "The Bad and the Beautiful," "Al Capone," and "Big Hand for a Little Lady," and wrote the music for TV shows "Ben Casey," "Medical Center," and other series.

Sue Randall

(Philadelphia b. 1935, d. 1984)

A busy actress and social activist, she appeared in hundreds of hours of TV in such shows as "Sea Hunt," "Leave It To Beaver," Bonanza," and "Death Valley Days."

Man Ray

(Philadelphia b. 1890, d. 1976)

A painter, filmmaker, and photographer, he's closely associated with the Dadaist and Surrealist movements in art. He directed a few surrealist films, including "Return to Reason" and "What Do Young Films Dream About." As a still photographer, he worked on "Pandora and the Flying Dutchman" and "Show Boat" (1951).

James Rebhorn

(Philadelphia b. 1948)
He's the skinny character actor you've seen everywhere from the mid 1970s on. Some of his credits include playing doctors in "Silkwood," "Regarding Henry," "Basic Instinct," "Meet the Parents," "Far from Heaven," and "Cold Mountain"; he's also worked opposite Al Pacino in "Carlito's Way" and "Scent of a Woman." Other key roles include "My Cousin Vinny" and "The Talented Mr. Ripley." Prominent TV assignments include episodes of "Law & Order" (as Charles Garnett); and as the district attorney in the last two "Seinfeld" episodes.

Peter Mark Richman

(Philadelphia b. 1927)
A graduate of South Philly High and the Philadelphia College of Pharmacy and Sciences, this busy actor has appeared in hundreds of hours of TV shows, dating back to the mid 1950s. He appeared on most major TV shows in the 1960s and 1970s, as well as the features "Friday the 13th Part VIII: Jason Takes Manhattan" and "4 Faces," an inspirational film he also wrote.

Susan Richardson

(Coatesville b. 1952)
She appeared in "American Graffiti," then several TV series before gaining a spot as Susan Bradford Stockwell on "Eight is Enough." Emotional problems and the claim she was kidnapped by filmmakers and held hostage in Korea may have something to do with her retirement from show business.

Stephen J. Rivele

(Philadelphia b. 1949)
A former student at Saint Joe's and Swarthmore, Rivele did missionary work with the Jesuits in the Congo before returning to Philadelphia where he penned plays for local theater companies. Teaming with Christopher Wilkinson, he's specialized in writing scripts with historical backdrops. Among his credits are "Nixon," "Ali," and "Copying Beethoven" with Ed Harris as the composer.

Daniel Roebuck

(Bethlehem b. 1963)
A horror movie fanatic and memorabilia collector, he produced and directed the "Monstermania" TV series. Roebuck started in standup and as a magician, but got his first big break as one of the troubled teens with Keanu Reeves, Crispin Glover, and Ione Skye in "River's Edge." Network TV stints in "Matlock" and "Nash Bridges" followed, as well as supporting parts in "Only You," "The Fugitive," and "Bubba Ho-Tep."

Norman Rose

(Philadelphia b. 1917, d. 2004)
The man who supplied the voice of the fictional coffee industry spokeman Juan Valdez, had a diverse show biz career. Along with starting a long-running off-Broadway theater company, Rose studied at the Actor's Studio, served as a radio announcer, supplied the voice of God in "Love and Death," narrated the English version of 1968's "War and Peace," and acted in such soaps as "Search for Tomorrow."

Mark Rosenthal

(Philadelphia b. 1951)

Temple University grad Rosenthal and writing partner Lawrence Konner sold the script for "The Legend of Billy Jean" (1985), which helped put them on the map. They soon got steady, high-profile work scripting sequels ("The Jewel of the Nile," "Superman IV: The Quest for Peace,"), remakes ("Mighty Joe Young," "The Desperate Hours," "Planet of the Apes"), TV-to-screen translations ("The Beverly Hillbillies," "Flicka"), and star vehicles ("Mona Lisa Smile" with Julia Roberts, "Mercury Rising" with Bruce Willis). Rosenthal also wrote and directed "The In Crowd" (1988), a nostalgic look at an "American Bandstand"-like show. He's also taught screenwriting at the University of Pennsylvania,.

Robert Rothbard

The director of "The Life and Times of Charlie Putz" has been working on films as a production manager and in other capacities since 1981's "Blow Out," and counts "The Rat Pack," "Super Mario Brothers," "CSI: Miami" and "Deuces Wild" (which he produced) among his other credits. He's the son of music agent and manager Bernie Rothbard.

Murray Rubinstein

(Philadelphia b. 1956)

A character actor whose TV credits range from "Frasier" to "The X-Files" to "The Practice" to "American Dreams."

Elizabeth Russell

(Philadelphia b. 1916, d. 2002)

She was a character actress who was cast regularly in the great Val Lewton thrillers of the 1940s, including "Cat People," "The Seventh Victim," "Curse of the Cat People," and "Bedlam." The only actress to play the wife of Bela Lugosi ("The Corpse Vanishes") and Boris Karloff ("Bedlam"). She was Rosalind Russell's sister-in-law.

Bobby Rydell

(Philadelphia b. 1942)

Born Robert Ridarelli, the South Philly "Bandstand Boy" had hits with "Wild One," "Sway," and "Volare," then made his mark in the screen version of "Bye Bye Birdie" in 1963, playing "Hugo," boyfriend of Kim McAfee (Ann-Margret). Unlike other Philly-born singers like Frankie Avalon and Fabian Forte, Rydell never tried to mix music and movies much, preferring instead to stick to the tunes rather than Tinseltown.

Bob Saget

(Philadelphia b. 1956)

A Temple University grad who attended Abington High School, comedy club veteran Saget made his mark in the long-running family-oriented sitcom "Full House," playing Danny Tanner, a widowed talk show host raising his three girls — two of whom were played by the oh-so-cute Olsen twins. Saget parlayed the family factor to become the host of the hit "America's Funniest Home Videos," and went on to direct sitcoms, TV movies (including one involving a woman with scleroderma, a disease which afflicted Saget's sister) and the feature "Dirty Work" with Norm McDonald. After a few years out of the limelight, Saget caught attention with his filthy and funny take on a dirty joke in "The Aristocrats," which lead to directing "Farce of the Penguins," a spoof of the hit documentary "March of the Penguins."

Alvin Sargent

(Philadelphia b. 1927)

For decades, Sargent has been considered one of Hollywood's top screenwriters. He started in TV, penning scripts for TV series "Alfred Hitchcock Presents," "Route 66," and "Ben Casey." In 1966, he then broke into movies with his work in the Shirley MacLaine-Michael Caine heist flick "Gambit." Subsequent work included adaptations of many novels and plays. Among his credits are: "The Sterile Cuckoo," "Paper Moon," "Julia" (for which he won the Oscar), "Ordinary People" (ditto), "Nuts," "Dominick and Eugene," "White Palace," "Other People's Money," "What About Bob?," "Unfaithful," and, rather uncharacteristically, "Spider-Man II" and "Spider-Man III." He's married to movie studio executive Laura Ziskin. He's also the brother of the late Herb Sargent.

Herb Sargent

(Philadelphia b. 1923, d. 2005)

Sargent grew up in Upper Darby and after serving in the Army during World War II, he began writing for radio. He eventually landed as a gig as a writer on "The Steve Allen Show" and adapted the novel "Bye Bye Braverman" for a darkly comic 1968 film by Sidney Lumet. Lorne Michaels enlisted Sargent to be one of the initial head writers of "Saturday Night Live," where he worked for 20 years. Sargent coined the term "Not Ready for Prime-Time Players," won six Emmy Awards, and cowrote "Lily," Lily Tomlin's first TV special, and "Annie: The Woman in the Life of a Man," a TV special with Anne Bancroft and Mel Brooks. He's the brother of Alvin Sargent.

William Schilling

(Philadelphia b. 1939)

Best known as Dr. Harold Samuels on "Head of the Class," this busy character actor has appeared in hundreds of TV shows — mostly comedies — including "Archie Bunker's Place," "M*A*S*H," and "The Jeffersons." He was a regular on "ER" in the mid 1980s, playing Richard, and was in the films "Ruthless People," "Space Jam," and "Jury Duty." But don't hold that last credit against him.

Leon Schlesinger

(Philadelphia b. 1884, d. 1949)

If the name's familiar, it's because it's appeared in front of scores of classic Warner Brothers cartoons featuring Bug Bunny, Porky Pig, and Daffy Duck. Schlesinger produced hundreds of them for the studio, employing Friz Freling, Bob Clampett, Tex Avery, Chuck Jones, and Frank Tashlin. He started making title cards for silent films, loaned the Warner studio money to complete 1927's "The Jazz Singer," and began his work in animation producing "Bosko" cartoons for Hugh Harman and Rudolf Isimg. An archrival to Walt Disney, Schlesinger was vehemently anti-union and notoriously stingy to his talented workers, but his no-nonsense management style kept Warner Brothers' creators cranking out his "Looney Tunes" and "Merrie Melodies" at a rapid clip throughout the 1930s and 1940s. Daffy Duck's lisp was reportedly based on Schlesinger's way of speaking.

Scott L. Schwartz

(Philadelphia)

A graduate of Washington High School, Schwartz is an imposing figure, standing 6'9 ½" and weighing over 300 pounds. He usually plays henchmen, bouncers, or tough guys, and has been seen in such films as "Oceans's Eleven" and "Ocean's Twelve" as Bruiser; "The Scorpion King" as "Torturer"; "Spider-Man" as Screaming Wrestler;

and "Fun With Dick and Jane" as Bigger Convenience Store Clerk. He's a former pro wrestler who once went by the name "Giant David" and wore Jewish stars on his boots.

Bill Scott
(Philadelphia b. 1920, d. 1985)
One of the unsung heroes of the animation world, Scott was the voice of "Bullwinkle," "Dudley Dooright," "Mr. Peabody," and "Fearless Leader." Collaborating with Jay Ward, he scripted the "Rocky and Bullwinkle Show," and earlier worked on "Mr. Magoo" cartoons for UPA Studios. Along with Ward, he also created "Fractured Flickers," a show in which silent films were dubbed for comic effect by himself, June Foray (the voice of "Rocky"), and others.

Lizabeth Scott
(Scranton b. 1922)
Born Emma Matzo to Czech parents, she became a model and headed to Broadway where she found work as Tallulah Bankhead's understudy in a play. She was then discovered by producer Hal B. Wallis, and cast in such films as "Since You Came Along" and "Desert Fury" by the Paramount-based executive. She was a fixture as the blonde "with something else going on" in such noir winners as "The Strange Love of Martha Ivers," "I Walk Alone," "Dead Reckoning," "Pitfall," and "The Racket." She never married and once sued a tabloid for reporting she had lesbian affairs.

Susan Seidelman
(Philadelphia b. 1952)
This Abington High School grad and Drexel University student also studied film at New York University and was an early pioneer of the independent film movement, female division. Her 1981 effort "Smithereens," about a slacker girl trying to make it among the Greenwich Village punk and art scene, made waves when it was accepted to be shown at the Cannes Film Festival. Her follow-up, 1985's "Desperately Seeking Susan," a riff on "The Prince and the Pauper," made Madonna and the director bankable as film entities,. Subsequent films — independent and studio backed — have included "Cookie," "Making Mr. Right," "She-Devil," "Gaudi Afternoon," and "The Boynton Beach Club," which was cowritten by her mother. She's also turned the camera on herself in the 1992 documentary "Confessions of a Suburban Girl" and helmed several episodes of "Sex and the City."

Amanda Seyfried
(Allentown b. 1985)
She was a teen model who got her first acting job on the soap operas "As the World Turns" and "All My Children" before landing the part of spaced-out Karen Smith in "Mean Girls." Since then, this doe-eyed blonde actress been in the TV shows "Wildfire," "Veronica Mars," and "Big Love," playing Sarah Henrickson, polygamist Bill Paxton's daughter with wife numero uno Jeanne Tripplehorn.

Martin Sherman
(Philadelphia b. 1938)
The author of the hit 1979 play and 1997 screenplay for "Bent," about a gay man's experiences in a concentration camp during World War II, Sherman has also scripted the 2003 TV version of Tennessee Williams' "The Roman Spring of Mrs. Stone" with Helen Mirren and 2005's "Mrs. Henderson Presents," featuring Bob Hoskins and Dame Judi Dench.

Jonathan Shestack

(Philadelphia)

The son of former KYW TV reporter Marciarose Shestack and lawyer Jerome Shestack, Jonathan has produced such films as "The Last Seduction," "Waiting," and the Harrison Ford thrillers "Air Force One" and "Firewall."

Craig Shoemaker

(Philadelphia b. 1962)

Like Bob Saget, this Philly funnyman attended Temple University and started out in local comedy clubs. He was a regular on PRISM and KYW's "Saturday Night Dead," featuring "that maneater from Manyunk-Stella." He then moved to L.A., where he won awards for his standup routines. He's acted in such series as "The Fresh Prince of Bel-Air" and "Family Law," and starred in the feature "The Lovemaster," based on his nightclub routine. Currently married to actress Carolyne Ann Clark, his former wife is Nancy Allen of "Blow Out" fame.

M. Night Shyamalan

(Mahe, Pondicherry, India b. 1970)

Philly's most famous filmmaker-in-residence, Shyamalan catapulted to international success writing and directing 1999's surprise hit "The Sixth Sense," a supernatural thriller shot locally and starring Bruce Willis and Haley Joel Osment. Born Manoj Nelliyattu Shyamalan to two doctors, he was raised in Penn Valley and attended Episcopal Academy and New York University. Before "The Sixth Sense," the filmmaker made "Praying with Anger," in which he starred, and "Wide Awake," a lighter take on some of the themes presented in "The Sixth Sense." Thanks to "The Sixth Sense's" surprise ending, audiences have expected — and received — more surprise finales in follow-ups "Unbreakable," "Signs," and "The Village." His latest feature is "Lady in the Water."

Kerr Smith

(Exton b. 1972)

This graduate of Henderson High School in West Chester had his scenes cut out of "Twelve Monkeys," but rebounded as a regular on "Dawson's Creek," playing Jack McPhee, and has had roles in such series as "Charmed" and "E-Ring." Film credits include the horror movies "Final Destination" and "The Forsaken."

Melanie Smith

(Scranton b. 1962)

She was Rachel Goldstein, Jerry's buxom girlfriend in several classic "Seinfeld" episodes in the fifth season of the show, then showed up in Larry David's "Curb Your Enthusiasm" as an incest survivor. In between, she played Tora Ziyal in "Star Trek: Deep Space Nine."

Will Smith

(Philadelphia b. 1968)

"The Fresh Prince" hails from Overbrook and attended West Philly High, made a name for himself as a rap artist with partner D.J. Jazzy Jeff until he took Hollywood by storm. Supporting parts in "Where the Day Takes You" and "Made in America" led to the sturdy major role in "Six Degrees of Separation," then a starring part in 1990 in the hit sitcom "Fresh Prince of Bel-Air," which ran until 1996. He shared the big screen with Martin Lawrence in "Bad Boys," played Agent J in two "Men in Black" films, "and starred in box-office hits "Enemy of the State," "Independence Day," "I, Robot," and "Hitch." He copped an Oscar nomination as "Ali." He now produces most of his own films. He's married to actress Jada Pinkett Smith.

Stacey Snider

(Philadelphia b. 1961)

A University of Pennsylvania graduate, Snider attended UCLA Law School, but opted instead to go into the film business, starting in the mailroom of talent agency triad artists. She's been President of Production at Tri-Star Studios, Chairperson of Universal Studios, and in June 2006 was named CEO of DreamWorks Pictures, after they were sold to Paramount.

George Spahn

(Philadelphia b. 1889, d. 1974)

He owned the Spahn Movie Ranch, a spot near Chatsworth in L.A.'s San Fernando Valley that looked like a vintage western town, which was used for several TV shows and movies. In exchange for help on the farm, he allowed Charles Manson and his disciples, to live there for free. In his latter years, the blind Spahn was cared for by Lynette "Squeaky" Fromme, who supposedly fed him and acted as his bedmate in order to keep him happy.

Anne Spielberg

(Philadelphia b. 1949)

Steven Spielberg's sister wrote and produced the hit "Big," then seems to have left show business. Her father-in-law was character actor David Opatoshu.

Timothy Stack

(Doylestown b. 1957)

A graduate of Central Bucks West, Stack drew attention for his performance as a smarmy talk show host Dick Deetrick in the syndicated TV parody "Night Stand." He' was also the star of F/X's Howard Stern-produced "Baywatch" spoof "Son of a Beach," playing lifeguard Notch Johnson. Along with lots of voice work and guest spots on TV shows, he's appeared in "Scary Movie 3" and "American Pie Presents Band Camp." He's also scripted a long-in-the-works remake of "Rock and Roll High School," to be produced by Stern.

Sylvester Stallone

(New York b. 1946)

Closely associated with the City of Brotherly Love because of the "Rocky" movies, Stallone was actually born in the tough Hell's Kitchen area of Manhattan, then moved to Maryland with family before settling into Philly as a young teen, and attending Lincoln High School among other local schools. After a role in the porn film "A Night at Kitty and Stud's," Stallone snagged supporting parts in "Bananas" and "Farewell My Lovely" and a major role in "The Lords of Flatbush," but was rejected for a part in "The Godfather" after an audition. The dismissal gave Stallone the fuel to write what would become his own meal ticket: "Rocky," about a Philadelphia club boxer who faces off against the world heavyweight champ, selling the script only with himself attached as star. Stallone scored big, as the film won Academy Awards for Best Picture and Best Original Screenplay, while he was nominated for Best Actor. After "Rocky," Stallone was bankable, and honed his working class hero persona acting in (and sometimes writing and directing) such films as "Paradise Alley," "F.I.S.T.," "Rocky II," and "Rocky III," and "Rambo: First Blood." The success of the "First Blood" film, in which he played a disgruntled Vietnam vet, seemed to push him in a different direction, as he took bigger-than-life parts that often went into comic book territory — "Rocky IV," Rambo II" and Rambo III," "Over the Top," and "Cobra." He also tried unsuccessfully to flex his comedic muscles with "Rhinestone," "Oscar," and "Stop! OR My Mom Will Shoot." After some box-office duds, Stallone went back to his roots, playing a sheriff in a North Jersey City populated by New York cops in 1997's "CopLand." Working opposite Robert De Niro, Harvey

Keitel, and Ray Liotta, Stallone received some of the best reviews of his career. After some cameo work in the heist flick "Shade" and "Spy Kids 3-D," and leads in a few direct-to-video thrillers, Stallone got back to his roots, starring and acting in 2006's "Rocky Balboa," the sixth film in the series. He was married to actress Brigitte Nielsen and is now married to model Jennifer Flavin.

Teller
(Philadelphia b. 1948)
The silent partner in the Penn & Teller magic act was born Raymond Joseph Teller, and went to Central High School. He began doing magic as a kid, performing at birthday parties. He continued with the tricks, working New Market corners, street fairs, and colleges, while earning a living as a Latin teacher in Trenton. He took a sabbatical from teaching at the age of 26, and joined forces with juggler Penn Jillette and Wier Chrisemer to form the Asparagus Valley Cultural Society, a magic/comedy review that had a popular run at the Walnut Street Theatre and in San Francisco. When Chrisemer, the son of a Lutheran minister, left because of his partners' atheist views, Penn, with his motor-mouthed delivery and imposing 6'6" frame and Teller, mute with a bemused demeanor, emerged as a comedy duo, staging elaborate magical feats and satirizing show business at the same time. Along with successful touring stints, shows on Broadway and in Vegas, a feature film ("Penn & Teller Get Killed") and a few popular TV series, Teller has appeared solo in the TV movie "Long Gone," on "The Drew Carey Show," and in the 2000 film "The Fantasticks."

Joseph Stefano
(Philadelphia b. 1922)
The man who scripted "Psycho" (based on a novel by Robert Bloch) has had a varied career in movies and TV, as both a writer and producer. A veteran of live TV of the 1950s, Stefano's success with the Hitchcock classic led to writing and producing the classic 1960s sci-fi series "The Outer Limits." He later wrote for the TV series "The Magician," "Star Trek: The Next Generation," and "Swamp Thing," and wrote "Psycho IV" for TV. Stefano also penned "Two Bits," the 1995 Philly-set drama starring Al Pacino.

Parker Stevenson
(Philadelphia b. 1952)
This graduate of Princeton, made his screen debut in the highly touted film version of "A Separate Peace" in 1972, appeared in the cult film "Lifeguard" in 1976, and drew attention as Shaun Cassidy's brother in "The Hardy Boys/Nancy Drew Mysteries" on NBC in the late 1970s. Along with marrying—then divorcing Stevenson — Kirstie Alley is also known for his work on "Baywatch," "Melrose Place," and "Falcon Crest."

Christine Taylor
(Allentown b. 1971)
The blonde actress was great as Marcia in "The Brady Bunch Movie," and played the lead in the short-lived TV version of the movie "Party Girl." Other TV credits include "Friends" and "Arrested Development." Also, she's costarred in "Zoolander" and "Dodgeball: A True Underdog Story" with hubby Ben Stiller.

Holland Taylor

(Philadelphia b. 1943)

Born in Philly but raised in Allentown where she attended Quaker schools, Taylor got her first big break as a regular on "Bosom Buddies" with Tom Hanks and Peter Scolari. Usually cast as a no-nonsense, somewhat cantankerous woman, Taylor won an Emmy for playing a judge who had an affair with lawyer Michael Balduicci on "The Practice" and plays Charlie Sheen and Jon Cryer's mother on "Two and a Half Men." Screen roles have included Kathleen Turner's publisher in "Romancing the Stone" and Jim Carrey's mother in "The Truman Show." She's also appeared in "Next Stop, Wonderland" and Happy Accidents" for director Brad Anderson, who is her nephew.

Harry Thomas

(Philadelphia b. 1909, d. 1996)

This Hollywood makeup artist specialized in B movie assignments, providing the faces for characters in such films as Ed Wood's "Glen or Glenda," "Cat Women of the Moon," and "Night of the Blood Beast."

Jonathan Taylor Thomas

(Bethlehem b. 1981)

He was the voice of Simba in Disney's "the Lion King," and became a "tweener" sensation as Tim Allen's son in the "Home Improvement" series from 1991 to 1998. Other roles have included the films "Man of the House" and "Tom and Huck," and TV stints on "Smallville" and "Eight Simple Rules ... for Dating My Teenage Daughter."

Michael Tollin

(Philadelphia b. 1956)

He started working for the Rotfield family, Philly-based producers of "Greatest Sports Legends" and writing "The Baseball Bunch" with Johnny Bench and the San Diego Chicken in the early 1980s. After moving to L.A., he teamed with former child star Brian Robbins for a kid's variety show called "All That," and they formed Tollin/Robbins Productions, which became a major contributor to Nickelodeon with "The Amanda Show" and "Good Burger." Tollin was nominated for an Academy Award for Best Documentary and won a Peabody Award for directing 1995's "Hank Aaron: Chasing the Dream." Other directing credits include "Summer Catch" and the surprise hit "Radio." His company's production credits include TV ("Smallville," "One Tree Hill," "Bonds on Bonds") and movies ("Varsity Blues," "Hard Ball," "Coach Carter," "Dreamer: Inspired by a True Story," and the Eddie Murphy vehicle "Norbit"). He's also planning a movie based on the annual "Wing Bowl" contest.

Robert Trebor

(Philadelphia b. 1953)

Northeast Philly native Trebor has worked steadily in character roles for decades. He first drew attention as David Berkowitz, the "Son of Sam" killer in the 1985 TV film "Out of the Darkness," and scored more points for his creepy portrayal of a hood in "52 Pick-Up." He played Salmoneus in the syndicated, Sam Raimi-produced "Hercules": The Legendary Journeys" and appeared in "Xena: Warrior Princess," and "The Young Indiana Jones Chronicles," He's also directed episodes of the "Hercules" series.

Bobby Troup

(Harrisburg b. 1918, d. 1999)

A University of Pennsylvania grad who served with the Marines during World War II, he went on to become a prolific actor and composer of such songs as "(Get Your Kicks on) Route 66" and "The Girl Can't Help It." His acting stints included playing Dr. Joe Early on "Emergency!," and he appeared on "Dragnet," "Adam-12," and "Rawhide," and he had one line in the film "M*A*S*H." He married singer Julie London after she split from "Dragnet" producer and star Jack Webb.

Larry Tucker

(Philadelphia b. 1934, d. 1999)

Best known as a comedy writer and producer who collaborated with director Paul Mazursky on "The Monkees" TV series, as well as on the feature films "Bob & Carol & Ted & & Alice" and "I Love You, Alice B. Toklas." His acting credits include "Advise & Consent" and "Shock Corridor."

Lorenzo Tucker

(Philadelphia b. 1907, d. 1986)

Nicknamed The Black Valentino, this handsome, African American actor attended Temple University, then appeared in several films directed by legendary black filmmaker Oscar Micheaux, including "When Men Betray" (1928), "Easy Street" (1930), and "Veiled Aristocrats" (1932).

Tom Verica

(Philadelphia b. 1964)

His mother danced on the Dick Clark-hosted "American Bandstand," which inspired him to cut loose on locally produced 1980s show "Dancin' on Air." After paying his dues off-Broadway, Verica got cast in six episodes of "L.A. Law," then appeared as a regular in such TV shows as "Central Park West," "Providence," "Citizen Baines," "Crossing Jordan" (with wife, writer-actress Kira Arne) and as Tom Pryor on "American Dreams," produced by Clark. Film roles include "Red Dragon," "Murder by Numbers," and Clint Eastwood's "Flags of Our Fathers."

Mike Vogel

(Abington b. 1979)

A regular on the WB series "Grounded for Life," Vogel has been on the rise since his supporting role in "The Texas Chainsaw Massacre." He's had high-profile roles in "The Sisterhood of the Traveling Pants," and he played Kevin Costner's son in "Rumor Has It …," and fielded a key supporting role in "Poseidon."

Thomas G. Waites

(Philadelphia)

He got a nice break with his second credit, playing a convict in 1978's "On the Yard." Then he made strong impressions as Fox in Walter Hill's "The Warriors"; as Windows, one of the terrified explorers in "John Carpenter's The Thing"; and as the bigoted Neanderthal Broud in "Clan of the Cave Bear." He also played Harry Stanton in several episodes of "Oz" on HBO.

Nancy Walker
(Philadelphia b. 1922, d. 1992)
The daughter of a vaudeville performing father, the former Anna Smoyer was a kid actor who worked on Broadway and for MGM in such films as "Best Foot Forward" and "Girl Crazy" with Judy Garland and Mickey Rooney. In the 1960s she became recognizable as the waitress Rosie on the long-running Bounty paper towel commercials. A series of parts playing agitated characters followed: on her own short-lived sitcom, as a maid on "McMillan and Wife," and as Valerie Harper's mother in "Rhoda." The only feature she directed was the 1980 campfest "Can't Stop the Music" with the Village People, Steve Guttenberg, Bruce Jenner, and Valerie Perrine.

Sydney Walker
(Philadelphia b. 1921, d. 1994)
A Broadway and theater veteran who appeared onstage in "Becket," "The Wild Duck," and "The Plough and the Stars," Walker played Dr. Shapely in "Love Story," a bus driver in "Mrs. Doubtfire," and the old man in 1992's "Prelude to a Kiss," a role which he also played onstage.

Richard Ward
(Glenside b. 1915, d. 1979)
This African-American character actor with a voice like sandpaper worked a lot during the 1970s, appearing in such films as "Across 110th Street," "Cops and Robbers," and "The Jerk."

Eric Wareheim (Audobon b. 1976)
Tim Heidicker (Allentown b. 1976)
The creative forces behind "Tom Goes to the Mayor," an inventive animated show that's part of Cartoon Network's "Adult Swim" about a newcomer to a small rundown town who joins forces with its mayor try to improve the place.

Paul Wendkos
(Philadelphia b. 1922)
The 1957 shot-in-Philly film noir "The Burglar" launched his prolific and diverse career that includes directing three "Gidget" movies (with Sandra Dee, Deborah Walley, and Cindy Carol, respectively); episodes of TV shows like "The Outer Limits," "The Rifleman," "The Untouchables," and "Ben Casey"; the classic TV movies "Brotherhood of the Bell" and "Honor thy Father"; and the features "The Mephisto Waltz" and "Guns of the Magnificent Seven."

Michael Whalen
(Wilkes-Barre b. 1902, d. 1974)
Prolific character player who was usually cast as an authority figure, like a sheriff, private investigator, or politician. TV work includes "The Lone Ranger," "The Cisco Kid," and "The Count of Monte Cristo"; in the movies he appeared in scores of B pictures, including "The Treasure of Monte Cristo" and "Missile to the Moon."

John Sylvester White
(Philadelphia b. 1919, d. 1988)
He was an original cast member of the soap "Search for Tomorrow" when it debuted in 1951, and later was featured in TV shows "The Gun," "The Law," and, as a regular, in "Welcome Back Kotter," playing Mr. Michael Woodman.

Michael Willis
(Lancaster b. 1949)
This Vietnam veteran has appeared as a regular on "Homicide" Life on the Street" (as Darin Russom) and on "The Wire" (as Andy Krawczyk). He can also be seen in two John Waters films, "Cecil V. DeMented" and "A Dirty Shame."

Hal Willner
(Philadelphia b. 1957)
A music producer who has been the music supervisor for "Saturday Night Live" since the early 1980s, Willner crafted tribute albums to film and theater composers Nino Rota, Harold Arlen, and Kurt Weill. He's also worked produced several tribute concerts and has acted as music supervisor for Robert Altman films "Kansas City" and "Short Cuts." In addition, he's put together the "Carl Stalling Project," a collection of Looney Tunes from the Warner Brothers cartoon composer.

Brian Anthony Wilson
(Philadelphia b. 1960)
This busy actor has appeared in such local productions as "The Good Thief" (aka Saint Christopher), "White Men Can't Rap," and "Prison Song," as well as the TV shows "The Corner," "The Sopranos," and "The Wire."

Carey Wilson
(Philadelphia b. 1889, d. 1962)
A founding member of the Academy of Motion Picture Arts and Sciences, Wilson scripted many films for MGM, including the classics "Gabriel Over the White House" (1933) and "Mutiny on the Bounty" (1935), as well as "Murder at the Vanities" (1934) and many "Andy Hardy" films with Mickey Rooney.

Thomas F. Wilson
(Philadelphia b. 1959)
Best known as the bully Biff Tannen in the "Back to the Future" films, Wilson has appeared regularly in TV or as a voice talent on many shows. He's had regular gigs on the TV series "Fired Up," "Freaks & Geeks," and "Ed," and has supplied voice work to "SpongeBob Square Pants" and "Pinky and the Brain."

Iggy Wolfington
(Philadelphia b. 1920, d. 2004)
A decorated World War II veteran who had success on Broadway playing Henry Hill's right-hand man in "The Music Man" (Buddy Hackett got the screen role), Wolfington had a varied and interesting career on the big screen and little screen. He did lots of live TV dramas in the 1950s, and such comedies as "Get Smart," "The Andy Griffith Show," and "Love, American Style" in the 1960s. On film, he can be seen in Disney's "Herbie Rides Again" and the thriller "Telefon."

Sam Wood
(Philadelphia b. 1883, d. 1949)
A former real estate broker and oil pipeline technician, Wood started as an assistant with Cecil B. DeMille in the silent days, and worked with such stars as Gloria Swanson and Rudolph Valentino in pre-talkie assignments. Many of the performers in his films gave top performances and, in many cases, received Oscar nominations. However, several of Wood's coworkers have gone on record claiming that Wood was tough — especially with overly theatrical actors whom he wore down with multiple takes until they seemed natural in front of the camera. Wood worked for many years for MGM, directing such films as "A Night at the Opera" and "A Day at the Races" with the Marx Brothers, "Waterloo Bridge," "Goodbye,

Mr. Chips," and portions of "Gone with the Wind." His other work includes "Kitty Foyle," "The Pride of the Yankees," "For Whom the Bell Tolls," and "The Stratton Story." Vehemently anti-communist, he testified with Robert Montgomery and Adolphe Menjou before the House Un-American Activities Committee in 1947, telling them how important it was for Hollywood to keep communists out of the movie business. Reportedly, Groucho Marx considered him a fascist.

Danny Woodburn

(Philadelphia b. 1964)

The diminutive actor played Kramer's pal Mickey Abbott on a few memorable episodes of the "Seinfeld" show and has also been seen on "Baywatch," "Becker," "Philly," "Charmed," and the syndicated "Conan" TV series.

Chuck Workman

(Philadelphia)

Anybody who has watched the Academy Awards show in the last 20 years or so, is familiar with the work of Chuck Workman; he's the master of the mini-documentaries that offer scores of clips in a few minutes of screen time. In addition to these efforts, , Workman has directed such interesting clip-oriented documentaries as "Superstar: The Life and Times of Andy Warhol," and "The Source," a look at the writers Jack Kerouac, Allen Ginsburg, and the rest of the Beats. He won an Academy Award for his clip-filled 1986 short "Precious Images," and also helmed 1986's "Stoogemania," which uses public domain footage of the comedy team in a story about a Stooges fan whose obsession has gone too far.

Ed Wynn

(Philadelphia b. 1886, d. 1966)

A vaudeville veteran and stage clown, the former Isiah Edwin Leopold worked for Ziegfeld Follies, and, known as The Perfect Fool, wrote his own shows, and hosted his own TV show in 1949. He turned down the lead in "The Wizard of Oz" ("too small" he said of the role), but later supplied the voice of "The Mad Hatter" in Disney's animated "Alice in Wonderland." Wynn also originated the role of the cut-man Army in the 1957 "Playhouse 90" production of "Requiem for a Heavyweight"; played Kris Kringle in a 1959 TV version of "Miracle on 34th Street"; got nominated as Oscar for Best Supporting Actor for "The Diary of Anne Frank" (1959); played the laugh-happy "Uncle Albert" in "Mary Poppins"; and was featured in two classic episodes of "The Twilight Zone"—in "One For The Angels," he's an elderly salesman who has to outsmart Mr. Death (Murray Hamilton) to save himself and a young girl; and in "Ninety Years Without Slumbering," Wynn plays an old man fearful of his grandfather clock stopping. His son was late character actor Keenan Wynn; writer Tracy Keenan Wynn ("The Longest Yard") and actor-writer Ned Wynn are his grandsons.

John Zacherley

(Philadelphia b. 1918)

This Germantown resident became a popular New York horror movie TV host and narrator as Zacherley, the Cool Ghoul. A regular on New York's WPIX TV, Zach had a late 1950s hit record called "Dinner with Drac."

Acknowledgments

Many people helped out putting this together.

Thanks to Blake Miller, Richard Rys, and Tom McGrath for getting the ball rolling with the original article that appeared in *Philadelphia Magazine*.

Special kudos to Geraldine Duclow of the Free Library of Philadelphia Theater Collection, Nicole Ross and Nicole Shiner of the Greater Philadelphia Film Office, and Scott Abbamonte of the Burlington County Community College library for their valuable research assistance,

At Movies Unlimited, thanks to Jerry Frebowitz, Ed Weiss, Jay Steinberg, Brian Burkart, George Allen, Jay Steinberg, Mark Wildfeuer, Mike Wunsch, Damian Flasser, Steve Fenton, Tony Malczon, Mike Wlodarcyk, Joe DiTella, Elaine Lipkin, Ava Leas, Andrea Seitchick, Charlotte Katz, John Tartaglia, Matt Torpey and Anthony Conrad, and the rest of the MU crew for their support.

Also, thanks to Glenn and Janet Gasser (*www.video-discounters.com*) and Jeremy Bruner of *www.nostalgiafamilyvideo.com* for helping me track down some impossible-to-find titles.

Lewis Beale, Alan Cylinder, Norm Klar, David Bleiler, Steve Austin, Paul Fishbein, Joel Gibbs, Jon Caroulis, Laurence Lerman, Alan Gasmer, Joe Baltake, Lou Gaul, Mitch Neiburg, Jack Blank, David Beck, Mark Scheffler, and Steve Rusk added insight and inspiration.

Family members Selma Chopinsky, Ellen and Mark Segal, and Ricky and Kayleen Slifkin offered encouragement and much-needed kicks in the pants. And Grandmom Rose helped start this whole movie thing for me.

The following publicists also helped: Monica Montalvo, Frank Chille, Paula Moritz, Patrick McHugh, Nick Tarnowski, and Ann Marie Nacchio from Allied Advertising; Jesse Cute from Terry Hines Associates; and, especially, Donna Baum from The Promotions Group.

A big hug to agent Sheree Bykofsky and Janet Rosen, the funniest author's rep in the world.

And, mucho gracias to the Koen family — Barry, Blake, and Pat — for inviting me aboard for the El ride.

Sources

The following sources were used in writing this book.

On the Internet:

All Movie Guides
www.allmovie.com

Internet Movie Database
www.imdb.com

TV Guide
www.tvguide.com

Movies Unlimited
www.moviesunlimited.com

TLA Video
www.tlavideo.com

Total Rocky
www.totalrocky.com

Directed by Brian DePalma
www.briandepalma.net

Greater Philadelphia Film Office
www.film.org

The Blob Site
www.theblobsite.filmbuffonline.com

Wikipedia Encyclopedia
www.wikipedia.org

Silents Is Golden
www.silentsisgolden.com

Movie Locations
www.movie-locations.com

The New Jersey Film Commission
www.njfilm.org

M. Night Shyamalan Online
www.mnight.com

M. Night Shyamalan Fans
www.mnightfans.com

These newspapers and magazines were used in the research of this book:

The Philadelphia Inquirer

The Philadelphia Daily News

Philadelphia Magazine

Camden Courier-Post

Burlington County Times

The following books were helpful in putting together this book:

Before Hollywood: Turn-of-the-Century American Film
(Hudson Hills Press, 1987)

Philadelphia Theaters: A Pictorial Architectural History
by Irvin R. Glazer (Dover Press/The Athenaeum, 1994)

The Three Stooges: The Triumphs and Tragedies of The Most Popular Comedy Team of All Time
by Jeff Forester and Tom Forrester (Donaldson Books, 2002)

The Worldwide Guide to Movie Locations
by Tony Reeves (Chicago Review Press, 2001)

The Film Encyclopedia
by Ephraim Katz (Collin, 2005)

The King of the Movies: Film Pioneer Sigmund Lubin
by Joseph P. Eckhardt (Fairleigh Dickenson University Press, 1998)

Accidental Genius: How John Cassavettes Invented the American Independent Film
by Marshall Fine (Miramax, 2006)

Stallone: A Rocky Life
by Frank Sanello (Mainstream Publishing, 1998)

Movies we Love: 100 Collectible Classics
by Frank Miller (Turner, 1996)

Film Noir: An Encyclopedic Reference to the American Style
by Alain Silver and Elizabeth Ward (Overlook Press, 1993)

Photo Credits

Page 14 photo courtesy of Buena Vista/The Kobal Collection

Page 50 top photo courtesy of 20th Century Fox/The Kobal Collection/Baldwin, Sidney
   left photo courtesy of Scott Weiner

Page 51 photo courtesy of Disney Enterprises/The Kobal Collection/Phillips, Ron

Page 80 photo courtesy of Scott Weiner

Page 83 photo courtesy of Columbia/The Kobal Collection/Regan, Ken

Page 92 photo courtesy of United Artists/The Kobal Collection

Page 95 photo courtesy of Sally Lindsay

Page 96 photo courtesy of Scott Weiner

Page 99 photo courtesy of Sally Lindsay

Page 112 photo courtesy of Paramoount/The Kobal Collection

Page 120 photo courtesy of Hollywood Pictures/The Kobal Collection

Page 122 photo courtesy of Touchstone/The Kobal Collection/Masi, Frank

Page 131 photo courtesy of Sally Lindsay

Author Biography

Irv Slifkin writes and edits the "Movie Buzz" webzine at *www.moviesunlimited.com*. For several years, he helped write and edit the acclaimed Movies Unlimited Video Catalog. He's also the author of "VideoHound's Groovy Movies: Far-Out films of the Psychedelic Era" (Visible Ink Press) and has written about movies for *Entertainment Weekly*, *Philadelphia Magazine*, *Video Business*, *The Los Angeles Times*, *The Hollywood Reporter*, and *The Chicago Tribune*. Slifkin has contributed to WIP Radio's morning show, reviewing films as "Movie Irv." Born in Wynnefield and raised in Northeast Philadelphia, he now lives with his wife and two daughters in Delran, New Jersey.

Gloucester County
Library System